D0891409

New Development Strategies

New Development Strategies

Beyond the Washington Consensus

Edited by

Akira Kohsaka
Osaka University
Japan

338.9009172
N5322

First published 2004 by
PALGRAVE MACMILLAN
Houndmills, Basingstoke, Hampshire RG21 6XS and
175 Fifth Avenue, New York, N.Y. 10010
Companies and representatives throughout the world

PALGRAVE MACMILLAN is the global academic imprint of the Palgrave
Macmillan division of St. Martin's Press, LLC and of Palgrave Macmillan Ltd.
Macmillan® is a registered trademark in the United States, United Kingdom
and other countries. Palgrave is a registered trademark in the European
Union and other countries.

ISBN 1–4039–2072–9

This book is printed on paper suitable for recycling and made from fully
managed and sustained forest sources.

A catalogue record for this book is available from the British Library.

Library of Congress Cataloging-in-Publication Data
New development strategies : beyond the Washington
consensus / edited by Akira Kohsaka.
        p. cm.
    "This book originated from the outcome of the international research
project on Development Policies Outlook conducted by JETRO Institute
of Developing Economies (IDE), Chiba, Japan for the fiscal years
2000–01"—P.
    Includes bibliographical references and index.
    ISBN 1–4039–2072–9 (cloth)
    1. Developing countries—Economic policy.   2. Economic development—
Political aspects.   3. Globalization—Economic aspects—Developing
countries.   I. Kohsaka, Akira.
    HC59.7.N376 2004
    338.9'009172'4—dc22   2003061147

10   9   8   7   6   5   4   3   2   1
13 12 11 10 09 08 07 06 05 04

Printed and bound in Great Britain by
Antony Rowe Ltd, Chippenham and Eastbourne

Contents

List of Tables

List of Figures

Notes on the Contributors

Kaushik Basu is C. Marks Professor of International Studies, Professor of Economics and Director of the Program on Comparative Economic Development at Cornell University.

Yoon Je Cho is Professor of Economics at Sogang University.

Barry Eichengreen is George C. Pardee and Helen N. Pardee Professor of Economics and Political Science at the University of California, Berkeley.

Stephan Haggard is Lawrence and Sallye Krause Professor of Korean Studies and Director of the Korea-Pacific Program at the University of California, San Diego.

Fukunari Kimura is Professor of Economics at Keio University.

Akira Kohsaka is Professor of Economics at Osaka University.

Koji Nishikimi is Senior Research Fellow at the Institute of Developing Economies, JETRO.

Jeffrey B. Nugent is Professor of Economics at the University of Southern California.

Koichi Ohno is Professor of Economics at Nagoya City University.

Dwight H. Perkins is Harold Hitchings Burbank Professor of Political Economy at Harvard University.

Dani Rodrik is Professor of International Political Economy at the John F. Kennedy School of Government, Harvard University.

Preface

This book emerged from an international joint research project on Development Policies Outlook, conducted by the Institute of Developing Economies, JETRO (IDE), in Chiba, Japan, for the fiscal years 2000–1. Based on developing economies' experiences and the expansion of development economics in the 1990s, we reexamined development strategies and tried to elaborate them for the future.

We are concerned about the recent *market fundamentalist* view on development strategy, which appears to regard the liberalization of trade, investment and financial flows as necessary and sufficient conditions for economic development. Furthermore we are not comfortable with the so-called *Washington Consensus*, which reduces the role of government to macroeconomic stabilization and the provision of public goods. Less than successful structural adjustments in developing and transition economies strongly reflect these two lines of policy thought, so something is obviously wrong with their prescriptions.

In our view that something is neglect of the relationship between market and government. We have seen that the East Asian miracle was at least partially the result of the positive roles played by governments in the region. More generally, it is easy to see that the market cannot work without government involvement. With the recent trend towards globalization, and because there is no such a thing as a world government, collective action by governments or states is needed.

Markets and governments are complementary, particularly in the case economic development, although the precise mechanics of this remain unclear. To clarify this is our ultimate goal, and towards that end this book provides a conceptual framework with which to assess development strategies and policy issues in the context of individual and/or regional economies' historical and political-economic experiences. The complementarity depends on them.

With these perceptions above in mind, we focus on the role and significance of governments in economic development, examine the effects of initial conditions and the development policies of developing economies on their structure and performance in the new international economic environment, and discuss policy interventions to promote economic development. Through these efforts we hope to offer alternative orientations towards future development policies and strategies. This book constitutes an interim report of our trial-and-error efforts and more remains to be done, so we would appreciate readers' comments.

As part of the IDE research project we held international workshops at the IDE and Keio University and seminars at Hiroshima University, Tohoku University and Shimane Prefecture University during the period 1999–2002. The discussions there deepened and enriched our arguments. We thank all the discussants and participants in those workshops and seminars for their valuable inputs.

Akira Kohsaka

1
New Development Strategies: Beyond the Washington Consensus

Akira Kohsaka

The state and development strategy

Development economics became an independent field of study in the 1950s. Since then we have witnessed differing views on the relationship between (nation) states and their economic development (Meier and Rauch, 2000, p. 421). In the early days, states were optimistically presumed to be represented by social-welfare-maximizing governments, but then the pessimistic view emerged that states were one of the largest hindrances to development and served only to maximize the profits of selected interest groups, politicians and/or bureaucrats.

Subsequently, a more neutral view came to prevail: that, since the performance of states has been quite diverse, not all states hinder development and could in fact aid development given the right policies. The next question was how to build up states' capacity to formulate and implement the right policies. Also, even if we can hardly have social-welfare-maximizing government, intervention by the government with good will, information and competence could be justified for market-failure cases in resource allocation and for equity purposes in income distribution.[1]

On one hand, the view that markets, and not states, should play the central role in economic development, recently appears to have become mainstream. The so-called Washington Consensus is most representative of this.[2] According to this view, such concepts as developmentalist states and industrial policies run counter to economic development. As a matter of fact, even the East Asian countries, once praised for their successful industrial policies, experienced severe economic crises in the 1990s and their reputation of successful developmentalist states appeared to have plummeted.

This view that government failure, rather than markets, hinders development may be unquestionable to those who have witnessed development experiences in Sub-Saharan Africa. Generally, if there is government intervention, it creates opportunities for rent seeking. No matter how benevolent the intervention, the behaviour of the private sector is distorted by rent seeking.

1

Moreover, private interest groups are motivated to lobby the government to create rent-seeking opportunities. In other words, government intervention necessarily calls for corruption.

Nonetheless, on the other hand, the growth performance of the East Asian Miracle countries (World Bank, 1993) was spectacular enough for many economists to admit activist role for the state and/or government. East Asia is far from homogeneous, especially in terms of political stability, law and order, infrastructure development, independence of the bureaucracy and so on. The East Asian countries exhibit a wide spectrum of arrangements, which in turn is reflected in their diverse economic performances. However, they have clearly demonstrated that states do not always maximize the profits of only a few selected interest groups.

Why have some states tried to maximize public interests more than others? Is it true that political independence and/or bureaucratic expertise tend to support the success of developmentalism? Why do information exchanges and communication between developmentalist bureaucracies and the private sector appear to be immune from corruption? Even if there is some consensus on the kinds of policies to be implemented by governments, how can we motivate them to adopt those policies?

As discussed in the Preface, we are concerned about the recent *market fundamentalist* view on development strategy and uncomfortable with the Washington Consensus. In our view, markets and governments are complementary, particularly in the case of economic development. To illustrate this, in this book we assess development strategies and policy issues in the context of individual and/or regional economies' history and political-economic reality. The complementarity just mentioned may be conditional on these.

The book consists of four parts. Part I (Markets, Governments and Institutions) considers some fundamental aspects of economic development, including the interaction between markets, governments and institutions. Part II (Development Strategies under Globalization) deals with the impact of globalization on development strategy. Part III (Policy Reforms and the Asian Financial Crisis) examines the Asian financial crisis from political, country-specific and sectoral points of view. Finally, two case studies of transition economies are presented in Part IV (Transition to a Market Economy).

Markets, governments and institutions

The collapse of the socialist centrally planned economies and the stalemate of capitalist welfare states revealed that nation states, if they neglect the market mechanism, can fail to improve national welfare and sustain national economies. We should not, however, jump to the conclusion that we need the market, but not the state any more, or that national economies are no longer relevant to people's welfare. Why? First, the welfare state was born because the market could not bring about distributional equity and adequate public good provision. Second, as demonstrated by some *marginalized* economies, the loss of state functions has led to the collapse of national economies, severely damaging people's welfare.

Lessons from the twentieth century

Along with a large swing in development strategy thinking, we have learned valuable lessons from events in the twentieth century, one of the most important of which is the complementarity between state and market. With this complementarity in mind, in Chapter 2, Dani Rodrik tries to build a groundwork for designing new development strategies for the twenty-first century. Particularly, the author focuses on the role of public institutions, which is inadequately addressed by the Washington Consensus. Evaluation of the successes and failures of development experiences suggests the need for more diverse combinations of state and market in different sociopolitical contexts and different historical phases.

In order for markets to work properly, public institutions must play specific roles with the support of capable governments. Knowing that the present mixed economies have successfully developed in quite different ways over extended periods, Rodrik argues that market incentives need to be underpinned by strong public institutions, that the public institutions could function in diverse arrangements, and that the arrangements would and should be formed as fitted to local practices and needs over a due time horizon.

Strategies for reforms and regime changes

Institutional changes are evolutionary and take time, and economic development is not always a smooth and continuous process. Rather, it is often accompanied by discontinuities such as regime changes and reforms in response to changes in views on development strategies and changes in the national or international political and economic environments.

Why do some countries take a long time to adjust to new development strategies and environments while others do not? What is needed is a set of strategies tailored to the circumstance of individual countries. In Chapter 3, Jeffrey B. Nugent examines how, and under what conditions, we can reorient policy and institutional regimes. Particularly, the author highlights not only the initiation but also the sustenance of policy reforms by looking at countries' experiences of two types of reform: the introduction of property rights and outward-oriented reforms.

Nugent tentatively suggests that the initiation of serious economic reform is enhanced by a regime change and a significant crisis. But at the same time, he argues that sustenance of the reform requires the new regime to be legitimate and the crisis not to be too large, and that, in general, economies with greater income inequality, lower literacy and higher natural resource endowments tend to have greater difficulty sustaining their reforms.

The increasing roles of government under globalization

There is an optimistic view that the increasing integration of the world economy will equalize opportunities of people and help poor countries to catch up with the rich, in terms of capital and technology. If that is the case, then globalization will substitute for some functions of national governments and the role of the nation state will dwindle. Reviewing the outcome of past development strategies, in Chapter 4, Akira Kohsaka examines possible inter-actions between state and market under globalization.

Since the accumulation of knowledge and technology takes time, uncer-tainties and asymmetric information are unavoidable and their allocation and accumulation tend to be inadequate. Moreover, technological innovation, a driving force of globalization, has external effects in terms of economies of scale and agglomeration. If such cumulative effects serve to marginalize some developing countries, national welfare will decline and income differences across countries will widen. Hence Kohsaka argues that there is every reason for governments to provide these knowledge-related factors and/or mini-mize uncertainties and incomplete information through risk sharing and information provision, but little reason for globalization to substitute for government roles.

Furthermore, globalization can exacerbate market failures by magnifying the effect of uncertainties and incomplete information, as happened in the Asian economic crisis in 1997. Enhanced capital mobility has brought increasing risks for emerging market economies, and more volatile financial flows is apparently one of the costs of globalization. Minimizing these negative externalities can be partly handled by national governments, for example by introducing more flexible exchange rate regimes and strengthening bank supervision, but it can be better addressed collectively through international efforts to establish a new international financial architecture and new debt work-out schemes.

Development strategies under globalization

Inequality and globalization

Enhanced capital, labour, knowledge and other factor mobility under global-ization may not necessarily benefit developing economies. Agglomeration could be one of the reasons for this. Enhanced factor mobility may well deprive developing countries of the opportunity to catch up with developed economies. Globalized standards or codes of conduct could be another reason, when they are formulated under circumstances of imperfect and asymmetric information. They may narrow the scope for national policy discretion of developing economies.

When analyzing the possible negative effects of globalization on labour markets and poverty reduction in developing economies, Kaushik Basu

(Chapter 5) argues for international efforts to counter the erosion of global democracy. Labour standards used to be a purely national matter but have become less so recently. In particular, the globalization of labour standards is likely to be used to protect workers in developed economies at the cost of those in developing economies. Hence, globalization could result in the marginalization of certain nation states and of certain social groups within nation states. Moreover, the author argues that global income inequality is reaching an intolerable level due to globalization, so special international initiatives are needed to redress this and ensure stability in the future.

Alternative industrialization strategies in Southeast Asia

Since the 1990s the international economic environment has changed significantly. One feature is acceleration of global economic interdependence, where both trade and investment flows have grown far faster than output across developed and developing economies. Another feature is a tightening of international policy coordination. Particularly remarkable changes can be found in trade and investment policy, with international rules constraining the room for domestic discretion in these policy fields.

In Chapter 6, Fukunari Kimura discusses the effects of these changes on the industrialization strategies of developing countries. Because of the international division of labour by multinational corporations and the disciplinary power of the WTO and other international institutions, the author argues that the conventional approaches to industrialization, such as whether to pursue import substitution or export promotion, have become irrelevant.

According to Kimura, the strategy of protecting infant industries which was a major factor in the development of Korea and Taiwan in East Asia, is now not only economically ineffective but also infeasible in a political-economic sense. Rather, the Southeast Asian model, in which foreign investment is actively introduced and trade and investment liberalization is promoted within the WTO framework, should make a reference for the future industrialization of developing economies.

However, Kimura points out that the Southeast Asian industrialization does not offer unconditional success. In fact, the Southeast Asian countries have suffered from such problems as technology gaps between foreign and local firms, and distortions brought by policies to attract footloose foreign firms. Nonetheless, because of these common experiences shared by other developing economies, the Southeast Asian example can still provide better reference than the East Asian model.

Getting policy intervention right

While the roles of market and state (government) can be complementary in economic development and development strategies, the argument for positive roles of government, even in a limited way, has been frowned on recently. In Chapter 7, Koichi Ohno sheds new light on the role of government intervention in economic development. He focuses on such fields that the structural adjustment approach appears to neglect a priori or for a political economic reason. The structural adjustment approach has not met with visible success in Sub-Saharan Africa or Latin America, and that it has confronted unexpected difficulties in transition economies in Central and Eastern Europe.

Ohno first examines the characteristics of market structures that tend to make structural adjustment difficult. He argues that the market structure intended to be achieved by the approach is so distant from the existing one, that the structural adjustment turns out to be basically inconsistent or irrelevant. Next, focusing on East Asia, he reevaluates the role of trade policy during the East Asian Miracle period by empirically scrutinizing the comparative advantage of industries. It is shown that the Miracle was due not to the use of static comparative advantages but to the creation of dynamic advantages through policy intervention. Learning effects, agglomeration effects and technology policies provide rationales for policy intervention in a framework of the recent theory of endogenous growth.

Policy reforms and the Asian financial crisis

The onset and management of the crisis: a political view

At the onset of the Asian financial crisis, some observers pointed to crony capitalism as a fundamental cause of the crisis. However, if this was the case, how could the preceding economic miracle be explained? Meanwhile, country studies of the crisis have found that political factors were crucial in the onset and management of the crisis, particularly, among them is business–government relations.

In Chapter 8, Stephen Haggard discusses three political and institutional aspects of the crisis and its management in the four crisis-hit Asian economies, Indonesia, Korea, Malaysia and Thailand. These three aspects are said to constitute political institutions that had supported the East Asian Miracle. First, government decision making under different political regimes and its economic outcomes are examined. The different regimes are proved to affect the outcomes because political uncertainties play some key roles. Second, close business–government relationships are scrutinized. While market liberalization has been regarded as an alternative development strategy, it turned out to lead to the abuse of private power. Third, as part of crisis as well as globalization management, the possible replacement of the region's traditionally thin social safety net (the social welfare bargain) is discussed.

Admitting that these political institutions had been in transition even before the crisis accelerated its pace, however, the author is not certain how these institutions metamorphose themselves from good, old Asian types.

Regime transition in Korea: an economic view

Contrary to the view that regards the Asian economic crisis as one of external origins, e.g. as a capital-account crisis, country studies have pointed to structural defects and the vulnerability of the economy as fundamental causes of the crisis. In Chapter 9, Yoon Je Cho discusses how deep-rooted structural problems were the main reasons for the crisis in Korea.

Examining the asymmetric financial restructuring of the bank and non-bank sectors and the lack of coordination between monetary and supervisory policies, the author argues that the speed of Korea's transition to a more open and more liberalized economy was far greater than market players expected, and also outpaced institutional development, which would have made a crisis unavoidable sooner or later. He adds that the transition to a more liberalized economy will continue to be bumpy and unstable because of the lack of necessary institutions, a social safety net and an economic incentive structure in Korea.

How to tame hedge funds

It was not only in Korea that the speeding up of capital mobility was far greater than market players expected and also outpaced institutional development. The same also applies to the world economy and the international capital market. Indeed, one could say that the *Asian flu and the Russian virus* (Forbes, 2000) was also unavoidable.

One example is the call for regulating hedge funds, whose speculative activities are often held responsible for the Asian financial crisis. In Chapter 10, Barry Eichengreen examines the role of hedge funds in international financial markets, with a particular focus on market manipulation and systemic stability. While being sceptical about their possible market manipulation, the author shares the concern about systemic stability and scrutinizes the pros and cons of alternative regulations on these funds. Policy options for emerging markets include higher margin requirements, entry and exit taxes on short round-trip transactions, and more flexible exchange rates, although all are far from perfect. The author also argues that regulations on hedge funds' counterparties, i.e. those on international banks' exposures to hedge funds, are more effective.

Globalization goes hand in hand with financial integration. Both phenomena result in, as well as result from, the growing number of high-income investors seeking to diversify their portfolios to include high-risk, high-return investments. As far as we live with this trend, the author suggests that emerging markets should protect themselves by adopting more flexible exchange rates and some less costly capital control measures such as those in Chile and Malaysia. He also advocates international collaboration in collecting information on bank exposures in investor countries.

Transition to a market economy

So far our focus on development strategies has been restricted to national economies with functioning market systems, albeit imperfect ones. Economic reforms in former centrally planned, transition economies have brought new challenges to our thinking on appropriate development strategies.

The policy advice given to transition economies by the IMF and other international financial institutions, was based on the experiences of developing economies such as those in Latin America. It is not difficult, however, to see that a straightforward application of the structural adjustment approach would raise serious problems. There are two reasons why transition economies face difficulties that have not been experienced by ordinary developing economies. First, in Eastern Europe many of the transition economies were once part of the Council for Mutual Economic Assistance (CMEA, or Comecon). The collapse of the CMEA in 1991 meant that they were abruptly thrown into the world of completely different comparative advantage. This shock, particularly to external sectors, would be unfathomably large and far beyond the difficulties encountered by the developing countries.

Second, the transition economies have had to build their economic and institutional systems from scratch. The reforms needed for transition to a market economy are not partial, but involve revolutionary changes to the entire institutional framework, including a new system of ownership based on private property rights, a new corporate system based on privatization, a new financial system to replace the *monobank*, and a new fiscal and social security system to replace the government–state enterprise relationship based on the 'soft budget' principle.

Building a market system from scratch

While a soft budget relationship between the government and state enterprises and/or repression of the financial system can be found in some capitalist developing countries, the latter nonetheless function on the basis of private property rights and decentralized decision making. The difference between developing economies under a capitalist regime and former planned economies is therefore not simply a matter of degree. For transition economies there is an enormous gap between the start and the goal of economic reforms, and therefore far more extensive reforms are needed than in developing economies.

In Chapter 11, Koji Nishikimi examines the difficulties involved in building a market system for agriculture in the case study of wheat production in Kazakhstan. The collapse of the centrally planned economy, through the collapse of the state credit system for financing and input materials, destroyed production linkages, and brought about an extreme output decline. The government failed to form an alternative production linkage, but the private sector has started institutional arrangements through trial-and-error processes of contractual and organizational reforms among farmers and distributors. The author's case study of Kazakhstan shows that the mere existence of exchanges does not necessarily enable the market system to function, and that market systems are barely supported by a complex combination of institutions and a network of trust between market participants.

Strategic choices for China and Vietnam

In contrast to the ex-CMEA economies, China and Vietnam have retained significant state-owned sectors since they began their transition to a market economy. As it turned out, it has not been a mistake to retain some control over the markets so far. Is it sustainable, though? Can they continue to progress by maintaining the strategies adopted in the 1990s even at the turn of the century?

In Chapter 12, Dwight H. Perkins argues that sooner or later the governments of the two countries will have to face serious decisions about the future of their economic systems and their role in the economy, but so far Vietnam, and to a lesser extent China, have appeared unwilling to minimize the role of government in ownership and control. They may refer to the successes of government intervention in Japan, Korea and Taiwan in the 1960s and 1970s, but the world has changed substantially since then, and the author argues that China and Vietnam are in sharp contrast to Japan, Korea and Taiwan in some respects on the national or domestic front.

First, nowadays there is a wide range of international codes of conduct that impose restrictions on government intervention. If China and Vietnam are to reap the fruits of globalization they must follow the new rules of the game in the world economy. Second, in order for government intervention to be successful, decision makers must be free from political and rent-seeking pressures, which may not the case in either country. Hence Perkins concludes that the two countries have little choice but to orient themselves towards more openness and less government intervention. However, he warns that constructing a new system will take at least a generation even if there is a strong will for reform, and that the transition to a market economy will not be smooth, but full of possible setbacks due to political, economic and other elements.

Concluding remarks

The argument that it is not the state but the market mechanism that should lead economic development has appeared to become mainstream. The collapse of centrally planned economies seemed to prove this. However, if we went one step further and said that the state was unnecessary for economic development we would have gone too far. Rather, we should consider how to establish a good division of labour between the state and the market. In order for the market to function effectively, it must be integrated properly and systematically. This requires not only good policies but also good institutional designs.

Designing institutions is a complicated job. While the basic unit for institutions would be a state, states are too diverse to have one-size-fits-all institutions. Moreover, we need to grasp the mechanisms of institutional change. Institutional change takes time. One reason for this is that it involves changes in income distribution among participants, and those who stand to lose will naturally resist the change. If this resistance becomes extreme, the resulting political instability will hinder any change. Meanwhile, the existing institutions may not be supported by the majority of people, and while the latter may demand reform they may be too ill-organized to bring it about. If the stalemate can be broken by effective leadership, institutional innovation can accelerate.

Institutions are constituted in a complex way as a system of mutually complementary subinstitutions. Thus, in the case of institutional reforms, we do not know a correct and consistent sequencing of introducing subinstitutions.

Apart from official institutions, unofficial institutions could play a significant role. Particularly in developing economies, where official institutions tend to be underdeveloped, custom-based unofficial institutions can be utilized at least as temporary substitutes for official ones. Not only national and local governments, but even international organizations are subject to institutional development. Finally, in the interest of development the market needs a strong and competent state, and not an arbitrary and corrupt one.

Notes

1. Here we include activities that are of public-good nature in the broad sense of non-rivalry and non-excludability, such as education, public health, national security, environmental protection and so on.
2. This is discussed in more detail in Chapters 2 and 3.

References

Forbes, Kristin (2000) 'The Asian Flu and Russian Virus: Firm-level Evidence on How Crises are Transmitted Internationally', *NBER Working Paper*, No. 7807, July.

Meier, Gerald M. and James E. Rauch (2000) *Leading Issues in Economic Development*, 7th edition (New York, Oxford University Press).

World Bank (1993) *The East Asian Miracle* (New York, Oxford University Press).

Part I

Markets, Governments and Institutions

2

Development Strategies for the Twenty-First Century[1]

Dani Rodrik

Introduction

The mixed economy is possibly the most valuable heritage that the twentieth century has bequeathed to the twenty-first in the realm of economic policy. The nineteenth century discovered capitalism. The twentieth century learned how to tame it and render it more productive by supplying the institutional ingredients needed for a self-sustaining market economy: central banking, stabilizing fiscal policy, antitrust legislation and regulation, social insurance and political democracy. It was during the twentieth century that these elements of the mixed economy took root in today's advanced industrial countries. The simple idea that markets and the state are complements – recognized in practice if not always in principle – enabled the unprecedented prosperity experienced by the United States, Western Europe and parts of East Asia during the second half of the century.

The truism that private initiative and collective action are both required for economic success was recognized rather late by developing countries. Most of them became independent in the 1950s and 1960s, and the apparently successful example of the Soviet Union and the antimarket ideology of national governing elites resulted in heavily statecentric development strategies. In Latin America, where countries had long been independent, the dominant 'structuralist' view was that market incentives would fail to elicit much of a supply response. Throughout the developing world the private sector was regarded with scepticism and private initiatives were severely circumscribed.

These views underwent a radical transformation during the 1980s under the joint influence of a protracted debt crisis and the teachings of the Bretton Woods institutions. The 'Washington Consensus', which emphasizes privatization, deregulation and trade liberalization, was embraced enthusiastically by policy makers in Latin America and postsocialist Eastern Europe. The reception was more guarded and cautious in Africa and Asia, but there too policies took a decided swing towards markets. These market-oriented

13

reforms at first paid very little attention to institutions and the complementarity between the private and public spheres of the economy. The
role assigned to the government did not go beyond that of maintaining
macroeconomic stability and providing education. The priority was on
rolling back the state, not on making it more effective.

A more balanced view began to emerge during the closing years of
the twentieth century as the Washington Consensus failed to deliver its
promises. The talk in Washington turned towards 'second-generation
reforms', 'governance' and 'reinvigorating the state's capability'.[2] Three
developments added fuel to the discontent about the orthodoxy. The first of
these was the dismal failure in Russia of price reform and privatization in
the absence of a supportive legal, regulatory and political apparatus. The
second was the widespread dissatisfaction with market-oriented reforms in
Latin America and the growing realization that these reforms had paid too
little attention to social insurance and safety nets. The third and most
recent was the Asian financial crisis, which revealed the danger of allowing
financial liberalization to run ahead of adequate regulation.

So we entered the twenty-first century with a better understanding of the
complementarity between markets and the state, and a greater appreciation
of the virtues of the mixed economy. That is the good news. The bad news is
that the operational implications of this for the design of development
strategy are not very clear. There are still plenty of opportunities for
renewed mischief on the policy front. As will be argued below, the state and
the market can be combined in different ways. There are many different
models of the mixed economy, and the major challenge facing developing
nations is to fashion their own particular versions.

This Chapter reviews some of the principles that should guide this quest,
beginning with a brief history of the growth performance of developing
countries since the Second World War. Because the reasons for disappointing
growth performances since the late 1970s are intricately linked with current
policy prescriptions, I shall present my own interpretation of what went
wrong. This interpretation highlights the importance of domestic institutions
and downplays the role of microeconomic factors (including trade policy)
in the post-1980 growth collapse.

The third section provides, a more detailed analysis of market-supporting
institutions. It discusses five functions that public institutions must serve
if markets are to work adequately: protection of property rights, market regulation, macroeconomic stabilization, social insurance and conflict management. However that section and the next emphasize that in principle a large
variety of institutional set-ups can fulfil these functions. We need to be sceptical
of the notion that a specific institution in a country (say, the United States)
is the type that is most compatible with a well-functioning market
economy. It is argued in the fifth section that partial and gradual reforms
have often worked better because reform programmes that are sensitive to

institutional preconditions are more likely to be successful than those which assume that new institutions can be erected wholesale overnight.

The sixth section considers some implications for international governance. A key conclusion is that international rules and International Financial Institutions (IFI) conditionality have to leave room for development policies that diverge from the dominant orthodoxies of the day. The seventh section evaluates the priority that openness to trade and capital flows should receive in the design of development strategies. It argues that trade and capital flows are important insofar as they provide developing countries with access to cheaper capital goods. But the links between a country's opening up to trade and capital flows and its subsequent growth are weak, uncertain and mediated through domestic institutions. The final section provides some concluding thoughts.

Some lessons from recent economic history[3]

In the postwar period, many developing countries experienced unprecedented rates of economic growth until the late 1970s. Until the first oil shock more than 40 of them grew at rates that exceeded 2.5 per cent per capita per annum. At this rate of growth, incomes would have doubled every 28 years or less – that is, every generation. The list of countries with this enviable record goes far beyond the usual handful of East Asian examples and covers all parts of the globe: 12 countries in South America, six in the Middle East and North Africa, and 15 in Sub-Saharan Africa (Rodrik, 1999a, table 4.1). There can be little doubt that economic growth led to substantial improvements in the living conditions of the vast majority of households in these countries.

The role of import substitution policies

Most of the countries that did well in this period followed import-substitution policies, which spurred growth and created protected and therefore profitable home markets in which domestic entrepreneurs could invest. Contrary to conventional wisdom the growth driven by import substitution did not produce huge inefficiencies on an economy-wide scale. In fact the productivity performance of many Latin American and Middle Eastern countries was, in comparative perspective, exemplary (ibid., table 4.2). In 1960–73 countries such as Brazil, the Dominican Republic and Ecuador in Latin America, Iran, Morocco and Tunisia in the Middle East, and Côte d'Ivoire and Kenya in Africa all experienced more rapid total factor productivity (TFP) growth than any of the East Asian countries (with the possible exception of Hong Kong, for which comparable data are not available). Mexico, Bolivia, Panama, Egypt, Algeria, Tanzania and Zaire experienced higher TFP growth than all but Taiwan. Productivity growth estimates of this type are not without problems, and one can quibble with the methodologies employed.

Nevertheless, there is little reason to believe that the estimates by Collins and Bosworth (1996), from which the above claims are drawn, are seriously biased in the way they rank different regions.

Hence, as a strategy of industrialization that was intended to increase domestic investment and enhance productivity, import substitution apparently worked very well in a very broad range of countries until at least the mid 1970s. Despite its problems, import substitution achieved a more than respectable record. Had the world come to an end in 1973, the strategy would not have acquired its dismal reputation, nor would East Asia have deserved its 'miracle' appellation.

Collapse of growth

After the oil shock of 1973, however, things began to look very different. The median growth rate for all developing countries fell from 2.6 per cent in 1960–73 to 0.9 per cent in 1973–84 and 0.8 per cent in 1984–94. The dispersion in performance across developing countries increased sharply, with the coefficient of variation for national growth rates increasing threefold after 1973 (Rodrik, 1999a, table 4.3). The Middle East and Latin America, which had led the developing world in TFP growth prior to 1973, not only fell behind but on average actually experienced negative TFP growth thereafter. TFP growth also turned negative in Sub-Saharan Africa, where productivity growth had been undistinguished but still positive. Only East Asia held its own in TFP growth, while South Asia actually improved its performance.

This was not the result of the 'exhaustion' of import-substitution policies, whatever that term actually means. Rather, the common timing implicates the turbulence experienced in the world economy after 1973 – the abandonment of the Bretton Woods system of fixed exchange rates, two major oil shocks, various other commodity boom-and-bust cycles, plus the Volcker interest rate shock of the early 1980s. Moreover, the fact that some of the most ardent followers of import substitution policies in South Asia (particularly India and Pakistan) managed either to maintain their growth rates after 1973 (Pakistan) or to increase them (India) also suggests that more than just import substitution was involved.

The actual story is straightforward. The main reason for the economic collapse was the inability to adjust macroeconomic policies appropriately in the wake of these external shocks. Macroeconomic maladjustment gave rise to a range of syndromes associated with macroeconomic instability – high or repressed inflation, scarcity of foreign exchange and large black market premia, external payments imbalances and debt crises – which greatly magnified the real costs of the shocks. Indeed there was a strong association between inflation and black market premia and the magnitude of the economic collapse experienced in different countries. The countries that suffered most were those with the largest increases in inflation and black market premia for foreign currency (ibid., fig. 4.1). The culprits were poor monetary and fiscal policies and inadequate adjustments in exchange rate policy, sometimes aggravated by the shortsighted policies of creditors and the Bretton Woods institutions. Trade and industrial policies had very little to do with bringing on the crisis.

Why were some countries quicker to adjust their macroeconomic policies than others? The deeper determinants of growth performance since the 1970s are rooted in the ability of domestic institutions to manage the distributional conflicts triggered by the external shocks of the period. Think of an economy that is suddenly and unexpectedly confronted with a drop in the price of its main export (or a sudden reversal of capital flows). The textbook prescription for this economy is a combination of expenditure-switching and expenditure-reducing policies – that is, devaluation and fiscal retrenchment. But the precise manner in which these policy changes are administered can have significant distributional implications. Should the devaluation be accompanied by wage controls? Should import tariffs be raised? Should the fiscal retrenchment take place through spending cuts or tax increases? If spending is to be cut, which types of expenditure should bear the brunt of the cuts? Should interest rates be raised to rein in private spending as well?

In general, macroeconomic theory does not have a clear preference among the available options. But since each of the options has predictable distributional consequences, in practice much depends on the severity of the social conflicts that lie beneath the surface. If the appropriate adjustments can be undertaken without an outbreak of distributional conflict or upsetting prevailing social bargains, the shock can be managed with few long-lasting effects on the economy. If they cannot, the economy can be paralyzed for years as inadequate adjustment condemns the country to foreign exchange bottlenecks, import compression, debt crises and bouts of high inflation. Furthermore, deep social divisions provide an incentive for governments to delay needed adjustments and take on excessive levels of foreign debt in the expectation that other social groups can be made to pay for the eventual costs.

In short, social conflicts and their management are key determinants of whether the effects of external shocks are transmitted to economic performance. Societies with deep social cleavages and poor institutions for conflict management tend not to be very good at handling shocks. In such societies the economic costs of exogenous shocks – such as a deterioration in the terms of trade – are magnified by the distributional conflicts that are triggered. Such conflicts diminish the productivity with which a society's resources are utilized by delaying necessary adjustments in fiscal policies and key relative prices (such as the real exchange rate or real wages) and by diverting activities away from the productive and entrepreneurial spheres. These is cross-national evidence to support this argument: macroeconomic disequilibrium and growth collapse have been more likely in countries with high degrees of income inequality and ethno-linguistic fragmentation, and less likely in countries with democratic institutions or high-quality public institutions (Rodrik, 1999b).

Lessons from the Asian financial crisis

The same logic played out in the Asian financial crisis. One lesson from the crisis is that international capital markets do a poor job of discriminating between good and bad risks. It is hard to believe that there was much collective rationality in investor behaviour prior to and during the crisis: financial markets got it badly wrong either in 1996 when they poured money into the region, or in 1997 when they pulled back *en masse*. The implication is that excessive reliance on liquid, short-term capital (as did all of the three worst affected countries) is a dangerous strategy.

Second, the crisis has demonstrated that trade orientation *per se* has very little to do with the propensity to be hit with severe liquidity problems. The Asian economies most affected by the reversal of capital flows were among the most outward-oriented economies in the world, routinely pointed out as examples for other countries to follow. The determinants of the crisis – as in the debt crisis of 1982 and the Mexican peso crisis of 1994 – were financial and macroeconomic. Trade and industrial policies were, at best, secondary.[4]

A third lesson from the crisis is that domestic conflict-management institutions are crucial for containing the adverse economic consequences of an initial shock. At the onset of the crisis, it seemed as though authoritarian governments would have a better chance of preventing the social explosions that the crisis had the potential to create, while 'messy' democracies would suffer. In fact, many critics of Western-style liberal democracy viewed the Thai and Korean troubles in the early stages of the crisis – and Indonesia's apparent resolve – as illustrations of the economic superiority of governments based on so-called 'Asian values'. The outcome was quite the opposite. Indonesia, an ethnically divided society ruled by an autocracy, eventually descended into chaos. South Korea and Thailand's democratic institutions, and their practices of consultation and cooperation among social partners, proved much more adept at generating the requisite policy adjustments. This recent experience has demonstrated once again the important part that can be played by institutions, and democratic institutions in particular, in dealing with external shocks.

While democratic institutions were a relatively recent phenomenon in Thailand and Korea, they were able to help these two countries adjust to the crisis in a number of ways. First, they facilitated a smooth transfer of power from a discredited set of politicians to a new group of government leaders. Second, democracy imposed the mechanisms of participation, consultation and bargaining, enabling policy makers to fashion the consensus needed to undertake the necessary policy adjustments. Third, because democracy provided institutionalized mechanisms for people to give voice to their concerns, the Korean and Thai institutions obviated the need for riots, protests and other disruptive actions by affected groups, as well as lowering the support for such behaviour by other groups in society.

Some conclusions

Many of the lessons that the development community has internalized from recent economic history are in need of revision. In my view the correct interpretation goes something as follows.

First, import substitution worked rather well for about two decades. It led to increased investment and brought unprecedented economic growth to scores of countries in Latin America, the Middle East and North Africa, and even to some in Sub-Saharan Africa. Second, when the economies of these same countries began to collapse in the second half of the 1970s, this had very little to do with import substitution policies *per se*, or to the extent of government intervention. The countries that weathered the storm were those whose governments rapidly and decisively made appropriate macroeconomic adjustments (in the areas of fiscal, monetary and exchange rate policy). Third, and more fundamentally, the success of these macroeconomic adjustments was linked to deeper social determinants. It was the ability to manage the domestic social conflicts triggered by the turbulence of the world economy during the 1970s that made the difference between continued growth and economic collapse. Countries with deeper social divisions and weaker institutions (particularly of conflict management) experienced greater economic deterioration in response to the external shocks of the 1970s.

Taken together, these points provide an interpretation of recent economic history that differs from much current thinking. By emphasizing the importance of social conflicts and institutions – at the expense of trade strategy and industrial policies – they also offer a quite different perspective on development policy. If I am right, the main difference between Latin America, say, and East Asia was not that the former remained closed and isolated while the latter integrated itself into the world economy. Rather, the main difference was that the former did a much worse job of dealing with the turbulence emanating from the world economy. The countries that got into trouble were those which could not manage openness, not those which were insufficiently open.

A taxonomy of market-substituting public institutions[5]

Institutions do not figure prominently in the training of economists. The standard Arrow–Debreu model, with a full set of complete and contingent markets extending indefinitely into the future, seems to require no assistance from non-market institutions. But of course, this is quite misleading even in the context of that model. The standard model assumes a well-defined set of property rights. It also assumes that contracts are signed with no fear that they will be revoked when this suits one of the parties. So, in the background there exist institutions that establish and protect property rights and enforce contracts. There has to be a system of laws and courts to make even 'perfect' markets function.

In turn, laws have to be written and to be backed up by the use of sanctioned force. This implies a legislator and a police force. The legislator's authority may derive from religion, family lineage or access to superior violence, but in each case she or he needs to ensure that her or his subjects are provided with the right mix of 'ideology' (a belief system) and the threat of violence to forestall rebellion from below. Or the authority may derive from the legitimacy provided by popular support, in which case she or he needs to be responsive to the voters' needs. In either case, we have the beginnings of a governmental structure that goes well beyond the narrow needs of the market.

One implication of all this is that the market economy is necessarily embedded in a set of non-market institutions. Another is that not all of these institutions are there first and foremost to serve the needs of the market economy, even if their presence is required by the internal logic of private property and contract enforcement. The fact that a governance structure is needed to ensure that markets can do their work does not imply that the governance structure serves only that end. Non-market institutions sometimes produce outcomes that are socially undesirable, such as the use of public office for private gain. They may also produce outcomes that restrict the free play of market forces in pursuit of a larger goal, such as social stability and cohesion.

The rest of this section discusses five market-supporting institutions: property rights, regulatory institutions, institutions for macroeconomic stabilization, institutions for social insurance and institutions of conflict management.

Property rights

In theory, it is possible to envisage a thriving socialist market economy, as established by the famous debates of the 1920s. But today's prosperous economies have all been built on the basis of private property. As North and Thomas (1973), North and Weingast (1989) and many others have argued, the establishment of secure and stable property rights have been a key element in the rise of the West and the onset of modern economic growth. Entrepreneurs do not have an incentive to accumulate and innovate unless they have adequate control over the returns from the assets that are thereby produced or improved.

Note that the key word here is 'control' rather than 'ownership'. Formal property rights do not count for much if they do not confer control rights. By the same token, sufficiently strong control rights can work adequately even in the absence of formal property rights. Present-day Russia represents a case where shareholders have property rights but often lack effective control over enterprises. Town and village enterprises (TVEs) in China are an example where control rights have spurred entrepreneurial activity despite the absence of clearly defined property rights. As these instances illustrate, the establishment of property rights is rarely a matter of just passing a piece of legislation. Legislation in itself is neither necessary nor sufficient for the provision of secure control rights. In practice, control rights are upheld by a combination of legislation, private enforcement, and custom and tradition. They may be distributed more narrowly or more diffusely than property rights. Stakeholders can matter as much as shareholders.

Moreover, property rights are rarely absolute, even when set formally in the law. The right to keep my neighbours out of my orchard does not normally extend to my right to shoot them if they actually enter it. Other laws or norms – such as those against murder – may trump property rights. Each society decides for itself the scope of allowable property rights and the acceptable restrictions on their exercise. Intellectual property rights are protected assiduously in the United States and most advanced societies, but not in many developing countries. On the other hand, zoning and environmental legislation restricts the ability of households and enterprises in rich countries to do as they please with their property to a much greater extent than is the case in developing countries. All societies recognize that private property rights should be curbed if doing so will serve a greater public purpose. It is the definition of what constitutes 'greater public purpose' that varies.

Regulatory institutions

Markets fail when participants engage in fraudulent or anticompetitive behaviour, when transaction costs prevent the internalization of technological and other non-pecuniary externalities, and when incomplete information results in moral hazard and adverse selection. Economists recognize this and have developed the necessary analytical tools to think systematically about their consequences and possible remedies. Theories of second best, imperfect competition, agency, mechanism design and many others offer an almost embarrassing choice of regulatory instruments to counter market failures, but theories of political economy and public choice offer cautions against unqualified reliance on these instruments.

In practice, every successful market economy is overseen by a panoply of regulatory institutions that regulate conduct in goods, services, labour, assets, and financial markets. A few acronyms from the United States are sufficient to give a sense of the range of institutions involved: FTC, FDIC, FCC, FAA, OSHA, SEC, EPA and so on. In fact the freer the markets the greater the burden on the regulatory institutions. It is no coincidence that the United States has the world's freest markets as well its toughest antitrust enforcement. It is hard to envisage in any country other than the United States that a hugely successful high-tech company such as Microsoft could be dragged through the courts for alleged anticompetitive practices. The lesson that market freedom requires regulatory vigilance has recently been driven home by the experience in East Asia. In South Korea and Thailand, as in so many other developing countries, financial liberalization and capital-account opening led to financial crisis precisely because there was inadequate prudential regulation and supervision.[6]

It is important to recognize that regulatory institutions may need to be extended beyond the standard list that covers antitrust regulation, financial supervision, securities regulation and a few others. This is especially true in developing countries where market failures may be more pervasive and the requisite market regulations more extensive. Recent models of coordination failure and capital market imperfections[7] make it clear that strategic government intervention may often be required to get out of low-level traps and elicit desirable private investment responses. The experience of South Korea and Taiwan in the 1960s and 1970s can be interpreted in that light. The extensive subsidization and government-led coordination of private investment in these two economies played a crucial role in setting the stage for self-sustaining growth (Rodrik, 1995). It is clear that many other countries have tried and failed to replicate these institutional arrangements. And even South Korea may have taken a good thing too far by maintaining the cozy institutional linkages between the government and the *chaebols* well into the 1990s, at which point they become dysfunctional. Once again, the lesson is that desirable institutional arrangements vary, and that they vary not only across countries but also within countries over time.

Institutions for macroeconomic stabilization

Since the time of Keynes, we have come to understand that capitalist economies are not necessarily self-stabilizing. Keynes and his followers worried about shortfalls in aggregate demand and the resulting unemployment. More recent views of macroeconomic instability stress the inherent instability of financial markets and the transmission of this instability to the real economy. All advanced economies have set up fiscal and monetary institutions that perform stabilizing functions, having learned the hard way about the consequences of not having them. Probably most important of these institutions is a lender of last resort – typically the central bank – to guard against self-fulfilling banking crises.

There is a strong current within macroeconomic thought – represented in its theoretically most sophisticated version by the real business cycle (RBC) approach – that disputes the possibility or effectiveness of stabilizing the macroeconomy through monetary and fiscal policies. There is also a sense in policy circles, particularly in Latin America, that fiscal and monetary institutions – as currently configured – have added to macroeconomic instability by following procyclical rather than anticyclical policies (Hausmann and Gavin, 1996). These developments have spurred the trend towards central bank independence and opened a new debate on the need for more robust fiscal institutions.

Some countries (Argentina being the most significant) have abandoned the idea of a domestic lender of last resort and replaced their central bank with a currency board. Argentina's thinking is that having a central bank that can *occasionally* stabilize the economy is not worth running the risk that it will *mostly* destabilize it. Argentine history provides plenty of reasons to think that this is not a bad bet. But can the same be said for Mexico or Brazil, or for that matter Turkey or Indonesia? A substantial real depreciation of the Indian rupee, engineered via nominal devaluations, was a key ingredient of India's superlative economic performance during the 1990s. What may work for Argentina may not work for the others. The debate on currency boards and dollarization illustrates the obvious but occasionally neglected fact that the institutions needed by a country are not independent of that country's history.

Institutions for social insurance

A modern market economy is one in which change is constant and where idiosyncratic risk (that is, specific to individuals) to incomes and employment is pervasive. Modern economic growth entails a transition from a static economy to a dynamic one in which the tasks that workers perform are in constant evolution and there are frequent movements up and down the income scale. One of the liberating effects of a dynamic market economy is that it frees individuals from their traditional entanglements – the kin group, the church, the village hierarchy. The downside is that it uproots them from traditional support systems and risk-sharing institutions. Gift exchanges, the fiesta and kinship ties – to cite just a few of the social arrangements for equalizing the distribution of resources in traditional societies – lose much of their social insurance function. And the risks that have to be insured against become much more difficult to manage in the traditional manner as markets spread.

The huge expansion of publicly provided social insurance programmes during the twentieth century was one of the most remarkable features of the evolution of advanced market economies. In the United States, it was the trauma of the Great Depression that paved the way for major institutional innovations in this area: social security, unemployment compensation, public works, public ownership, deposit insurance and legislation that favoured unions (see Bordo *et al.*, 1998, p. 6). As Jacoby (1998) notes, prior to the Great Depression the middle classes were generally able to self-insure or buy insurance from private intermediaries. As these private forms of insurance collapsed, the middle classes threw their considerable political weight behind the extension of social insurance and the creation of what would later be called the welfare state. In some European countries the seeds of the welfare state were sown at the tail end of the nineteenth century. But the striking expansion of social insurance programmes, particularly in the smaller economies that were most open to foreign trade, was a post-Second World War phenomenon (Rodrik, 1998a). Despite the considerable political backlash against the welfare state since the 1980s, neither the United States nor Europe has significantly scaled back these programmes.

Social insurance need not always take the form of transfer programmes funded by fiscal resources. In the East Asian model, represented well by the Japanese case, social insurance is provided through a combination of enterprise practices (such as lifetime employment and enterprise-provided social benefits), sheltered and regulated sectors (small family-owned shops) and an incremental approach to liberalization and external opening. Certain aspects of Japanese society that seem inefficient to outside observers – such as the preference for small-scale retail shops and extensive regulation of product markets – can be viewed as substitutes for the transfer programmes that would otherwise have to be provided (as in most European countries) by a welfare state. Such complementarities among the various institutional arrangements in a society imply that it is very difficult to alter national systems in a piecemeal fashion. One cannot (and should not) ask the Japanese to get rid of their lifetime employment practice or inefficient retail arrangements without ensuring that alternative safety nets are in place. Another implication is that substantial institutional changes come only in the aftermath of large dislocations, such as those created by the Great Depression and the Second World War.

Social insurance legitimizes a market economy by rendering it compatible with social stability and social cohesion. At the same time, the welfare states in Western Europe and the United States have engendered a number of increasingly apparent economic and social costs – mounting fiscal outlays, an 'entitlement' culture and long-term unemployment. Partly because of this, those developing countries which adopted a market-oriented approach following the debt crisis of the 1980s, such as those in Latin America, have paid insufficient attention to the creation of institutions of social insurance, thus provoking economic insecurity and a backlash against the reforms. How these countries will maintain social cohesion in the face of large inequalities and volatile outcomes, both of which are aggravated by the growing reliance on market forces, is a question without an obvious answer at the moment. But if Latin America and the other developing regions are to follow a different social insurance path than that followed by Europe or North America, they will have to develop their own means of overcoming the tension between market forces and the yearning for economic security.

Institutions of conflict management

Societies differ in their cleavages. Some are made up of an ethnically and linguistically homogeneous population marked by a relatively egalitarian distribution of resources. Others are characterized by deep cleavages along ethnic or income lines. These divisions hamper social cooperation and prevent the undertaking of mutually beneficial projects. Social conflict is harmful both because it diverts resources from economically productive activities and because it discourages such activities by the uncertainty it generates. Economists have used models of social conflict to shed light on questions such as the following. Why do governments delay stabilization when this imposes costs on all groups (Alesina and Drazen, 1991)? Why do countries that are rich in natural resources often do worse than countries that have few (Tornell and Lane, 1999)? Why do external shocks often lead to protracted economic crises that are out of proportion to the direct costs of the shocks themselves (Rodrik, 1999b)?

All of these can be thought of as instances of coordination failure, in which social factions fail to act together to bring about mutually beneficial outcomes. Healthy societies have a range of institutions that reduce the likelihood of such colossal coordination failures. The rule of law, a high-quality judiciary, representative political institutions, free elections, independent trade unions, social partnerships, institutionalized representation of minority groups and social insurance are examples of such institutions. What makes these arrangements function as institutions of conflict management is that they entail a double 'commitment technology': they warn the potential winners of social conflict that their gains will be limited, and they assure the potential losers that they will not suffer expropriation. They tend to increase the incentive for social groups to cooperate by reducing the payoff to socially uncooperative strategies.

What role for institutional diversity?

As shown in the preceding section, a market economy relies on a wide array of non-market institutions that perform regulatory, stabilizing and legitimizing functions. Once these institutions are accepted as part and parcel of a market-based economy the traditional dichotomies between market and state or *laissez faire* and intervention begin to make less sense. These are not competing ways of organizing a society's economic affairs; they are complementary elements that render the system sustainable. Every well-functioning market economy is a mix of state and market, *laissez faire* and intervention.

Another implication of the discussion in the previous section is that the institutional basis for a market economy is not uniquely determined. Formally, there is no single mapping between the market and the set of non-market institutions required to sustain it. This is reflected in the wide variety of regulatory, stabilizing and legitimizing institutions in today's advanced industrial societies. The American style of capitalism is very different from the Japanese style of capitalism, and both differ from the European style.

And even within Europe there are large differences between the institutional arrangements in, say, Sweden and Germany.

It is a common error to suppose that one set of institutional arrangements must dominate the others in terms of overall performance. Hence the fads of recent decades: because of its low unemployment, high growth and thriving culture, Europe was the continent to emulate throughout much of the 1970s; during the trade-conscious 1980s Japan became the exemplar of choice; and the 1990s were the decade of US-style freewheeling capitalism. It is anybody's guess which set of countries will capture the imagination if and when a substantial correction hits the US stock market.[8]

The point about institutional diversity in fact has a more fundamental implication. The institutional arrangements that are operating today, varied as they are, themselves constitute a subset of the full range of institutional possibilities. This is a point that has been forcefully and usefully argued by Unger (1998). There is no reason to suppose that modern societies have already managed to exhaust all the useful institutional variations that could underpin a healthy and vibrant economy. Even if we accept that market-based economies require certain types of institution, as listed in the previous section, 'such imperatives do not select from a closed list of institutional possibilities. The possibilities do not come in the form of indivisible systems, standing or falling together. There are always alternative sets of arrangements capable of meeting the same practical tests' (ibid., pp. 24–5). We need to maintain a healthy scepticism towards the idea that a specific type of institution – a particular mode of corporate governance, social security system or labour market legislation, for example – is the only one that is compatible with a well-functioning market economy.

Market incentives and institutions

It is individual initiative that ultimately accounts for all economic progress. The market system is unparalleled in its efficacy at directing individual effort towards the goal of material advancement of society. Early thinking on development policy, as mentioned in the introduction to this chapter, did not take sufficient account of this. Structuralists downplayed market incentives because they viewed them as ineffective in the presence of pervasive supply and other structural constraints. Socialists downplayed market incentives because they viewed them as inconsistent with the attainment of equity and other social goals.

Both positions have proved to be incorrect. Farmers, entrepreneurs and investors all over the world, regardless of income and education, have shown themselves to be quite responsive to price incentives. In South Korea and Taiwan, the private sector's strong response to the tax and credit incentives that were put in place during the early 1960s was a crucial factor in these countries' growth miracle (Rodrik, 1995). In China, the dual-track system that allowed farmers to sell their crops in free markets (once their quota obligations were fulfilled) resulted in a large increase in agricultural output and sparked the high growth that has continued to this day. After India reformed its cumbersome industrial licensing system, reduced the cost of imported capital goods and altered relative prices in favour of tradables in the early 1990s, it was rewarded with a sharp increase in investment, exports and growth. While inequality has worsened in some of these countries, the poverty level has been reduced in all of them.

So market incentives work. If this were the entire story the policy conclusion would be straightforward: liberalize all markets as fast as you can, which indeed was the message internalized by the advocates of the Washington Consensus and the policy makers who listened to them. However, the history of development over the past 50 years has revealed a striking fact: the best-performing countries are those which have liberalized partially and gradually. China, of course, stands out in this respect as its astonishing success since 1978 has been due to its dual-track strategy based on gradualism and experimentation. Apart from Hong Kong, which has always been a *laissez faire* haven, all the East Asian success cases have followed a gradualist reform path. India, which did very well in the 1990s, has also liberalized only partially. All these countries have unleashed the energy of their private sectors, but have done so in a cautious, controlled manner.

An important reason why gradualist strategies worked in the above cases is that they were tailored to pre-existing domestic institutions, and therefore the countries in question were able to economize on institution building.[9] South Korea used its repressed, heavily controlled financial system to channel credit to industrial firms that were willing to undertake capital investment. The textbook alternative – financial liberalization coupled with investment tax credits – might have been more efficient on paper, but it was unlikely to have worked well in the Korea of the 1960s and 1970s, nor to have paid off so quickly. Instead of relying on dual-track pricing, China could have fully liberalized agricultural prices and compensated urban dwellers and the treasury through tax reforms, but it would have taken years if not decades to establish the necessary institutions.

Compare these examples with the wholesale reforms implemented in Latin America and the former socialist countries. Because the latter were so radical and borrowed *en masse* from other countries, their success hinged on the creation of a wide range of new institutions in short order and from scratch. This was a Herculean task, and it is perhaps not surprising that the transition proved more difficult than many economists had anticipated. Indeed the most successful cases were those where capitalist institutions had not been entirely destroyed or their memory was recent (as in Poland).

Therefore, the designers of market-oriented reform strategies must recognize not only that institutions matter, but also that it takes time and effort to alter existing institutions. The latter fact presents both a constraint and an opportunity. It is a constraint because it implies that 'optimal' price reforms may not be feasible. It is an opportunity because it allows imaginative policy makers to try profitable alternatives (as with the dual-track system and TVEs in China).

Implications for international governance and conditionality

The arguments so far can be summarized as follows:

- Market incentives are crucial to economic development.
- Market incentives must be underpinned by strong public institutions.
- Market economies are compatible with a diverse range of institutional arrangements.
- The better the fit between market-oriented reforms and pre-existing institutional capabilities, the greater the probability of success.

The first two propositions are now widely accepted and form the basis of the augmented Washington Consensus. According to the revised Consensus, liberalization, privatization and global integration are still important, but they need to be supplemented with and supported by reforms in the area of governance. However, the importance of the third and fourth points is not adequately recognized.

The new Consensus can be seen in operation in a number of areas. For example in the aftermath of the Asian crisis, IMF programmes in the region proscribed a long list of structural reforms in the areas of business–government relations, banking, corporate governance, bankruptcy laws, labour market institutions and industrial policy. A key component of the new international financial architecture is a set of codes and standards – on fiscal transparency, monetary and financial policy, banking supervision, data dissemination, corporate governance and structure, and accounting standards – that are designed to be applied in all countries but are targeted especially at developing countries. And ever since the Uruguay Round of GATT, global trade negotiations have resulted in a number of agreements – on intellectual property rights, subsidies and investment-related measures – that harmonize practices in developing countries with those in more advanced countries.

Hence, as it has come into operation, the new view of development has resulted in a ratcheting up of conditionality and a narrowing of the space within which policy can be conducted. In general, this is undesirable for a number of reasons. First, it is ironic that this is happening at precisely the moment when our comprehension of how the global economy works and what small countries need to do to prosper within it has been shown to be sorely lacking. It was not so long ago that East Asia's export orientation and high investment rates were assumed to provide protection against the kind of external crisis that periodically rocked Latin America. A common exercise in the aftermath of the 1995 tequila crisis was to compare the two regions in terms of their current account deficits, real exchange rates, export–GDP ratios and investment rates to show how East Asia, for the most part, looked 'better'. East Asia had its critics of course, but what the critics predicted was a gradual running out of steam and not the meltdown that transpired.[10]

Second, as already emphasized (the third point above), market capitalism is compatible with a variety of institutional arrangements. The new Washington Consensus either rejects this view (the extreme convergence view) or underestimates its significance in practice. The new set of external disciplines come hand in hand with a particular model of economic development that has remained untested even in today's advanced countries. These disciplines foreclose some development strategies that have worked in the past, and others that could work in the future. The narrowing of national autonomy in the formulation of development strategy is a cost for which developing countries are unlikely to receive an adequate reward.

Third, the practical difficulties of implementing many of the institutional reforms under discussion are severely underestimated. Today's developed countries did not establish their regulatory and legal institutions overnight. It would be nice if Third World countries could somehow acquire First World institutions, but it is safe to bet that this will happen only when they are no longer Third World countries. A strategy that tailors market-based reforms to existing institutional capabilities is more likely to bear fruit in the short term (the fourth point above).

None of this is meant to suggest that the specific institutional reforms that dominate the agendas of the Bretton Woods institutions are without merit. No one can be seriously against the introduction of proper accounting standards or improved prudential supervision of financial intermediaries. While some of the standards are likely to backfire in practice, the more serious concerns are twofold. First, these standards are the wedge with which a broader set of policy and institutional preferences – in favour of open capital accounts, deregulated labour markets, arms-length finance and American-style corporate governance, and hostile towards industrial policies – are imposed on the recipient countries. Second, the agenda focuses too much on the institutional reforms that are needed to make the world safe for capital flows, and therefore it diverts political capital and attention from institutional reforms in other areas. The risk is that such an approach will privilege freedom of international trade and capital mobility in the name of 'sound' economic policy, and that it will do so at the cost of neglecting other goals of development policy that have the potential to clash with it.

Whatever shape is taken by the evolving architecture of the international economy, therefore, it is important to give developing countries the space to experiment with their own strategies.

How important is international economic integration?

As indicated in the previous section, the requirements of global economic integration have come to exert a long shadow over the design of development policies. Developing countries are incessantly lectured about the long list of requirements they have to meet in order to integrate into the world economy. The trouble with the current discourse on globalization is that it confuses ends with means. A truly development-oriented strategy requires a shift in emphasis. Integration into the world economy has to be viewed as an instrument for achieving economic growth and development, not as an ultimate goal. Maximizing trade and capital flows is not and should not be the objective of development policy.

No country has developed successfully by turning its back on international trade and long-term capital flows. Very few countries have grown over a long period of time without experiencing an increase in the share of foreign trade in their national product. As Yamazawa (2000, p. 2) puts it, 'no developing economy can develop within its protected wall'. In practice the most compelling reason why trade is linked to growth in developing countries is that imported capital goods are likely to be significantly cheaper than those manufactured at home. Policies that restrict imports of capital equipment raise the price of capital goods at home, and therefore reduced real investment levels have to be viewed as undesirable, *prima facie*. In turn exports are important since they provide the wherewithal to purchase imported capital equipment.

But it is equally true that no country has developed simply by opening itself up to foreign trade and investment. The trick in successful countries has been to combine the opportunities offered by world markets with a domestic investment strategy to stimulate the animal spirit of domestic entrepreneurs. As mentioned earlier, almost all of the outstanding examples have partially and gradually opened up to imports and foreign investment. There is simply no evidence that across-the-board trade liberalization is systematically associated with higher growth rates. Multilateral institutions such as the World Bank, the IMF and the OECD regularly promulgate advice predicated on the belief that openness generates predictable and positive consequences for growth. In fact the evidence on this is not nearly as strong as it is made out to be.

The evidence on trade liberalization

A few years ago Rodríguez and Rodrik (2000) reviewed the extensive body of empirical literature on the relationship between trade policy and growth, and concluded that there was a significant gap between the message that the consumers of this literature had derived and the facts that the literature had actually demonstrated. This gap was due to a number of factors. In many cases the indicators of 'openness' used by researchers were problematic as measures of trade barriers or were highly correlated with other sources of poor economic performance. In other cases the empirical strategies used to ascertain the link between trade policy and growth had serious shortcomings, the removal of which had resulted in significantly weaker findings.[11]

The nature of the relationship between trade policy and economic growth remains very much an open question and the issue is far from being settled on empirical grounds. In fact, there are reasons to be sceptical that a general, unambiguous relationship between trade openness and growth is waiting to be discovered. The relationship is likely to be contingent on a host of country and external characteristics. The fact that practically all of today's advanced countries embarked on their growth path behind the security of tariff barriers, and only subsequently reduced their degree of protection, surely offers a clue of sorts. Note also that the modern theory of endogenous growth yields an ambiguous answer to the question of whether trade liberalization promotes growth. The answer varies according to whether the forces of comparative advantage push the economy's resources in the direction of activities that generate long-term growth (via externalities in research and development, the expansion of product variety, the upgrading of product quality and so on) or divert them from such activities.

Indeed, the complementarity between market incentives and public institutions that has been repeatedly emphasized above has been no less important in the area of trade performance. In East Asia, the part played by governments in getting exports out during the early stages of growth has been extensively studied and documented (Amsden, 1989; Wade, 1990). Even in Chile – the exemplar of free-market orientation – post-1985 export success has depended on a wide range of government policies, including subsidies, tax exemptions, duty drawback schemes, publicly provided market research and public initiatives to foster scientific expertise. After listing some of the pre- and post-1973 public policies to promote the fruit, fishery and forestry sectors in Chile, Maloney (1997, pp. 59–60) concludes that 'It is fair to wonder if these ... dynamic export sectors, could have responded to the play of market forces in the manner they have without the earlier and concurrent government support.'

The appropriate conclusion to draw from all this is not that trade protection should be preferred to trade liberalization as a rule. There is no credible evidence from the events of the past 50 years that trade protection is systematically associated with higher growth. The point is simply that the benefits of trade openness should not be oversold. When other worthwhile policy objectives compete for scarce administrative resources and political capital, deep trade liberalization often does not deserve the high priority it typically receives in development strategies. This lesson is of particular importance to countries that are in the early stages of reform, such as those in Africa.

The evidence on capital-account liberalization

The evidence on the benefits of capital-account liberalization is even weaker.[12] On paper, the appeal of capital mobility is obvious. In the absence of market imperfections, freedom to trade enhances efficiency, and this is as true of trade in paper assets as it is of trade in widgets. But financial markets suffer from various syndromes – informational asymmetries, agency problems, self-fulfilling expectations, bubbles (rational and otherwise) and myopia – to an extent that makes their economic analysis inherently second-best. No amount of institutional tinkering is likely to make a significant difference to that basic fact.

The question of whether developing nations should be pushed to open their capital accounts (in an 'orderly and progressive' manner, as recommended by the IMF) can ultimately be answered only on the basis of empirical evidence. While there is plenty of evidence that financial crashes often follow financial liberalization (see Williamson and Mahar, 1998, for a survey), there is very little evidence to suggest that higher rates of economic growth follow capital account liberalization. Quinn (1997) reports a positive association between capital account liberalization and long-term growth, while Grilli and Milesi-Ferretti (1995), Rodrik (1998b) and Kraay (1998) – the last of these authors using Quinn's (1997) indicator of capital account restrictions – can find no relationship. Klein and Olivei (1999) report a positive relationship, but one largely driven by the experiences of the developed countries in their sample. This field of inquiry is still in its infancy, and there is clearly much more to be learned. The least that can be said at present is that convincing evidence of the benefits of capital account liberalization has yet to be produced.

Of all the arguments in favour of international capital mobility, perhaps the most appealing one is that such mobility serves a useful disciplinary function in terms of government policy. Governments that have to be responsive to investors cannot easily squander their society's resources. As Summers (1998) puts it, 'market discipline is the best means the world has found to ensure that capital is well used'.

While this idea is attractive, once again one has to question its empirical relevance. When foreign creditors suffer from the syndromes noted above, a government that is intent on irresponsible spending finds it easier to finance its expenditure when it can borrow from abroad. Moreover, for such a government even domestic borrowing is politically less costly because, in a world of free capital mobility, there is no crowding out of private investors (since the latter can borrow from abroad). In both instances, international financial markets allow reckless spending that might not have taken place in their absence. Conversely the discipline that markets exert in the aftermath of crises can be excessive and arbitrary, as discussed previously. As Willett (2000) points out, the appropriate characterization of market discipline is that it comes too late, and when it does come it is typically too much.

Mukand (1998) has nicely developed the analytics of such situations. Consider the following stylized set-up suggested by Mukand's framework. Suppose there are two actors – a government (G) and a foreign investor (F) – who have to decide what actions to pursue when the underlying state of the world is not observable. The state of the world can be either neat or messy. G receives a private signal about which state prevails and then chooses a policy, which is observed by F. The policy can be either orthodox or heterodox. Assume that the orthodox (heterodox) policy produces larger aggregate surplus when the state of the world is neat (messy). The foreign investor, F, wants to invest only when there is a match between policy and the expected state (orthodox/neat or heterodox/messy). F also believes (perhaps incorrectly) that the productivity of the investment will be higher under the orthodox/neat combination than under the heterodox/messy combination, and will invest more when the first scenario is expected.

Mukand (1998) demonstrates that the government may have two reasons to follow the orthodox policy in these circumstances, even when it receives a signal that the underlying state is messy (and therefore the heterodox policy would be more appropriate). He calls the resulting biases 'conformity bias' and 'good-news bias'. These can be explained as follows.

- *Conformity bias.* Let F have a strong and unmovable prior that the state is neat. Even if G's posterior is sufficiently strong that the state is messy, G may want to follow the orthodox policy anyway because it will not be able to sway F's beliefs (posterior), and G may be better off making the investment and following the wrong policy than not making the investment and following the right (that is, aggregate surplus-maximizing) policy.
- *Good-news bias.* When F's posterior can be affected by G's choice of policy, G may want to follow the orthodox policy to signal a neat state and move F's state expectation to neat, because more investment will be forthcoming if F expects a neat state rather than a messy one (assuming there is a match between expected state and policy in both cases).

Note that for the second scenario to materialize it is not necessary for the productivity of the investment actually to be higher under orthodox/neat than under heterodox/messy. All that is needed is that the foreign investor believes it is so. In either case the government is driven by market sentiment to follow policies that are inappropriate and fall short of the optimum.

Governments do need discipline of course. However in modern societies this discipline is provided by democratic institutions – elections, opposition parties, independent courts, parliamentary debate, a free press and various civil liberties. Governments that make a mess of their economies are punished at the polls. The broad cross-national evidence suggests that democratic nations tend to be good at maintaining responsible fiscal and monetary policies. Most of the significant cases of fiscal profligacy have occurred under authoritarian regimes rather than democratic ones. It was military dictatorships that plunged Latin American countries into their debt crises, and democracies that cleaned up the mess. In Asia, democratic countries such as India and Sri Lanka have exemplary macroeconomic records by Latin American and African standards. Africa's only two long-running democracies (Mauritius and Botswana) have done an excellent job of managing booms and busts in the price of their main exports (sugar and diamonds). Among the transitional economies, the most successful stabilizations have occurred in the most democratic countries. There is a strong negative association between the Freedom House index of democracy and the average inflation rate in a sample of more than 100 countries, after controlling for per capita income. The 'international capital mobility as discipline' position embodies a view of politics that is at best partial and at worst harmful to democracy.

Finally, as pointed out above, pursuit of the capital account liberalization agenda has the effect of crowding out policy makers' agenda and diverting them from national development efforts. Finance ministers who spend all their time mollifying investor sentiment and marketing the economy to foreign bankers have no time to spend on traditional development concerns: reducing poverty, mobilizing resources and setting investment priorities. In the end it is global markets that end up dictating policy, not domestic priorities.

Concluding remarks

The lesson of the twentieth century is that successful development requires markets to be underpinned by solid public institutions. Today's advanced industrial countries – the United States, the Western European countries and Japan – owe their success to their ability to develop their own workable models of the mixed economy. While these countries are alike in the emphasis they place on private property, sound money and the rule of law, their practices differ substantially in the areas of labour market relations, social insurance, corporate governance, product market regulation and taxation.

All of these models have been in constant evolution, and none has been without its problems. European-style welfare capitalism seemed especially appealing during the 1970s, Japan became the model to emulate during the 1980s, and the 1990s were clearly the decade of freewheeling American-style capitalism. Evaluated in an historical perspective, all of these models have been equally successful. The evidence from the second half of the twentieth century is that none of these models clearly dominates the others, and it would be a mistake to hold up American-style capitalism as the model to which the rest of the world must aspire.

Of course all successful societies are open to learning, especially from useful precedents in other societies. Japan is a good example of this. When its legal system was reformed and codified under the Meiji restoration it was Germany's civil and commercial law that served as the primary model. So the emphasis here on institutional diversity and non-convergence should not be viewed as rejection of institutional innovation via imitation. What is important is to adapt imported blueprints to local practices and needs. Once again Japan provides the example. As Berkowitz *et al.* (1999, p. 11) point out, Japan's decision to adopt the German legal system was an informed choice, not an imposition from abroad: 'extensive debates about the adoption of English or French law, and several drafts based on the French model preceded the promulgation of codes that were largely based on the German model'. In other words the Japanese reformers consciously selected from the available codes those which seemed most suited to their circumstances.

What is true of today's advanced countries is also true of developing countries. Economic development ultimately derives from a home-grown strategy, and not from the world market. Policy makers in developing countries should avoid fads, put globalization into perspective and focus on domestic institution building. They should have more confidence in themselves and domestic institutions and place less faith in the global economy and the blueprints that emanate therefrom.

Notes

1. The paper on which this chapter is based was presented at the conference on 'Developing Economies in the 21st Century', held at the Institute for Developing Economies, Japan External Trade Organization, Chiba, 26–27 January 2000. I am grateful to the conference organizers and participants for valuable comments.
2. The last term is from World Bank (1997), p. 27.
3. This section draws on Rodrik (1999a, ch. 4).
4. This point is disputed by many and goes against the official view of the IMF (Fischer, 1998). The argument that structural aspects of the East Asian model were not at the root of the crisis is well put by Stiglitz (1998) and Radelet and Sachs (1998). This is not to say that these economies did not have structural weaknesses, and in particular an overreliance on a governmental steering of the economy that had probably outlived its usefulness. But as Stiglitz points out, financial crises break out with some regularity in countries that have very different types of economic management and standards of transparency, ranging from the Scandinavian countries to the United States.
5. This section borrows heavily from Rodrik (1999c).
6. See also Johnson and Shleifer (1999), who attribute the more impressive development of equity markets in Poland, compared with the Czech Republic, to the stronger regulations in the former country in terms of upholding minority shareholder rights and guarding against fraud.

7. See Hoff and Stiglitz (1999) for a useful survey and discussion.
8. Perhaps Europe will come back into fashion. On 8 October 1999 the *New York Times* published a major feature article entitled 'Sweden, the Welfare State, Basks in a New Prosperity'.
9. See Qian (1999) for a good account of China's experience along these lines.
10. '"I have learned more about how this new international financial system works in the last twelve months than in the previous 20 years," Alan Greenspan acknowledged recently' (Thomas L. Friedman, 'A Manifesto for the Fast World', *New York Times Magazine*, 28 March 1999, p. 71).
11. The detailed analysis covered the four papers that are probably the best known in the field: Dollar (1992), Ben-David (1993), Sachs and Warner (1995) and Edwards (1998).
12. The discussion on capital-account convertibility is based on Rodrik (2000).

References

Alesina, A., and A. Drazen (1991) 'Why Are Stabilizations Delayed?', *American Economic Review*, vol. 81, pp. 1170–88.

Amsden, A. H. (1989) *Asia's Next Giant: South Korea and Late Industrialization* (New York: Oxford University Press).

Ben-David, D. (1993) 'Equalizing Exchange: Trade Liberalization and Income Convergence', *Quarterly Journal of Economics*, vol. 108, no. 3, pp. 653–79.

Berkowitz, D., K. Pistor and J.-F. Richard (1999) 'Economic Development, Legality and the Transplant Effect', unpublished paper.

Bordo, M. D., C. Goldin and E. N. White (eds) (1998) *The Defining Moment: The Great Depression and the American Economy in the Twentieth Century* (Chicago, Ill.: University of Chicago Press).

Collins, S., and B. Bosworth (1996) 'Economic Growth in East Asia: Accumulation versus Assimilation', *Brookings Papers on Economic Activity*, vol. 2, pp. 135–91.

Dollar, D. (1992) 'Outward-Oriented Developing Economies Really Do Grow More Rapidly: Evidence from 95 LDCs, 1976–85', *Economic Development and Cultural Change*, vol. 40(3) pp. 523–44.

Edwards, S. (1998) 'Openness, Productivity and Growth: What Do We Really Know?', *Economic Journal*, vol. 108, pp. 383–98.

Fischer, S. (1998) 'In Defense of the IMF', *Foreign Affairs*, July/August pp. 103–6.

Grilli, V. and G. M. Milesi-Ferretti (1995) 'Economic Effects and Structural Determinants of Capital Controls', *IMF Staff Papers*, no. 42 (Washington, DC: IMF) pp. 517–51.

Hausmann, R., and M. Gavin (1996) *Securing Stability and Growth in a Shock Prone Region: The Policy Challenge for Latin America*, Working Paper (Washington, DC: Inter-American Development Bank).

Hoff, K. and J. E. Stiglitz (1999) *Modern Economic Theory and Development* (Washington, DC: World Bank).

Jacoby, S. M. (1998) *Risk and the Labor Market: Societal Past as Economic Prologue* (Los Angeles, CA: Institute of Industrial Relations, UCLA).

Johnson, S. and A. Shleifer (1999) *Coase v. the Coasians: The Regulation and Development of Securities Markets in Poland and the Czech Republic* (Cambridge, Mass.: MIT and Harvard).

Klein, M. and G. Olivei (1999) 'Capital Account Liberalization, Financial Deepening, and Economic Growth', *NBER Working Paper* W7384 (Cambridge, Mass.: NBER).

Kraay, A. (1998) *In Search of the Macroeconomic Effects of Capital Account Liberalization* (Washington, DC: World Bank).

Maloney, W. F. (1997) 'Chile', in Laura Randall (ed.), *The Political Economy of Latin America in the Postwar Period* (Austin, Tex.: University of Texas Press).

Mukand, S. W. (1998) 'Globalization and the "Confidence Game": Policy Making in the Open Economy', unpublished paper, Department of Economics, Tufts University, Boston MA, USA.

North, D. C., and R. Thomas (1973) *The Rise of the Western World: A New Economic History* (Cambridge: Cambridge University Press).

North, D. C., and B. Weingast (1989) 'Constitutions and Commitment: The Evolution of Institutions Governing Public Choice in Seventeenth Century England', *Journal of Economic History*, vol. XLIX, pp. 803–32.

Qian, Y. (1999) 'Institutional Foundations of China's Market Transition', unpublished paper, Stanford University, California.

Quinn, D. (1997) 'The Correlates of Change in International Financial Regulation', *American Political Science Review*, vol. 91, pp. 531–51.

Radelet, S., and J. Sachs (1998) 'The Onset of the Asian Financial Crisis', unpublished paper, Harvard University, Cambridge, Mass.

Rodríguez, F. and D. Rodrik (2000) 'Trade Policy and Economic Growth: A Skeptic's Guide to the Cross-National Evidence', in B. Bernanke and K. Rogoff (eds), *NBER Macroeconomics Annual 2000* (Cambridge, Mass.: MIT Press for the NBER).

Rodrik, D. (1995) 'Getting Interventions Right: How South Korea and Taiwan Grew Rich', *Economic Policy*, vol. 20, pp. 55–107.

Rodrik, D. (1998a) 'Why Do More Open Economies Have Bigger Governments?', *Journal of Political Economy*, vol. 106, pp. 997–1032.

Rodrik, D. (1998b) 'Who Needs Capital-Account Convertibility?', in Fischer, S., Cooper, R. N., Dornbusch, R., Garber, C., Massad, C., Polak, J.J., Rodrik, D. and Tarapore, S. S. *Should the IMF Pursue Capital-Account Convertibility?*, Essays in International Finance no. 207, (Princeton, NJ: International Finance Section, Department of Economics, Princeton University).

Rodrik, D. (1999a) *The New Global Economy and Developing Countries: Making Openness Work* (Washington, DC: Overseas Development Council).

Rodrik, D. (1999b) 'Where Did All the Growth Go? External Shocks, Social Conflict, and Growth Collapses', *Journal of Economic Growth*, 4(4), pp. 385–412.

Rodrik, D. (1999c) 'Institutions for High-Quality Growth: What They Are and How to Acquire Them', unpublished paper, November.

Rodrik, D. (2000) 'Governing the World Economy: Does One Architectural Style Fit All?', *Brookings Trade Policy Forum* (1999) Collins, S. and Lawrence, R., (Washington, D.C.: Brookings Institution).

Sachs, J. and A. Warner (1995) 'Economic Reform and the Process of Global Integration', *Brookings Papers on Economic Activity*, vol. 1, pp. 1–118.

Stiglitz, J. (1998) 'Knowledge and Development: Economic Science, Economic Policy, and Economic Advice', paper presented at the Annual World Bank Conference on Development Economics, Washington, DC, 20–1 April.

Summers, L. H. (1998) 'Building an International Financial Architecture for the 21st Century', remarks to the Cato Institute, Washington, DC.

Tornell, A., and P. R. Lane (1999) 'The Voracity Effect', *American Economic Review*, vol. 89, pp. 22–46.

Unger, R. M. (1998) *Democracy Realized: The Progressive Alternative* (London and New York: Verso).

Wade, R. (1990) *Governing the Market: Economic Theory and the Role of Government in East Asian Industrialization* (Princeton, NJ: Princeton University Press).

Willett, T. D. (2000) *International Financial Markets as Sources of Crises or Discipline: The Too Much, Too Late Hypothesis* Essays in International Finance (Princeton, NJ: Princeton University, May).

Williamson, J. and M. Mahar (1998) *A Survey of Financial Liberalization*, Essays in International Finance no. 211 (Princeton, NJ: Princeton University, November).

World Bank (1997) *World Development Report, 1997* (Washington, DC: World Bank).

Yamazawa, I. (2000) 'Regional Cooperation in a Changing Global Environment: Success and Failure of East Asia', paper presented at the UNCTAD X High-Level Round-Table on Trade and Development, February.

3
Re-examination of Development Policies and Strategies: Some Political Economy Lessons[1]

Jeffrey B. Nugent

Introduction

Views on which policies and strategies are good for development have changed radically over the last half century. So too have the prevailing circumstances, particularly the national and international political and economic environments in which development policies are chosen. Not surprisingly, there have been two lags of considerable length in the adjustment process. First, views on desirable development policies have lagged behind the experience in development and the realization of changing circumstances. Second, the policies chosen have lagged considerably behind the views on good policy.

Even the standard development textbooks and the literature of international organizations, which tend to change only very slowly, have long revealed an appreciation of the need for development policy to be more aligned with strengthening market forces. They have also seen the need for a much lighter touch in interventions in product and factor markets and have called attention to the importance of incentives, good governance (associated with transparency in decision making, accountability of the executive branch for its actions, the quality of the bureaucracy and the provision of better information to decision makers and the public), clearly defined property rights, an appropriate legal framework and a strong civil society to limit the possibility that the benefits of chosen policies will be captured only by a narrow group of rent seekers. This is a dramatic change from the planning, physical capital, import-substituting industrialization policies, heavy-handed tax and regulatory policies, public-sector-led and expansionary monetary and fiscal policies that were implied by some of the most important treatises on and practitioners of development economics in the 1940s and 1950s.

The story of how the failures of the first generation of heavy-handed development policies adopted by many of the newly independent countries in the Third World, all the 'socialized' countries of the Second World and even some countries of the First World were learned is well known. Poor growth performance can usually be traced back to bad, or at least inappropriate, policies and strategies. In some cases, policies and institutions that might once have been suitable eventually proved themselves quite unsuitable in the light of changed circumstances. While some elements of desired institutions could be brought about quite quickly, such as the removal of exchange controls, others, such as the development of competitive markets and clearly defined property rights, could take more time – indeed as much as two hundred years rather than a couple of years or a decade.

What is less understood is why some countries took so long to adjust to changed circumstances and development ideas while others did not. Knowledge of this is important not only for positive purposes (that is, explaining the transitions in and patterns of policy and institutional orientations) but also for normative ones, that is, identifying the optimal development strategies for a given country and time period. By and large, development economists and practitioners are at least as keen as other economists, social scientists and policy makers to see economic performance improved in the countries they work on or in. Many of them have long argued for reforms, but with little to show for it. What is needed is a set of implementation strategies that are suited to the conditions that prevail in the country or countries in question. How and under what conditions can policy and institutional regimes be changed in the desired directions?

Because of the interest in and importance of the questions of how, why and when some countries make regime changes while others do not, there is a rapidly growing body of literature on the subject. Most of the recent publications in economics, however, are almost exclusively theoretical. Typically a model is developed to explain a particular case or an assumed set of stylized facts.

But without empirically testing individual cases or the general applicability of findings from single cases, any conclusions drawn may be dangerously misleading. For this reason it is important to obtain a broad view of the similarities and differences in the relevant conditions, reform programmes and outcomes. To capture more fully the lessons from past experiences that will aid the identification of suitable development strategies, this chapter starts with a broader review of alternative explanations than is usually undertaken by economists. It includes not only explanations of contemporary successes and failures but also some of the attempts to explain broad historical differences. It then looks at attempts to operationalize some of the explanations and to compare them with relevant data, and finally draws some conclusions for development policy implementation strategies in the next century.

The next section begins by identifying the policy and other regime changes we have in mind. This is followed in the third section with some recent explanations of important early transitions in policy and institutional regimes that may have contributed to long-term differences in economic growth rates across countries. The fourth section reviews the theoretical and applied literature on contemporary policy reform in developing countries. While no attempt is made formally to test the alternative explanations, the fifth section reconsiders some empirical assessments of determinants of the initiation and sustenance of development policies and institutional reforms. The sixth section concludes the chapter with some implications for implementation strategies and further research.

Identifying desirable policy and institutional regimes

Naturally there is considerable disagreement among economists about the optimal mix of policies for developing countries. Moreover, country conditions vary considerably, implying that even if there were universal agreement on the optimal policies in a given country or on general principles, it would not follow that the same policies should be prescribed for all countries or that similar reforms should be adopted everywhere. Moreover, because there are various dimensions of policy, there are also many directions in which reforms can proceed: tax reform, exchange rate policy, monetary policy reforms, reforms of expenditure and transfer policy, trade policy, agricultural and industrial regulations, banking, telecommunications and other service sector reforms. There can also be various sequences of such reforms.

Nevertheless, during the 1990s there was increasing agreement on some of the basic components needed for developing or less developed countries (LDCs). One of the best-known and most referenced lists of reform components is the one labelled by Williamson (1994) as the 'Washington Consensus on Reform':

1. Fiscal discipline.
2. Reorientation of public expenditure towards the building of human capital and infrastructure.
3. Tax reform: broaden base and cut marginal rates.
4. Financial liberalization: end interest rate controls and so on.
5. Exchange rates: unified and competitive.
6. Trade liberalization: reduce tariffs and eliminate NTBs.
7. Foreign direct investment: welcome.
8. Privatization: do.
9. Deregulation: stop only for environmental, safety or prudential (banking) reasons.
10. Property rights: secure.

As can be seen, this list includes fiscal measures such as fiscal discipline as well as expenditure and tax reforms. The expenditure reforms would redirect government expenditure primarily into growth-stimulating functions such as human capital formation and infrastructure. The list also includes the liberalization of transactions on the current account and of at least some items in the capital account, including greater openness to FDI and the unification and freeing of exchange rates. Financial liberalization, decontrol of interest rates and general deregulation (to limit regulations to those related to the environment, safety and prudential banking) are also important components as are the privatization of public enterprises and government-run activities and the creation of clear and secure property rights.

This list of reform objectives will be considered throughout the chapter. While some of the items are microeconomic in nature and others macroeconomic, and there is strong disagreement about the relative importance of the individual reforms and their sequencing and necessity,[2] the list is likely to remain relevant for some time. Actual reforms, moreover, tend to come in packages in which a number of these elements are included at the same time, and it is often the case that microeconomic reforms are undertaken to mitigate certain unwanted effects of stabilization and other macroeconomic reforms. This does not mean, however, that we should consider only reforms in which every item on the list is included. In this chapter we shall consider reforms that go beyond mere stabilization and include a degree of current account liberalization.

Explanations of early institutional and policy transitions

Economic historians have long noted that several of the items on the Washington Consensus list are important to if not prerequisites for long-term development. Especially prominent among the identified prerequisites has been the importance of secure property rights, liberal trade policies, competitive and unified exchange rates and the provision of infrastructure. Yet until relatively recently little attention has been given to how, when and where these policies and institutions are adopted. Among the various explanations of the differences between the relatively developed countries (DCs) and LDCs that have been offered in recent years are technological, cultural-historical, geographical and political economy explanations.

Technology

Economic historians Engerman and Sokoloff (1997, 2000) have used what are essentially technological differences to explain why North America grew much more rapidly than Latin America from the late eighteenth century, when the two regions' per capita incomes were quite similar. In particular they note that the crops that can be grown in tropical Latin America, such as sugar, coffee, cocoa, bananas, cotton and tobacco, are different from those grown in North America, mainly grains and vegetables. The former are alleg-edly subject to economies of scale while the latter are not. This makes it economic to organize agricultural production in Latin America and the American south on large-scale plantations, but in the rest of North America on small farms.

It is claimed that this difference in technology led to different institu-tional trajectories over time. In Latin America, to make plantations econom-ically viable and their exports internationally competitive, it led to the setting up of institutions to suppress the organization and mobility of labour. It also fostered slavery and *encomiendas* and provided little incentive for education. Meanwhile, in North America the small farm orientation encouraged the development of secure property rights. These rights fostered investment in land and the shortage of labour encouraged the development of labour-saving innovations, which in turn encouraged the extension of private property to intellectual property so as to internalize the benefits there from. Finally, these innovations and the expansion of non-agricultural activi-ties stimulated educational investment.

This explanation has two shortcomings. First, detailed studies of productive technologies for tropical agriculture have usually failed to find economies of scale in production (Binswanger and Rozensweig, 1986). Second, the character of technological change may well be seriously affected by the way in which technology is developed, for example by private individuals or firms, or by public institutions with different sets of rules and incentives (de Janvry *et al.*, 1989). It may also be affected by factor endowments (Hayami and Ruttan, 1971; Ruttan, 2001).

Cultural background and colonial institutions

Another explanation of the differences between the development paths of Latin America and North America hinges on their different colonial and cultural backgrounds. Most of the Latin American countries were colonies of Spain and Portugal, whereas Canada and the United States were for the most part colonized by Great Britain. For this reason they had different legal and other institutional regimes, and because of the path dependence of institutions this resulted in very different growth paths (North, 1990; North *et al.*, 1998; Landes, 1998). In particular, North America's legal and other insti-tutions were based on English common law, whereas those of Latin America were built on the foundations of Spanish and Portuguese civil law. The former were consistent with decentralized government and liberal trade and regulatory regimes, whereas the latter were more consistent with centraliza-tion and heavy-handed regulation (La Porta *et al.*, 1998). The religious and cultural differences between Catholic Latin America and Protestant North America might also have played a part in the differences in hierarchy and centralization (Landes, 1998).

Geography

A third explanation of the differences in long-term growth rates and levels of development hinges on geography. There are a number of variants of this explanation, one of which is the long-term evolutionary view espoused by Diamond (1997). Diamond argues that the inhabitants of the Eurasian land mass were favoured geographically by the very wide east–west land continuity, the easterly direction of the prevailing winds and the climatic similarity across the central regions. This facilitated the natural breeding of similar seeds and their subsequent spread across the land mass, and then technological diffusion since the same technological innovations could be applied throughout the geographical area. (The same technologies could also have been used in North America as it too was quite wide.) In contrast Africa and Central and South America were not favoured because they were more long than wide, that is, they largely ran from north to south rather than east to west, with substantial differences in climate taking place in the move from north to south. This greatly limited the usefulness of technological transfer, communication and trade along the more important north–south axes of these continents.

Another variant is the 'tropics breed germs, and germs make human and animal health and development more difficult' hypothesis. In other words, the climatic and other conditions of the African, South American and other tropical areas combined to make them vulnerable to vectors of disease, which impeded the successful raising of livestock and certain commercial crops, and subjected humans to debilitating illnesses. The African tropics were additionally disfavoured by the fact that heavy vegetation made transportation difficult and costly, except along rivers (Sachs and Warner, 1995; Sachs, 2001).

A more sophisticated version of the geography hypothesis combines geography with technological change. According to this hypothesis, while the tropics may have been favourable to development in the very early years (say prior to 1500) because of the relative ease of exploiting natural resources and the existence of abundant rainfall, the agricultural and other innovations that were developed over time tended to be more appropriate for drier, less highly populated areas (Bloch, 1966; Mokyr, 1990).

Political economy

The fourth explanation for the creation of property rights and other institutions deemed conducive to long-term development revolves around political economy. One thesis that has been applied quite specifically to the emergence of private property rights is the appearance of a split in the elite as a result of intra-elite competition. In such circumstances, individual members of the elite may have needed to make credible offers to non-members in order to persuade them to participate in common defence or serve some other purpose. While other kinds of offer, such as promises of employment, credit or future public goods, could also have been used to lure people to an area to work or fight, these could easily be rescinded and therefore may not have been credible. The granting of private property rights over well-defined parcels of land, authenticated by formally registered titles, clearly carried greater credibility and could have been deemed necessary for the very survival of a divided elite.

Evidence in support of this argument has been provided by Volckart (1999) in the case of medieval Germany and by Nugent and Robinson (2000) for Costa Rica and Colombia. The latter refute the general validity of the technological, geographical and cultural explanations by contrasting the institutional and development trajectories of Costa Rica and Colombia with those of Guatemala and El Salvador. All four countries were colonies of Spain, and therefore acquired the same institutions, were located in the same region and came to specialize in production of the same crop, namely coffee. However, they did so in different ways – Colombia and Costa Rica with small farms and Guatemala and El Salvador with large plantations. The authors argue that the earlier development of property rights for smallholders in Costa Rica and Colombia resulted in these countries becoming more democratic earlier and investing more in education than the other two countries. The difference between the two pairs of countries has also been attributed to elite fragmentation in Costa Rica and Colombia but solidarity in the other two countries. A prerequisite for this argument to be valid is that workers and soldiers would have to have been in relatively short supply, so the argument cannot be easily applied to labour-abundant countries such as India and China.

Acemoglu *et al.* (2001) have developed a political economy argument that overlaps the geographical explanation. They attempt to disprove the validity of the cultural background thesis by showing that even the same colonial power had quite different institutional orientations in different colonies. In particular they show that where relatively healthy conditions prevailed and people from the home country chose to settle there, the latter introduced property rights and other institutions that were favourable to development. But in unhealthy areas the inferior institutions were left in place. The authors substantiate the hypothesized long-term effects of these differences in colonial institutions by showing a positive correlation between the initial conditions and the quality of current institutions and levels of development.

In a related paper, Acemoglu *et al.* (2001) argue in favour of the political economy explanation and against the geographical argument. Since geography is constant, this suggests continuity over time in terms of growth rates, whereas the political economy of institutional change view suggests that differentials in growth rates could have been reversed after institutional changes were introduced. The authors demonstrate that the highly populated, more urbanized and developed areas were left with their existing inferior institutions and/or had new extractive regimes imposed on them. In contrast the areas with lower population density, urbanization and development were more attractive to colonial settlers since they could take advantage of land and other resources without necessarily coming into conflict with indigenous inhabitants. They therefore had a greater incentive to establish their superior institutions in these areas. The previously less developed areas outgrew the more developed ones during the subsequent 500 years because of their superior institutions, which over time brought about a reversal of fortunes.

Political economy factors have also been connected to growth and development in two other ways: via income inequality and sociocultural heterogeneity. Easterly and Levine (1997) suggest that the slow economic growth of African countries can be attributed to their greater ethnic and linguistic (tribal) differences, which have made it difficult to arrive at a consensus on public goods production (hence less education provision, fewer roads, restricted electricity supply and poor governance institutions), the result being greater policy distortions. Others (Persson and Tabellini, 1992, 1994; Alesina and Perotti, 1996) suggest that income inequality may have similarly harmful effects on public goods production, efficiency in resource allocation, the diversion of public expenditure away from infrastructure towards distribution and so on. Numerous studies have been devoted to the effect of income inequality on growth and possible interactions between other variables, such as between income inequality and democracy, income inequality and political instability, and between these and physical or human capital formation and growth.

Legal systems are rarely accommodating enough to recognize officially the very informal property rights claimed by the poor. According to de Soto (2000), in effect the failure to recognize these rights renders the assets of the poor worthless or 'dead'. Hence, they cannot be used as collateral to generate new capital. This results in the poor being much poorer than they should be, and unable to put their capital to use. De Soto argues that, again mostly in the nineteenth century, the rich countries gradually incorporated informal systems into their formal systems. Among the vehicles for this were land and mine claim associations, laws of preemption and the common law principle of accepting common practices as legal. De Soto argues that today this process should be facilitated by non-governmental organizations and more willingly accepted by formal legal institutions in LDCs.

Additional evidence in support of some of the political economy, geographical and institutional explanations for intercountry differences in growth rates has been provided by growth regressions. For example, Sachs and Warner (1995) and Hall and Jones (1999) have included geographical variables such as 'distance from the equator' and 'land-locked' in such regressions. Others have included political variables such as democracy, constraints on the chief executive and various measures of political instability (Alesina and Perotti, 1996; Alesina *et al.*, 1996; Campos and Nugent, 2001). Mauro (1995), Easterly and Levine (1997), Knack and Keefer (1995), Campos and Nugent (1999) and others have included such indicators as corruption, bureaucratic efficiency, various indicators of property rights, openness to trade and capital movements, the legal and other foundations of financial markets, policy distortions such as the black market premium and interest rate spreads, and governance. Several of these studies have found links between geographical, technological, cultural and political economy factors, each with both direct and indirect effects on growth.

Outward-oriented reforms in the contemporary world

As discussed above, property rights, governance, stabilization and outward-oriented reforms (OORs) are important components of the Washington Consensus reforms listed earlier. While the importance and determinants of property rights have been demonstrated in historical terms, the other components, and in particular the OORs, can best be examined in terms of the post-1950 experience of such reforms. There are two steps in reform implementation: initiation and maintenance. Success in each stage is related to various conditions and factors.

External and internal environmental conditions

OORs are more likely to be successful if they are undertaken under relatively favourable environmental conditions, both external and internal. With regard to external conditions, the most important seem to be the following:

- Relatively rapid growth in the world demand for products from LDCs that are conducting OORs.
- A limited number of countries attempting OORs at the same time (otherwise the exchange rate component of OORs may cause a serious deterioration of the terms of trade).
- Stable world financial and other markets.
- No restrictions on the exportation by DCs of advanced technology to the more technologically advanced LDCs with OORs.

Since DCs were enjoying higher GNP and import growth rates in the 1950s and 1960s than in the 1970s and 1980s, fewer LDCs were undergoing OORs at the same time, the magnitude of default and delay in the repayment of LDC debt was much smaller and DC financial markets were more stable than in later years, the odds of any given LDC meeting success with its OORs programme might be considered as being lower in the 1970s and 1980s, *ceteris paribus*, than in the earlier decades. On the other hand, because in the earlier period policy makers and strategists may have been imbued with greater export pessimism and belief in the import substitution regime, and had insufficient experience with OORs to draw on, it cannot be certain that this is true. Since unfavourable external environmental conditions at the global level would have had their primary effect at the level of LDCs as a whole, they would not necessarily have applied in full force to any particular LDC exporter. As a result, the success or failure of OORs in an LDC may have depended more on internal than on external conditions.

Among the internal or individual country characteristics that may impair the chances of OOR success are the following:

- A substantial endowment of natural resources or long-term dependence on capital transfers or remittances, which allow a country to postpone necessary adjustments.[3]
- A large stock of external debt, which may impede the reforming country from attracting new credit and raise the cost of devaluation (another component of OORs) because it raises the domestic currency cost of any given debt service cost in US dollar terms (McKinnon, 1973; Shaw, 1973).
- Large country size, which may imply a greater ability to absorb shocks and delay reforms.
- Sizable budgetary imbalances and consequent inflation, which may render the tariff reduction components of OORs less likely to be accepted and sustained.[4]
- Low literacy and low intersectoral mobility of labour, entrepreneurial resources and capital, which may impede the structural adjustment components of OORs.
- In the early stages of import substitution the low social costs of the strategy may undermine the rationale for replacing it with OORs.[5]

Institutional and political economy considerations

Many writers on OORs make two critical assumptions: that OORs almost inevitably involve short-term costs, and that there will be many losers (as well as winners) from the reforms, with the losers being naturally inclined to try to block the reforms. These two assumptions imply that such reforms will not be easy to accomplish and that success can be achieved only by curtailing the operation of these obstacles in particular circumstances. There are three alternative political mechanisms for doing so:

- The OORs can be imposed by a military government, or at least a strong state that can, if necessary, crush opposition to the reforms and discipline private sector interest groups.
- A strong leader committed to the reforms emerges. While leadership is hard to define without being tautological, Harberger (1993) identifies one or more persons with 'vision' (defined as having a game plan for what needed to be done) who led each of the countries that were most successful with early OORs. While Harberger stresses the leadership strength of these individuals, he does not explain how this strength emerged, especially as the individuals had widely varying backgrounds.

- The leaders or administrators of economic policies are technocrats who can offer greater resistance to the pressures of unhappy interest groups than can professional politicians. Indeed the fact that several of the key leaders identified by Harberger were technocrats gives some plausibility to this hypothesis.[6]

Given the assumption that in the short run the net benefits of OORs will be negative, the failure of OORs is attributed to the myopia of LDC leaders in the face of, for example, social and political instability. With myopic leaders, another strategy for overcoming the assumed short-term costs of OORs is to exaggerate the long-term costs of failing to introduce reforms. The key here is for the actual or perceived situation to be a large crisis, implying that the long-term benefits will definitely outweigh the short-term costs. Hence, the greater the perceived crisis the greater the likelihood that even ordinary leaders will be successful in sustaining OORs.

Although the crisis hypothesis is one of the most popular in the political economy of reform, there are several problems with it. First, both genuine reform and failed reform can be justified by a crisis. Second, the larger the crisis the more complex and comprehensive the reform is likely to be, making it difficult to ensure its internal consistency and quite possibly increasing the likelihood that less conventional, less well tested and riskier measures will be included in the OOR package.

Nevertheless, doubts can be raised about the validity of the assumptions made here, and therefore about the suggested means of overcoming myopia and other problems. First, since military regimes are often viewed as less legitimate than democratically elected ones and monarchies, it is by no means clear that military governments should in general be any less sensitive to interest group pressures than non-military ones. Second, Rodrik (1996) has challenged the assumption that properly designed OORs will have negative net benefits in the short term. Several such reforms have been associated with consumption booms. But even if they were not and there were many short-term losers, if the long-term benefits were sufficiently positive the losers could be compensated for their losses and hence their opposition bought off.[7] Rodrik also argues that stabilization can be accomplished very quickly with little in the way of backlash, so OORs that push for stabilization early in the process should be relatively free of such problems.

Haber and Razo (1998), Campos and Nugent (2001) and others have challenged the idea that social and political instability is generally high in LDCs and that such instability results in bad policies and slow economic growth. For example, Haber and Razo (1998) show that Mexico had very good policies and rapid growth during a period of exceptionally high instability, while Campos *et al.* (2000) show that the relationship between instability, policy and growth is often highly non-linear, with very low instability being associated with failure to reform and slow growth. Without political competition a regime has little incentive to do what is good for society as a whole. Third, Campos and Nugent (2001) demonstrate that causality may if anything go the other way, that is, from slow growth to instability rather than from instability to bad policy and slow growth.

Naturally, if social and political instability is not the problem it has been presented as in the reform literature, this radically changes the preconditions for successful reform. For example, crises and military or other strong governments may be less necessary for success than hitherto believed. This does not mean that there are no ways of overcoming some of these arguments. It merely suggests that one needs to delve more deeply into the political economy of the context in question. For example, Alesina and Drazen (1991) argue that when different political-economic groups are sufficiently polarized, even without myopia, it may be rational for each group to hold back from a cooperative solution in a 'war of attrition' for as long as possible, especially if the benefits of holding out and joining the coalition late will be greater than those of joining it early. Situations characterized by greater income inequality might well make coalition formation and reform more difficult, but changes in the political rules to shift compensation in favour of early joiners to coalitions could be very helpful in ensuring success with OORs.

In a similar fashion, Fernandez and Rodrik (1991) suggest that many people and groups may be uncertain as to whether they will be net gainers or losers from the reform, and therefore procrastinate about formating a democratic plurality coalition, thereby quite rationally delaying reform.

Just as some analysts of the creation of private property rights point to the role of elite fission, analysts of successful OORs have pointed to splits in a once dominant party or coalition. Nelson (1989), Bates and Krueger (1993) and especially Tornell (1998) highlight cases such as Chile (under Pinochet) and Mexico (under de la Madrid), where reform was pushed by elements within the elite who were willing to sacrifice some of the rent earned under the *status quo* (for example, protection) in order to stifle what they viewed as a more serious threat, namely the expropriation of property by statist or labour groups. Tornell formalizes this as a dynamic pre-emption game, where any part of the elite that does away with the *status quo* regime in the presence of social and political instability loses the rents accruing to it from its protected investments and jobs. Yet by introducing OORs, the first mover group can assure itself of a less bad situation than if the reforms were undertaken by another element of the elite. Tornell therefore identifies the existence of a fiscal crisis and a radical spit in the elite (resulting in a severe political change) as necessary joint conditions for successful OORs. (see also Papageorgiou *et al.*, 1991).

One form of elite fission is when a dominant populist party takes the economic reform position of classic conservative economists and parties. Indeed, Williamson and Haggard (1994) attribute 10 of the 13 most market-oriented reforms to populist left of centre governments such as Menem's in Argentina and Fujimori's in Peru. One way of understanding this is to view it as a way of orchestrating the outcome in a better way than it would be if it was left to the others (the approach described in the previous paragraph). Cukierman and Tommasi (1998) argue that such cross-over leaders are in a better position to put their policies across to the public than the more natural supporters of market-oriented policies (the 'Nixon to China' or 'Clinton to welfare reform' syndrome). Murphy and Sturzenegger (1996) argue that politicians can affect voters' beliefs about the situation by showing flexibility or sacrificing their own preferences when responding to external and unforeseen shocks.

Interest group politics

While the rationale for some of these theories is based on the median voter principle of stable democracies, where the location of the median voter determines everything, many LDCs are not stable democracies. For this reason we shall now turn our attention to interest group considerations that may be more relevant.

Institutional problems arise in virtually all aspects of OORs. First, the adoption of an OOR may require successful collective action, which in turn requires the overcoming of the free rider problem that is inherent in any such reform due to its public good character.[8] Second, they arise when monitoring the implementation of OORs. Finally, they arise even in the sanctioning process, that is, when responding to any observed defects in the design or implementation of OORs and when creating and maintaining an appropriate sanctioning system. In the following paragraphs each of these problems is addressed in turn.

Except in the case of primary exporters, whose ability to export may not require a fully fledged OOR anyway, very few organized interest groups are likely to support OORs. Managers and owners of import-competing industries certainly have little to gain and potentially have much to lose from OORs. Workers in these industries may have even more to lose inasmuch as OORs often involve policies (for example devaluations) that bring about a substantial reduction in real wages and/or require costly relocations in order to find jobs. The primary sectors may not give their support to, or may even oppose, OORs because they have easier and more direct means of achieving their objectives. That essentially leaves only non-traditional exporters as an identifiable interest group that might take collective action in support of an OOR. However, the potential support from this group is undermined by (a) considerable uncertainty about just what kinds of producer would benefit from an OOR in the country under consideration, and (b) the relatively long lapse between the time at which the costs (of both collective action and any required private investment) are incurred and that at which the benefits (in terms of future non-traditional exports) are realized.

Even if both traditional and non-traditional exporters could be encouraged to support OORs, the characteristics of such groups (a large number of members, geographical dispersal, heterogeneous backgrounds, lack of personal acquaintance and so on) are hardly likely to make for effective collective action in defence of their interests. By contrast, the opposing groups – public sector managers, private managers, owners of import-competing industries and workers in these industries – typically possess many of the characteristics that are favourable to collective action.[9] That leaves only the state or bureaucratic sector and international agencies (to be discussed below) as potentially important sources of collective action.

Even this brief review of interest group considerations goes a long way towards explaining why so few OORs are implemented with any vigour and why fewer still are successful in the long term.[10] This is not to say, however, that there are no situations in which the forces in support of OORs are somewhat stronger and those opposed are somewhat weaker. Indeed, since this means that the prospect of success with OORs is relatively bright, it is important to identify such situations.

Several factors are relevant in this regard, the first of which is the matter of timing. Significant changes in the prospects for collective action in support of OORs can be expected over time. In the earliest stage of import-substituting industrialization, which is rather labour intensive and labour is highly mobile because of the lack of skill requirements, any interest groups that rally in defence of import substitution are unlikely to be very strong. Some might even see a good future in exporting and thus become supporters of OORs. Over time, however, capital intensity, length of association and other characteristics that favour collective action build up, with concomitant growth in the strength of groups that oppose OORs. Later still – given (1) the small size of and the inevitable deceleraton of growth in the domestic market for domestically produced manufactures, (2) the increasing difficulty of import substitution over time as the capital, skill, technology and import intensities of such production increase, and (3) the priority given by bureaucrats to allocating investment and licences to investors in sectors with either large export or domestic market potential – the ranks of domestic producers are likely to include some who are disadvantaged by some aspects of import substitution. Moreover, since latecomers are likely to be in relatively concentrated industries (because of the relatively high capital and technology requirements of production), they are likely to possess characteristics that are favourable to collective action. Hence the prospects for OORs may improve somewhat after a relatively lengthy experience with import substitution (Nabli, 1990). This turning point may be reached earlier in small countries than in large ones.

Second, in situations where exports are relatively diversified by product and industry (including a variety of agricultural, mining and manufactured products – perhaps those of latecomers to manufacturing who have to export in order to receive their investment and foreign exchange licences and tax benefits) or services, the potential for collective action is likely to be increased by the heterogeneity of interests. Moreover, the more heterogeneous the interests among the group of exporters, or for that matter the group of late endrants, the lower the incentive for free riding by group members.

Another factor that can be important in determining the strength of collective action by any given group is the perceived cost of inaction to members of the group. For example, the poorer a country's resource endowment the higher the cost of failing to adjust (such as by adopting an OOR) to negative external shock, and hence the more likely it will be that an OOR will succeed.

OORs are more likely to be initiated and sustained in situations where a coalition of groups that favour them can be easily put together. As a result, factors that affect the likelihood of groups forming coalitions are relevant to and potentially important for success with OORs. The more polarized the political-economic setting the more difficult coalition formation will be, and hence the less likely it will be that an OOR will succeed. Democratic rules facilitate the communication and political exchanges that are vital to coalition formation, and therefore coalition formation and hence success with OORs is easier to accomplish in democratic societies than in non-democratic ones (Haggard and Kaufman, 1989).

Coalition formation is usually a dynamic process in which the expressed preferences or actions of one group at one point in time subsequently affect those of others. Since the willingness of some groups to join a coalition may be contingent on the participation of certain other groups, some aspects of coalition formation may be more successful than others. The existence of such interdependencies and the need for a critical mass in coalition formation imply that externalities are present, thereby providing justification for the use of selective incentives.

The fact that by their very nature OORs must be adopted at the national (rather than local) level exacerbates the coalition formation problem. Whereas at the local level people tend to know each other well, geographical and social distance between groups at the national level make it difficult for some groups to know the true preferences of individual members of other groups. As a result, their knowledge may be limited to the preferences revealed in the official organs of or by the spokespersons for such groups. Preferences revealed in this way may not reflect the true preferences of the individual members, and support for the *status quo* may seem more positive and pervasive than it really is (Kuran, 1987, 1995).

These considerations help explain why even reforms that are deemed positive by the vast majority of the citizens of a country may be very slow in coming. They also explain why reform proposals that are rejected at one point in time are accepted later without any real changes in the terms. Finally, because of the interdependency of preferences, they also explain how and why it is that once a few people change their minds many others do likewise and the reform process, once begun, proceeds very quickly (Alesina and Drazen, 1991; Kuran, 1995).

The role of the state and foreign agents in OORs

The above discussion has largely ignored the potentially important roles played by state and international agents and agencies in OORs. Clearly both foreign creditors to and investors in an LDC have a considerable interest in OORs as the latter can significantly increase the prospect of currency convertibility and loan repayment. Depending on the sector in which they have invested and the comparative profitability of sales to the domestic and foreign markets, foreign investors may either favour or oppose OORs.

Since considerable start-up costs are incurred by any organization dedicated to OOR, the state – because of its power and the scope of its activities – is likely to be subject to pressure by individuals and groups that either favour or oppose OORs. In some cases, weak states may react passively to collective pressure by non-state groups, but in certain situations the state and its bureaucracy may play very active initiating roles. While the direction of pressure (pro or con) will necessarily depend on the circumstances of the country in question, most state agents are likely to have an interest in the maintenance of import substitution because of their share of the rents generated by protection. However, the more unfavourable the economic conditions and the poorer the prospect of continued growth via import substitution, the more likely it is that some elements of the state bureaucracy will be willing to back OORs. Indeed if the situation is sufficiently bad, certain bureaucrats or military leaders may be willing to commit themselves to providing strong leadership in the drive for OORs, even if this involves considerable political risk.

Since technocrats may be more immune to interest group pressure than career politicians, and because on balance that pressure is likely to be against OORs, one might hypothesize that technocratic governments will be more likely than political ones to experiment with OORs. Also, the more merit-oriented (as opposed to loyalty oriented) the bureaucracy the more likely it is that some bureaucrats will be inclined to innovate.[11]

Empirical assessment

To date there have been few empirical analyses of the success of OORs. Most of the studies that have been conducted are case studies of individual countries' experiences with reform, including a series of two-country comparisons by Lal and Myint (1996) and the rather informal comparisons of non-randomly selected case studies by Krueger (1978), Harberger (1984), Papageorgiou *et al.* (1991), Bates and Krueger (1993) and Little *et al.* (1993). Bates and Krueger (1993) reached the following conclusions:

- Crisis is a necessary but not sufficient condition for reform. The critical magnitude at which a problem becomes a crisis varies from case to case, as does the form of the crisis.
- The relationships between the crisis and the nature or strength of the policy response, and between interest group analysis and the policy responses, are weak, partly because groups do not anticipate how they will be affected, and even if they do they are often not good at organizing themselves and articulating their views.
- What does seem to matter in the policy responses are political rules, such as those on elections, re-election and how operatives within the political system are promoted.
- Reform leads to a restructuring of the relationship between government and interest groups. When this is done in a way that generates learning, continuous policy refinements and better implementation, then the reforms can be sustained. Dynamic adjustments of this sort are more important than the correctness of the original 'game plan' or detailed policy programme.
- The empowerment of technocrats can contribute to the success of these dynamic adjustments and of the reforms as technocrats possess private information on how the economy works and how it will respond to various policy and other changes.

In addition the following can be concluded:[12]

- Country characteristics matter: small and medium-sized countries that are not well endowed with natural resources are more likely to be successful in sustaining liberalization.
- Political stability seems to be important to the undertaking and sustenance of liberalization.
- Liberalization that is conducted in a series of bold steps seems to be more sustainable than liberalization that involves tentative and partial steps. Bold steps are more important the longer that import restrictions have been in place.
- While a country's balance of payments position prior to and immediately after a reform has little effect on the likelihood or sustainability of the reform, sharp deteriorations, such as from a sharp decline in export prices, can cause policy reversals.

More quantitative analyses have been conducted by Nabli (1990), Tornell (1998) and Nugent (2002). Tornell (1998) defined an OOR event as a year in which there was not only a trade liberalization programme but also the volume of trade rose by 2–20 per cent relative to the previous year. This was to ensure that liberalization had occurred in reality and not just on paper. Yet the inclusion of this latter condition implies that luck or other exogenous factors could have played a role in increasing exports and thereby in identifying OORs. Tornell's study concentrated on the initiation of an OOR event in countries that according to Sachs and Warner (1995) were 'closed' in 1970. The sample consisted of 1225 country observations (the vast majority of which were not in reform years). A probit model was used to test for the 'crisis cum severe political change hypothesis' mentioned above. A major finding was the coincidence of major political regime changes with the initiation of reforms. This is sometimes called the 'honeymoon hypothesis': reforms are more likely if they undertaken soon in the tenure of a new government.

Nabli (1990) and Nugent (2002) investigated the sustenance of reform efforts rather than their initiation and considered several determinants of structural and political economy types. Nabli's (1990) study was based on 51 different country cases of OORs initiated between 1950 and 1980, most of which were drawn from the abovementioned case studies. When attempting to explain why some OOR efforts were sustained for least five years while others were not, Nabli highlighted interest group considerations and the degree of diversification away from traditional exports in determining the success or failure of OORs.

Nugent (2002) built upon Nabli's analysis by (1) enlarging its coverage to include attempts at reform in the late 1980s and early 1990s for a total of 100 OOR attempts, and (2) broadening its scope by including additional political and structural considerations, such as the relative importance of technocrats, the countries' natural resource endowments and income inequality, and previous experience with OOR. Nugent found that the most important determinant of success in OORs were the relative importance of technocrats (those with PhDs in economics from North America or Britain) in key ministerial positions, and their previous experience in international organizations (which could have instilled them with a strong pro-OOR orientation). Both of these factors (though highly correlated) significantly increased the probability of success. Other determinants of success were the relative importance of manufactures in exports (positive), the magnitude of the preceding current account deficit (negative), the income inequality index (negative), the natural resource endowment (negative) and lack of previous national experience with OORs (negative).

The explanatory power of these cross-country empirical studies is not very great. At best, the relevant determinants included in the models explain only about one third of the variation in the variable in question. Many of the measures employed are less than ideal and the cut-off point between the success and failure of OORs is very arbitrary. Conceivably, other researchers using different measures would obtain different results.

Conclusions

Clearly, success in reform requires not only economically sound programmes but also well-chosen strategies for implementing the reforms. Some elements of reforms may take a long time to accomplish. Inevitably, success or failure will depend heavily on political economy considerations. Country circumstances differ substantially, so the same reforms will not work everywhere and implementation strategies will have to take these differing circumstances into account.

One of the studies reported here (Tornell, 1998) investigated only the initiation of reform, while the other two (Nabli, 1990; Nugent, 2002) took the initiation of reforms as given and investigated the sustenance of reforms. Ideally the two stages should be combined into a single analysis, the first step being a self-selection analysis. In this way the effect of self-selection bias could be controlled. Also, the studies reported here looked at the success of only two types of reform: property rights and OORs. Yet the success of both types might well depend on other reforms being conducted at the same time, or on the sequence of such reforms. These are important issues that should be examined in future research.

While the findings reported here should be treated with caution until they can be shown to hold up to further testing, they at least provide tentative support for certain propositions. First, there is the idea that the initiation of serious economic reform usually follows a change of regime and a rather large crisis. In countries where a large and powerful interest group is aligned against reform, it may be necessary to find a way to split this group and to make the different elements compete with each other in some or other way. A regime change tends to be favourable to the adoption of substantial reforms, but the reforms often need to be conducted quickly and boldly to take advantage of the limited honeymoon period the new regime is likely to be allowed.

Yet for the reforms to be sustained, the crisis that prompts them should not be too large, and the presumed advantages of military or other 'hard' governments should not be exaggerated since perceptions of fairness and due process and transparency in decision making lend weight to the legitimacy of the government and the credibility of its pronouncements. There is at least some evidence to suggest that countries with greater income inequality, lower literacy and higher natural resource endowments tend to have greater difficulty with implementing and sustaining reforms. To some extent, governments may be able to overcome these disadvantages by placing technocrats imbued with proreform economic thinking in key ministerial positions, as they will be less subject to political pressure by interest groups than are politicians, and perhaps better able to explain the rationale for the reforms.

The success of development policies and strategies in the twenty-first century will depend heavily on how well the policy lessons of the past and present are learned and built into implementation strategies.

Notes

1. This chapter is a revised version of a paper presented at a workshop, held at the Institute of Developing Economies (JETRO), Chiba, Japan, on 29 January 2002. The author expresses his gratitude to Grace Lim, Justin Lam and Paul Hughes for their help in obtaining information and preparing materials for the paper, and to Mustapha K. Nabli for permission to draw on an earlier paper of his.
2. For example, Rodrik (1996) argues that it is important to distinguish between reforms that are macroeconomic in scope (that is, stabilization reforms) and reforms that are microeconomic in scope, such as trade policy, taxation policy and regulatory policies. This is because the latter may be much more difficult to achieve politically and may have less certain outcomes, with many more 'losers' to offset the 'winners'.
3. It is suggested that this is one reason why oil-rich countries such as Saudi Arabia, Venezuela and Nigeria have been especially slow to adjust their fiscal deficits and address their other problems, and conversely why the Republic of Korea, Singapore and Taiwan were particularly quick to adjust to oil price and other shocks and were early to undertake OORs.
4. On the other hand, since success in agreeing on and sustaining a reform package may be enhanced by the popularity that accrues from reducing the inflation rate, the presence of a fiscal deficit problem or inflation can provide a good rationale for undertaking and sustaining a reform package that includes both stabilization and OOR.
5. Nevertheless, as Krueger (1993) has stressed, these costs build up. In each successive stage of import substitution the import content and capital requirements are likely to rise, thereby raising both the social costs of further important substitution and the net benefits of OOR. Hence the longer that import substitution has been in place the brighter the prospects for OOR.
6. In particular, Sergio De Castro and Hernan Buchi were economists from Chile's Catholic University, and Cavallo, the architect of Argentina's reforms, was a PhD economist from Harvard.
7. If a government has difficulty coming up with funds in the short run to do this, Sachs (2001) and others argue that foreign loans could solve the problem, which is indeed one of the functions of structural adjustment loans from international agencies. Yet foreign loans can also postpone the need for reform so its actual effectiveness in this respect is an empirical question.
8. OORs have a public good character since the benefits that derive from them accrue to everyone, regardless of whether or not they have contributed to the costs of their creation and implementation. While in principle the same could be said of efforts to generate protection, such as the imposition of tariffs, in practice protection quotas are often used and import licences are tied to domestic producers that participate in the collective action, or to credit.
9. For a demonstration of the applicability of such Olsonian propositions to a typical developing country see Nabli and Nugent (1989, ch. 3), and for an international cross-sectional setting see Nabli (1990).
10. Somewhat similar conclusions could presumably be derived from a majority voting model with voting costs, factor ownership distributions and other realistic features. See Baldwin (1982); Mayer (1984).
11. Naturally, this will depend on the extent to which those who manage successful innovations are rewarded through promotion and other means and without

excessive interference from the top. These very characteristics appear to have been very important (though still underappreciated) ingredients of Korea's successful OORs – Korea's civil service is extremely merit-oriented and civil servants who have been successful in promoting successful innovations have even been promoted to high political ranks.

12. While these conclusions are not exactly comparable because they are based on overall indexes of liberalization, and not just on trade reforms or OORs, in fact in most countries trade reforms have been the single most important ingredient of overall reform.

References

Acemoglu, D., S. Johnson and J. A. Robinson (2001) 'Reversal of Fortune: Geography and Institutions in the Making of the Modern World Income Distribution', *NBER Working Paper*, no. 8460 (Cambridge, Mass.: NBER).

Acemoglu, D., S. Johnson and J. A. Robinson (2001) 'The Colonial Origins of Comparative Development: An Empirical Investigation', *American Economic Review*, 92 (5), pp. 1369–1401.

Alesina, A. and A. Drazen (1991) 'Why are Stabilizations Delayed?', *American Economic Review*, vol. 81, pp. 1170–88.

Alesina, A., S. Ozler, N. Roubini and P. Swagel, (1996) 'Political Instability and Economic Growth', *Journal of Economic Growth*, vol. 1, pp. 193–215.

Alesina, A. and R. Perotti (1996) 'Income Distribution, Political Instability and Investment', *European Economic Review*, vol. 40, pp. 1203–28.

Baldwin, R. E. (1982) 'The Political Economy of Protection', in J. N. Bhagwati and T. N. Srinivasan (eds), *Import Competition and Response* (Chicago, Ill.: University of Chicago Press), pp. 263–86.

Bates, R. H. and A. O. Krueger (1993) *Political and Economic Interactions in Economic Policy Reform* (Oxford: Blackwell).

Binswanger, H. P. and M. Rosenzweig (1986) 'Behavioral and Material Determinants of Production Relations in Agriculture', *Journal of Development Studies*, vol. 22, pp. 503–39.

Bloch, M. (1966) *Land and Work in Medieval Europe* (New York: Harper and Row).

Campos, N. F. and J. B. Nugent (1999) 'Development Performance and the Institutions of Governance: Evidence from East Asia and Latin America', *World Development*, vol. 27, pp. 439–52.

Campos, N. F. and J. B. Nugent (2001) 'Who Is Afraid of Political Instability?', *Journal of Development Economics*, vol. 67, pp. 157–72.

Campos, N. F., J. B. Nugent and J. A. Robinson (2000) 'Can Instability Be Good for Growth?', Working Paper, Los Angeles Department of Economics, University of Southern California.

Cukierman, A. and M. Tommasi (1998) 'Credibility of Policy Makers and Policy Reforms', in Sturzenegger, F. and M. Tommasi, (eds), *The Political Economy of Reform* (Cambridge, Mass.: MIT Press), pp. 329–48.

de Janvry, A., E. Sadoulet and M. Fafchamps (1989) 'Agrarian Structure, Technological Innovations and the State', in P. Bardhan (ed.), *The Economic Theory of Agrarian Institutions* (Oxford: Clarendon Press), pp. 356–82.

de Soto, H. (2000) *The Mystery of Capital* (New York: Basic Books).

Diamond, J. M. (1997) *Guns, Germs and Steel: The Fate of Human Societies* (New York: W.W. Norton).

Easterly, W. and R. Levine (1997) 'Africa's Growth Tragedy: Policies and Ethnic Divisions', *Quarterly Journal of Economics*, vol. 112, pp. 1203–50.

Engerman, S. L. and K. L. Sokoloff (1997) 'Factor Endowments, Institutions, and Differential Paths of Growth among New World Economies', in S. H. Haber (ed.), *How Latin America Fell Behind* (Stanford, CA: Stanford University Press).

Engerman, S. L. and K. L. Sokoloff (2000) 'Institutions, Factor Endowments, and Paths of Development in the New World', *Journal of Economic Perspectives*, vol. 3, pp. 217–32.

Fernandez, R. and D. Rodrik (1991) 'Resistance to Reform: Status Quo Bias in the Presence of Individual-Specific Uncertainty', *American Economic Review*, vol. 81, pp. 1146–55.

Haber, S. and A. Razo (1998) 'Political Instability and Economic Performance: Evidence from Revolutionary Mexico', *World Politics*, vol. 51, pp. 99–143.

Haggard, S. and R. Kaufman (1989) 'Economic Adjustment in New Democracies', in J. Nelson (ed.), *Fragile Coalitions: The Politics of Stabilization and Structural Adjustment* (New Brunswick: Transaction Books).

Hall, R. and C. I. Jones (1999) 'Why Do Some Countries Produce Much More Output per Capita than Others?', *Quarterly Journal of Economics*, vol. 114, pp. 83–116.

Harberger, A. C. (1984) 'Economic Policy and Economic Growth', in A. C. Harberger (ed.), *World Economic Growth: Case Studies of Developed and Developing Nations* (San Francisco, CA: Institute for Contemporary Studies).

Harberger, A. C. (1993) 'Secrets of Success: A Handful of Heroes', *American Economic Review*, vol. 83, pp. 343–50.

Hayami, Y. and V. W. Ruttan (1971) *Agricultural Development: In International Perspective* (Baltimore, MD: Johns Hopkins University Press).

Knack, S. and P. Keefer (1995) 'Institutions and Economic Performance: Cross-Country Tests Using Alternative Institutional Measures', *Economics and Politics*, vol. 7, pp. 207–27.

Krueger, A. O. (1978) *Foreign Trade Regimes and Economic Development: Liberalization Attempts and Consequences* (Lexington, Mass.: Ballinger).

Krueger, A. O. (1993) *Political Economy of Policy Reform in Developing Countries* (Cambridge, Mass.: MIT Press).

Krueger, A. O. (1995) *Trade Policies and Developing Nations* (Washington, DC: Brookings Institution).

Kuran, T. (1987) 'Preference Falsification, Policy Continuity and Collective Conservatism', *Economic Journal*, vol. 97, pp. 642–65.

Kuran, T. (1995) *Private Truths, Public Lies: The Social Consequences of Preference Falsification* (Cambridge, Mass.: Harvard University Press).

Lal, D. (1987) 'The Political Economy of Economic Liberalization', *World Bank Economic Review* (Washington, DC: World Bank), pp. 273–99.

Lal, D. and S. Rajapatirana (1987) 'Foreign Trade Regimes and Economic Growth in Developing Countries', *World Bank Research Observer*, vol. 2, pp. 189–217.

Lal, D. and H. Myint (1996) 'The Political Economy of Poverty, Equity and Growth: A Comparative Study', (New York: Oxford University Press).

Landes, D. S. (1998) *The Wealth and Poverty of Nations: Why Some Are So Rich and Some Are So Poor* (New York: W.W. Norton).

la Porta, R., F. Lopez-de-Silanes, A. Shleifer and R. W. Vishny (1998) 'Law and Finance', *Journal of Political Economy*, vol. 106, pp. 1113–55.

Little, I. M. D., R. Cooper, W. M. Corden and S. Rajapatirana (1993) *Boom, Crisis, and Adjustment: The Macroeconomic Experience of Developing Countries* (New York: Oxford University Press).

Luciani, G. (1992) 'Allocation vs. Production States: A Theoretical Framework', in H. Beblawi and G. Luciani (eds), *The Rentier State* (London: Croom Helm).

Mauro, P. (1995) 'Corruption and Growth', *Quarterly Journal of Economics*, vol. 110, pp. 681–712.

Mayer, W. (1984) 'Endogenous Tariff Formation', *American Economic Review*, vol. 74, pp. 970–85.

McKinnon, R. I. (1973) *Money and Capital in Economic Development* (Washington, DC: Brookings Institution).

Mokyr, J. (1990) *Lever of Riches: Technological Creativity and Economic Progress* (New York: Oxford University Press).

Murphy, L. R. and F. Sturzenegger (1996) 'The Feasibility of Low Inflation: Theory with an Application to the Argentine Case', *Policy Reform*, vol. 1, pp. 47–73.

Nabli, M. K. (1990) 'The Political Economy of Trade Liberalization in Developing Countries', *Open Economies Review* vol. 1, pp. 111–145.

Nabli, M. K. and J. B. Nugent (1989) 'Collective Action, Institutions and Development', in M. Nabli and J. B. Nugent (eds), *The New Institutional Economics and Development* (Amsterdam: North-Holland), pp. 80–137.

Nelson, J. (1989) *Fragile Coalitions: The Politics of Economic Adjustment* (New Brunswick: Transaction Books).

North, D. C. (1990) *Institutions, Institutional Change and Economic Performance* (New York: Cambridge University Press).

North, D. C., W. Summerhill and B. R. Weingast (1998) 'Order, Disorder and Economic Change: Latin America vs North America', unpublished manuscript, Hoover Institution, Stanford University, California.

Nugent, J. B. (2002) 'Technocracy, Income Distribution and the Sustainability of Outward Oriented Reforms', Los Angeles: Department of Economics, University of Southern California.

Nugent, J. B. and J. A. Robinson (2000) 'Are Endowments Fate?', working paper, Department of Economics Los Angeles: University of Southern California.

Papageorgiou, D., M. Michaely and A. M. Choksi (eds) (1991) *Liberalizing Foreign Trade* (Cambridge, MA: Blackwell).

Persson, T. and G. Tabellini (1992) 'Growth, Distribution and Politics', in A. Cukierman, Z. Hercowitz and L. Leiderman (eds), *Political Economy, Growth and Business Cycles* (Cambridge, Mass.: MIT Press).

Persson, T. and G. Tabellini (1994) 'Is Inequality Harmful for Growth? Theory and Evidence', *American Economic Review*, vol. 84, pp. 600–21.

Rodrik, D. (1996) 'Understanding Economic Policy Reform', *Journal of Economic Literature*, vol. 34, pp. 9–41.

Ruttan, V. W. (2001) *Technology, Growth and Development: An Induced Innovation Perspective* (New York: Oxford University Press).

Sachs, J. D. (2001) 'Tropical Underdevelopment', *National Bureau of Economic Research Paper* no. 8119 (Cambridge, Mass.: NBER).

Sachs, J. D. and A. Warner (1995) 'Economic Reform and the Process of Global Integration', *Brookings Papers on Economic Activity*, vol. 1, pp. 1–95.

Shaw, E. S. (1973) *Financial Deepening in Economic Development* (New York: Oxford University Press).

Thomas, V. (1991) 'Trade Policy Reform', in V. Thomas, A. Chhibber, M. Dailami and J. de Melo (eds), *Restructuring Economies in Distress: Policy Reform and the World Bank* (Oxford: Oxford University Press).

Tornell, A. (1998) 'Reform from Within', *NBER Working Paper*, no. w6497 (Cambridge, Mass.: NBER).

Volckart, O. (1999) 'Political Fragmentation and the Emergence of Market Economies: the Case of Germany, c1000–1800 AD', discussion paper (Jena: Max Planck Institute for Research into Economic Systems).

Williamson, J. (ed.), (1994) *The Political Economy of Policy Reform* (Washington, DC: Institute for International Economics).

Williamson, J. and S. Haggard (1994) 'Introduction', in J. Williamson (ed.), *The Political Economy of Policy Reform* (Washington, DC: Institute for International Economics).

4
National Economies under Globalization: A Quest for New Development Strategies
Akira Kohsaka

Introduction

Since the late 1980s the pace of economic globalization has accelerated. International trade has grown twice as fast as world GDP, and international capital flows have increased the speed of this expansion. Although the Asian economic crisis put a brake on the phenomenon, when we look at the recovery process, we find that globalization has not slowed, let alone reversed.

In view of the crisis, it is apparent that globalization is a double-edged sword in terms of both benefits and costs. There is no doubt that there were vulnerabilities in the domestic economic structures of the crisis-hit countries of East Asia. After all, however, these vulnerabilities had existed for years. So that the crisis would never have happened without structural changes in the international economic environment, and particularly globalization.

Globalization involves the international movement of goods, services and production factors such as capital, knowledge and labour. One major impediment to such movements is regulations by the governments of nation states.[1] We have often been told that reduced government intervention will lead to freer goods and factor mobility, which will promote people's income growth and enhance their living standards. But is this true?

What effects does globalization have on the policy management and economic performance of developing economies? Do they benefit from the increased international trade and capital flows? Is the deepening of economic interdependence reducing the income differences between North and South? And can the globalized market allocate resources efficiently and enhance global welfare without intervention by national governments?

This chapter reviews the outcomes of past development strategies and examines possible correlations between the globalization trend and development performance. The chapter will not present particularly new evidence on these subjects, but will consider the pros and cons of the effects of globalization on catching-up processes. It will also touch upon the impact of structural reforms on institutions under globalization.

The following section reviews the impact of globalization on developing economies. It looks first at developments in the cross-border movement of goods and services, and of capital in developing countries, and then reviews the long-run growth performance of both developing and developed countries. Despite the various postwar development efforts, incomes have not only continued to diverge between North and South, but have also diverged within the South.

Two channels through which income convergence can be expected are discussed in the subsequent two sections. As is well known, the production networks of multinational corporations (MNCs) extend beyond national boundaries. The third section discusses the effects of this on the welfare of developing countries and examines the potential roles of states or governments. The transfer of knowledge and technology has proved to be more difficult than was presumed because of the lack of appropriate institutional infrastructure. The fourth section discusses the expansion of knowledge gaps and public policies to address the problem.

Two costs that have accrued from globalization are examined in the next two sections. The fifth section discusses the necessity of government intervention to deal with volatile capital flows under globalization. As discussed in the sixth section, globalization requires institutional changes in emerging and other developing countries, and these changes can be costly and require government involvement. Noting the possible magnification of market failures by globalization, the seventh section argues that only national governments can remedy them.

Globalization and income convergence

The international movement of goods and services, capital, labour and knowledge is not a new phenomenon. Some argue, however, that towards the end of the twentieth century such movements not only accelerated but were also qualitatively different from earlier ones (Bordo *et al.*, 1998). It seems that the world economy is changing from a collection of autonomous national economies to a giant closed economy where producers and consumers are connected via the Internet across borders.

After the Second World War, development strategies were formulated by the governments of newly born nation states. Markets were underdeveloped and states were autonomous and strong, or at least they appeared to be so. However as markets evolved the autonomy of governments became more and more constrained. Today, for example, because MNCs base their location decisions on the taxation regimes of and regulations in host countries. This *regulatory arbitrage* behaviour may determine, or at least affect, related government policies.

International trade and capital flows have outgrown output, in which developing economies as a whole have increased their shares. Furthermore, these economies have deepened and diversified their linkages with the rest of the world through trade flows. With regard to trading partners, the share of trade between developing countries has expanded, and with regard to the composition of trade, the share of manufacturing with more forward and backward linkages of production has increased rapidly.

However, this general trend masks regional differences. Figure 4.1 shows the shares of world trade by region. As can be seen, only Asia and parts of Latin America have expanded their shares and enhanced their linkages with international markets. The other regions have been slow in this respect.

In addition, developing countries have become increasingly integrated into the international capital market. We can see the size and composition of capital inflows to developing countries by region in Figure 4.2. In 1996 capital flows to developing countries amounted to almost US$200 billion, six times more than the average in the 1980s and four times as large as the ratio to GDP. The composition of the flow changed significantly during the period. In the 1970s, bank and other loans were the first to expand, replaced by foreign direct investment (FDI) by the mid 1990s and portfolio flows increased in weight most recently in the 1990s. FDI has overwhelmingly concentrated in the emerging markets in Asia and some Latin American countries. In fact, flows to Asia amounted to more than ten times those to Africa in dollars, and twice as much as a ratio to GDP during the period 1990–96.

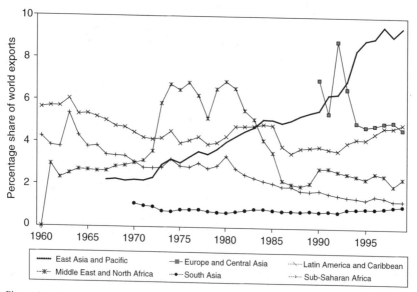

Figure 4.1 Trade shares of developing countries, by region, 1960–1999

66

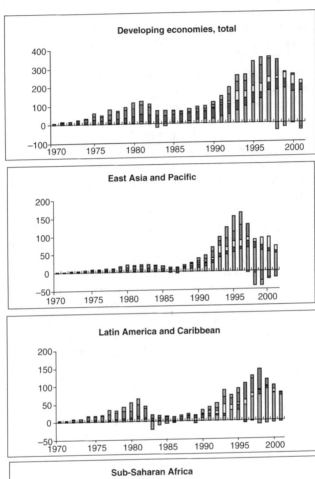

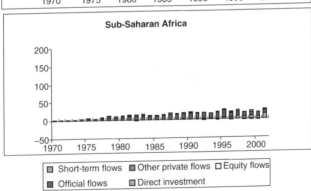

Figure 4.2 Net capital flows to developing countries, by region, 1970–2000 (billion US dollars)

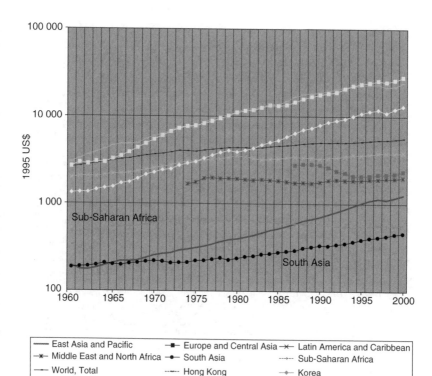

Figure 4.3 Per capita income, by region (PPP), 1960–2000 (constant 1995 US dollars)

So globalization has been felt all over the world, but its penetration has not necessarily been uniform across countries. How has this affected overall income levels and economic growth patterns? Figure 4.3 shows per capita income by region in terms of purchasing power parity (PPP). Real incomes in developing countries in all regions have doubled over the past 30 years. Therefore, in absolute terms, there can be no doubt that most developing countries have improved their standard of living. In particular, the Asian NIEs (Korea, Taiwan, Hong Kong and Singapore) have enjoyed miraculous income growth while income growth has stagnated since the 1980s in Latin America and Africa.

Regrettably, however, most developing countries are failing to close the income gap between themselves and the developed countries (Figure 4.4). Outside the Asian NIEs, only Chile, China, Malaysia and Thailand have caught up with developed countries. A similar regional pattern can be found in respect of the degree of integration into the global economy through

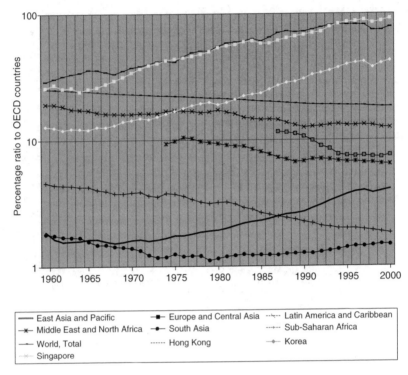

Figure 4.4 Relative per capita real income (PPP), 1960–2000

trade and capital flows. Low-income countries must grow faster than high-income ones in order to achieve income convergence, but in reality there has been no such trend. Income gaps do not necessarily dwindle, that is, there is no absolute income convergence. Indeed, although East Asia has demonstrated that developing countries can catch up with developed ones, the current situation suggests that *catch-up is possible, but neither easy nor automatic.*

It was once believed that the following mechanisms caused income convergence, and that globalization would reinforce these mechanisms. First, since capital is relatively scarce in developing countries, capital–labour ratios are lower and therefore expected rates of return on investment are higher. Consequently, the increased capital inflows that would result from integration into the international capital market would enhance the productivity and economic growth of developing countries. Second, since there is a large knowledge and technology gap between developing and developed countries, increased technology transfers and the accompanying spillover effects of integration into the global market through trade and FDI flows would aid technological catch-up.

Why, then, has there been no income convergence? According to new growth theory, other things being equal, low-income countries grow faster than high-income ones (conditional convergence). The question then is, which things or conditions are not equal, and how can we remedy this? The relevant conditions often cited in international cross-section analyses include human capital formation, price distortions, the openness of the economy, macroeconomic stability, and political and social stability. The theory asserts that the long-run, steady-state level of income is not unique, but depends on these conditions, and that the speed of convergence depends on the difference between this steady state and the initial income levels. In other words, the larger the gap the faster the catch-up. However, unless these conditions are improved, absolute income convergence cannot be expected to take place.

The following sections discuss the two catch-up mechanisms in more detail.

Catching up through the globalization of production

While multinational corporations (MNCs) attracted attention in the 1960s as leaders of world industrialization, it was not until the end of the 1960s that their subsidiaries began to practice international vertical specialization, with more emphasis being placed on the production of intermediate goods rather than final ones. By 2001 there were about 65 000 MNCs, most of them located in the United States, Japan and Europe, but some in developing regions such as East Asia and Latin America (UNCTAD, 2002). According to an UNCTAD estimate, in 2001 MNCs accounted for more than 10 per cent of world output, one third of host countries' output and almost 50 per cent of international trade (Table 4.1). While the majority of their activities in developed countries involved services, in developing countries they engaged in both manufacturing and services.

The expansion of MNC activities was a main cause of the increase in international current and capital transactions. First, external trade related to MNCs made up two thirds of the total, with intrafirm trade accounting for the other third. Second, MNC-related transactions led to an expansion of technology trade through capital goods trade, technology licence fees, technological training programmes and so on, with growth in this area exceeding that of FDI. Since research and development activities tend to take place at MNC headquarters, the growth of technology trade has been largest among developed countries. Third, with regard to financial flows that accompany the establishment, acquisition and expansion of subsidiaries (FDI), such flows have increased in the case of developed countries more dynamically than in the developing ones. In summary, MNCs have significantly

Table 4.1 International production, 1982–2000

item	Value at current prices (billion dollars)				Annual growth rate (per cent)		
	1982	1990	2000	2001	1986–90	1991–95	1996–2000
FDI inflows	57	202	1 271	735	23.6	20.0	40.1
FDI outflows	37	235	1 150	621	24.3	15.8	36.7
Gross product of MNCs	565	1 420	3 167	3 495	18.8	6.7	12.9
Total assets of MNCs	1 888	5 744	21 102	24 952	19.8	13.4	19.0
Exports of MNCs	637	1 166	3 572	2 600	14.9	7.4	9.7
GDP at factor cost	10 612	21 475	31 895	31 900	11.5	6.5	1.2
Exports of goods and services	2 124	4 381	7 036	7 430	15.8	8.7	4.2

Source: UNCTAD (2002).

contributed to the increased the international flow of goods and services, technology and financial resources.

Global FDI increased by 40 per cent a year during 1996–2000, a record high since the 1980s. However it should be noted that the net increase was mainly due to FDI among developed countries. The majority involved mergers and acquisitions, presumably driven by the urgent need to increase company size and market power in order to cope with the intensified competition that followed deregulation and market integration.

Globalization has led to rapid changes in the international economic environment by accelerating technological innovation and virtually shrinking economic space. What does this imply for the development strategies of developing countries? Let us consider this from the viewpoint of dynamic learning effects.

According to the theory of foreign direct investment, MNCs compete with local firms by making use of the location advantage of the host country and the ownership advantage of their managerial resources, as well as the internalization advantage of their intrafirm transactions. Since MNCs can deploy their mobile resources on a global scale in pursuit of optimal locations, their decisions on location depend on whether host countries can provide the necessary immobile resources or factors. In other words MNCs tend to utilize the static comparative advantages of a host country at the moment when they make investment decisions.[2]

The issue, then, is whether such behaviour affects the host countries' welfare. There are three types of market failure. First, incomplete information may result in inadequate investment. Second, the private benefits for MNCs may be different from the host countries' social benefits. Third, MNCs may have more bargaining power than host country governments and take the lion's share of the benefits that accrue from the enlarged international division of labour.

The first case occurs when incomplete information results in excessive investment by MNCs and the distortion of factor prices. This can lead not only to income transfers to MNCs, but also to the secondary burden of crowding out local firms. Excessive incentives for FDI can cause similar problems.

The second case becomes relevant when the learning effects are smaller for MNCs than for local firms. While FDI is supposed to be a major channel for technology transfers, this is not always the case. Internationally extended production networks have brought about a meticulous *process* division of labour (or *fragmentation* of production processes) in which MNCs tend to lock in the present static comparative advantage of a host country. This can retard changes in its dynamic advantages.

Examples of the third case arise when competition among host countries is so intense that factor prices are distorted by the provision of investment incentives, and transfer pricing by MNCs using market power and internalization advantages generates income transfers out of the host countries. In such cases, the presence of MNCs obviously results in a welfare loss to host countries.

In the course of globalizing production activities, firms make decisions about international locations and specialization just as they do in the case of domestic markets. It is firms that choose a country (a national economy), not *vice versa*, so that national borders tend to become more irrelevant to corporations. By contrast, cross-border movements by labour are quite limited, particularly those involving residence. It is estimated that at the beginning of the twenty-first century there were 130 million migrants (people residing outside their country of birth), and it is estimated that this figure will grow by 2 per cent a year. Yet their share of the total population only amounts to 2.3 per cent, concentrated mainly in North America, Western Europe, Oceania and the Middle East. In this sense, in contrast to goods and services and capital, it can be said that labour is immobile.

In order to maximize national welfare and achieve sustainable national income growth it is necessary to mobilize these immobile resources efficiently, to enhance their quality and to nurture the higher value added sectors that use them. National governments have a significant role to play in this. Essentially, they must develop and manage the institutional framework, including legal systems and economic rules, that form the basis of the market mechanism. They must also provide public goods and services in areas such as industrial infrastructure and human capital formation, where market failures are very likely. Particularly in the present context, in order to bring about dynamic comparative advantages national governments must compensate for the incompleteness of information by using their functions of signalling and insurance. At times, they must play the role of a negotiator delegated by the people to cope with the market power of MNCs.

Catching up through the globalization of knowledge

Natural resource endowments are not fundamental to economic development. This is made clear by the fact that economic development started from the need to overcome resource limitations, and that many countries with few natural resources have attained remarkable economic development. Economic development depends on the extent to which physical and human capital can be effectively organized and utilized in order to maximize output per unit of capital input. Knowledge can improve the quality of capital inputs as well as enhance the efficiency of organizing and utilizing them.

Developed countries' postwar experience of industrialization suggests that in the course of economic development, knowledge becomes more important than capital input (King and Levine, 1994).[3] Education, research and development, technological innovation and application, at both the individual and corporate levels, are sources of productivity growth. The globalization and integration of the world economy have promoted efforts these in areas. In fact, the output and trade shares of high-technology industries increased without exception in the OECD countries in the period 1970–94 (Table 4.2). In developed countries, more than half of GDP comes from goods and services in knowledge-based industries. Since the IT revolution has accelerated the creation of new knowledge, without proper investment in knowledge even developed countries will lose their competitive edge and their development will stall.

For individual developing countries, the globalization trend is a reality that, like it or not, they must accept. In order to develop in this new environment they have to acquire knowledge and improve their ability to utilize it to the full. Knowledge, however, is different from ordinary goods and services that can be bought on the market. Since it has the characteristics of a public good, including non-rivalry and non-exclusion, private markets cannot provide an adequate supply. Moreover, while it needs to be disseminated among people in order to contribute to economic development, this dissemination is not automatic and requires a variety of institutional infrastructure to facilitate it.

Thus in order to create and disseminate knowledge, developing countries should establish public institutions to provide the private sector with incentives. First, the protection of intellectual property rights is necessary not only for promoting technology transfers but also for creating local knowledge and adapting foreign technology. Second, human capital formation is indispensable for acquiring and utilizing knowledge. Specifically, public policies should play a very significant role in primary, secondary and tertiary education in order to maintain equality of educational opportunity, reap the spillover effects of education and compensate for market failures in

Table 4.2 Share of high-technology industries in manufacturing value added and exports in high-income economies, 1970–94 (per cent)

	Value added		Exports	
	1970	*1994*	*1970*	*1993*
Australia	8.9	12.2	2.8	10.3
Canada	10.2	12.6	9	13.4
France	12.8	18.7	14	24.2
Germany	15.3	20.1	15.8	21.4
Japan	16.4	22.2	20.2	36.7
United Kingdom	16.6	22.2	17.1	32.6
United States	18.2	24.2	25.9	37.3

Source: UNCTAD (1999).

educational services. Also, in fields where large social benefits can be expected, such as agriculture in developing countries, it would be useful for the public sector on its own to implement and support research and development activities.

Since acquiring established technologies is believed to be less costly than innovation, it was thought that developing countries would be able to enjoy the 'advantage of backwardness' in their effort to catch up *vis-à-vis* with developed countries. Indeed in the fields of public health and agriculture there has been a significant decline in infant mortality and a remarkable increase in grain production through the efficient utilization and dissemination of established knowledge. Nevertheless, knowledge gaps are widening in many fields, and it is likely that the acceleration of technological innovation that is driving globalization will hasten this process. Developing countries need not only to accumulate factor inputs through physical and human investment, but also to develop the ability to utilize best-practice knowledge efficiently. This is because the rents from reducing knowledge gaps can be very large. If developing countries rely on their present static comparative advantage and put little efforts into creating a dynamic advantage, their living standards will decline because technological progress tends to lead to lower returns from unskilled labour.

Costs of globalization: volatile capital flows

The recent trend towards financial globalization has revealed the opportunities and risks of capital account liberalization in developing economies. The opportunities include increased investment possibilities, the creation of technology spillovers and the deepening of domestic capital markets. The risks include increasing instability in small open economies that are highly exposed to extraneous shocks, such as a sudden reversal of foreign capital flows. This can lead to serious difficulties not only in macroeconomic management but also in financial systems as a whole.

In fact, small open economies in the developing world have never been as open as developed economies. Figure 4.5 shows the relative ratio of gross capital flows to GDP across regions. Due to the steady growth of foreign direct investment and other capital flows, reliance on foreign capital flows has increased in developing economies as a whole. Their situation is, however, not comparable to that of developed economies in terms of either levels or trends. It is obvious from the figure that developing economies, as well as Asian economies, have been far less open than developed economies relative to GDP levels.

To what extent are developing economies less open than developed ones, and why? The IMF (2001b) has two complementary measures of capital account liberalization. The 'restriction measure' is based on the number of restrictions on capital flows, as reported to the IMF by national authorities

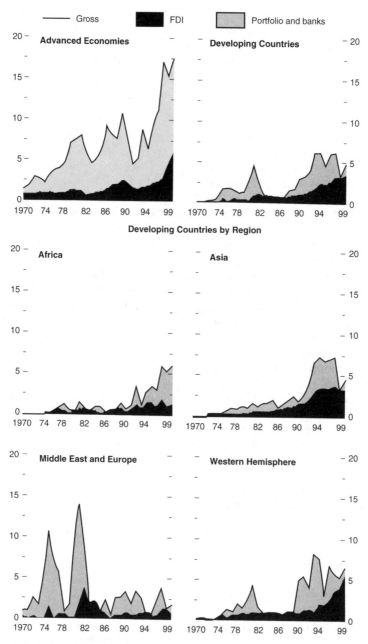

Figure 4.5 Gross capital flows, by region, 1970–1999
Source: IMF, *International Financial Statistics* and IMF staff estimates.

(note, however, that this measure does not adequately capture the degree of liberalization). The 'openness measure' is based on gross stocks of foreign assets and liabilities as a ratio to GDP. This indicates the depth of external finance. The degree of regions' capital account liberalization, according to these two measures, is illustrated in Figure 4.6.

One notable observation is that while in developed economies there were parallel movements in the two measures (towards more openness in the capital account), the measures diverged over time in developing economies. In more recent periods in particular, the degree of openness continued to increase despite the fact that restriction measures remained unchanged. In the case of Asia it is likely that this partly reflects the opening up of China and the rapid growth of East Asia.

This suggests either that the restrictions in developing countries are not particularly effective or up to date, or that the exogenous pressure of capital flows is very strong, or both. Either way, there is a need for institutional rearrangements and/or for capital flow management to be adjusted to the reality of accelerating global financial integration.

Market liberalization *per se* does not guarantee that the market mechanism will be fully functional, especially in the case of capital markets, which are characterized by incomplete and asymmetric information. Indeed various studies have found mixed evidence across economies in respect of whether simple capital account liberalization can generate economic growth, either through increased domestic investment, spillovers from technology transfers or deepened domestic financial markets (see IMF, 2001b, and the references therein). This suggests that the impact of capital account liberalization on economic growth depends crucially on the initial conditions in and policies of the economy in question. In other words, for liberalization to bring the expected benefits with minimum costs, institutional conditions must be improved in a way that suits an individual economy's context.

In the long term, the globalization of financial markets may lead to increased opportunities due to more efficient resource allocation and better risk diversification. Emerging markets, however, are only marginal to the global capital market, and they tend to be vulnerable to large swings in international investor sentiments, which are subject to herd behaviour and contagion.

The IMF (2001a) refers to the 'on-off' nature of international investors in emerging market financing. This is not news and is well recognized as being intrinsic to the international capital market. At present, on top of this, the 'increased asset price volatility in matured markets and the prospects of a slowdown in global growth combined with market turbulence in key emerging markets (ibid, p. 40)' will make it difficult for emerging markets, including East Asian economies, to tap external finance in either portfolio investment or loans in comparison with the early 1990s.

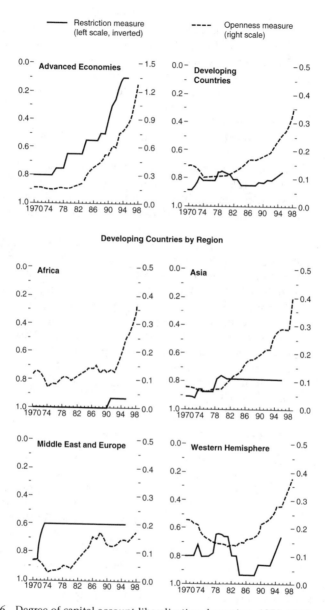

Figure 4.6 Degree of capital account liberalization, by region, 1970–1998

Note: The restriction measure is calculated and the average value of the on/off measure for the country group. The openness measure is calculated as the average stock of accumulated capital flows (as per cent of GDP) in a country group.

Source: IMF Annual Report on Exchange Arrangements and Exchange Restrictions various issues international financial statistics and IMF staff calculations.

Market failure can occur in all capital markets. To address this, in domestic markets a variety of safety nets have been devised, such as the central bank as lender of last resort and deposit insurance schemes, but there are no safety nets in the international market. Obviously, as illustrated by the Asian crisis, systemic risks are beyond the control of individual monetary authorities in developing countries, which is one reason why a new international financial architecture is desperately needed.

Of course, the short-term benefits from bailouts and the long-term costs and risks of moral hazard must be accounted for when devising any new safety net scheme. With this trade-off in mind, it is necessary to proceed on two fronts: short-term debt workouts and long-term crisis minimization. With regard to debt workouts, it is necessary not only to resolve debts on a case-by-case basis, with some debt relief, but also to establish rules for risk sharing between private debtors and creditors. Crisis prevention requires action in three areas.

First, there is a need to strengthen the supervision of both debtors and creditors, given proper consideration to comparative advantages and international cooperation. Second, expanded liquidity provision and stand-by arrangements could be helpful in at least partially containing sudden capital reversals. Considering the relatively slow pace of crisis spillovers in the Asian crisis, the existence of an Asian Monetary Fund might have been useful if the timing had been right. Third, increasing transparency and enhancing the disclosure of information in the private as well as the public sector could be of some use in reducing uncertainties, although this would take time and would have to proceed hand in hand with the institutional evolution of individual economies.[4]

Costs of globalization: institutional changes

Experiences during the past 50 years indicate that development is far from easy. Among the developing regions, only East Asia is catching up with the developed countries, while the income gaps between the others, and the developed economies have continued to widen. In the 1950s and 1960s, development strategies were intended to achieve industrialization through trade protection and government intervention (because of a loss of belief in the market mechanism), but these ended up as government failures. In the 1970s, the mainstream development strategy was to limit the government's role in macroeconomic stabilization and public good provision and to make full use of private markets in other domains. The former can be labelled 'interventionism' and the latter 'marketism'.

Let us look at the only successful region, East Asia.[5] The region's high investment and saving ratios, large investment in basic education, openness to the world economy and macroeconomic stability were the result of policy choices that were favourable to and efficient for economic development.

As is well known, the governments of East Asia never limited their role to the provision of macroeconomic stability and public goods. Rather, they intervened actively in the international trade and domestic capital markets, although one can say that they never deviated very far from market criteria. Good economic performance was the yardstick for the legitimacy of national governments as well as for strategic sectors and firms. It could be said that it was connection-based, informal discretionary rules rather than market-based, formal and transparent rules that constituted their institutional infrastructure.[6]

In this sense, the success of East Asia was not due to marketism. The choice between marketism and interventionism is not, however, at issue. Institutional infrastructure is never an outcome of social welfare maximization; it is the result of political-economic conflicts over the allocation of resources in a society. East Asia was no exception in this regard. Nevertheless, the chosen policies did not deviate far from market criteria, or at least not in comparison with those of other developing countries. As a result, people appeared to more or less enjoy improved living standards and were able to trust the general orientation of policy management. Indeed the aim of development strategies was not only to adopt the correct policies, but also to create the necessary institutional infrastructure to motivate it. This turned out to be the most difficult challenge.

In the case of East Asia, the existing institutional infrastructures were formed under political regimes that were, to a lesser or greater extent, closer to developmental dictatorships than to democracy. Through trial and error they arrived at comparatively effective policies. This was not marketism, but neither did their interventionism neglect the market mechanism. Although developmental objectives and priorities differed across countries as well as periods, governments coordinated the interests of the various constituents of their national economies. The constituents, for their part, minded their own business, as they had some trust in their governments' management capabilities. These practices resulted in the improvement of national welfare. Such networks of mutual trust are the very foundation of economic development, and who else can provide them but national governments?

The Asian economic crisis is said to have heralded sea changes not only in corporate governance but also in the social contracts between the governments and people of East Asia (World Bank, 2000). Indeed, after the crisis the East Asian governments launched serious institutional reforms in pursuit for the resumption of growth. It is claimed that the first stage of this was rewarded by rapid economic recovery, despite the slow pace of the structural reforms. Is this true? Will the East Asian recovery lead to the renewal of rapid growth based on the new institutional infrastructure?

It is thought that the 'East Asian Miracle' was due to high capital accumulation, continuous educational investment and a market-friendly institutional infrastructure (World Bank, 1993). However, the first two may no longer be able to support future growth, as the economies mature. If this is the case, growth will have to be supported by enhanced factor productivity. What is at issue, then, is how the past and current institutional infrastructure can adapt to globalization and whether the current reform efforts will lead to the institutional changes needed to support the growth of productivity.

It is ironic that the Asian economic crisis led to a greater role for government, since recent thinking – as in the Washington Consensus – tends to be negative towards government intervention in general. In fact, postcrisis macroeconomic adjustments that required fiscal resources to cope with significant private debts were carried out successfully by national governments, even without formal government guarantees.

In addition to cyclical or transitory needs, bigger governments or government involvement may be a necessity under globalization and increased market orientation, and for economic development itself. First, the risks brought about by globalization are increasing the need for social safety nets. Programmes that incorporate additional public employment, agricultural development, social security funds and income-guarantee mechanisms have been introduced to protect workers from these risks. Second, the knowledge-based economy and the acceleration of technical progress require increased educational expenditure and the upgrading of tertiary education. Third, to cope with globalization and intense international competition, infrastructure such as transportation, communication and urbanization must be strengthened. Through increasing income levels, urbanization, enhanced education and the ageing of society economic development itself is generating a need for public services such as environmental protection and social security.

The current reforms include the strengthening of government regulations and supervision and the reform of formal institutions and rules (such as accounting rules) and judicial institutions (such as bankruptcy laws). It is not at all clear whether or to what extent these reforms will be enforced and/or complied with in practice, and whether they may curtail transaction and information costs compared with those which prevailed with previous institutions. Generally, it is difficult for predesigned laws and organizations to become as 'institutionalized' (that is, accepted as self-binding rules within a society or a nation-state) as they are supposed to (Aoki, 2002). Furthermore, even if they are eventually institutionalized, this will take a great deal of time.[7]

Broadening the role of national governments

Is the integration of the world economy rendering nation-states and national economies useless? As we have seen, MNCs have extended their networks of optimal production by combining their own advantages with those of host countries. For MNCs, national economies are objects to choose between, not to develop. This holds true not only for real capital but for financial capital as well. With both bank loans and portfolio investments they will choose those with the highest expected rate of return in the same risk classes across countries. They never invest in order to increase the expected rates of return of host countries as a whole.

Even so, if the expected rates of return are higher in developing countries with a relative shortage of capital, capital will tend to flow – in accordance with differences in the rates of return – from capital-abundant to capital-scarce countries, equalizing the marginal rates of return. In practice, however, since uncertainties are generally more numerous in less developed countries with a shortage of capital, foreign capital tends to concentrate in just a few developing countries, such as the emerging markets. This helps the development of the host countries if it is used efficiently. If it is not, however, it may cause a reversal of capital flows, leading to a currency crisis. Financial globalization does not necessarily eliminate the failures that are inherent to capital markets, and may even magnify them.

The purpose of any development strategy is to nurture the national economy and improve social welfare. Hence the national government, as the delegated agency, is ultimately responsible for the welfare of the people. The financial crisis of 1997 highlighted the urgent need to restructure domestic capital markets and the regulatory and supervisory regimes. The Asian economic crisis occurred not because of inadequate intervention by national governments, but because of lack of adequate interventions.

Another cause of the crisis was an international capital market failure, as reflected in excess inflows of foreign capital, especially short-term capital, their reversal and the subsequent contagion. Such events are beyond the control of individual national governments, so there is a need for them to join forces in a cooperative effort to restructure the international financial arrangements. We should note, here, that international cooperation cannot be executed without support from the governments of nation-states.

With regard to technology (or knowledge) transfers to developing countries, if transfers are promoted under globalization through external trade, foreign direct investment and the licensing of technologies, and if the IT revolution facilitates access to global best-practice technologies, then it is possible that, taking advantage of their status as latecomers, developing countries could rapidly reduce their knowledge and technology gaps with the developed countries. In practice, however, it is not only difficult to acquire knowledge and technology, but it is also difficult to disseminate it. Acquiring knowledge requires an accumulation of knowledge capital (that is, large-scale fixed capital) and the protection of intellectual property rights. This can be expected to motivate knowledge creation, but tends to make the acquisition of knowledge more costly. The transfer and efficient dissemination of knowledge requires an institutional infrastructure that developing countries tend to lack. Hence, the current acceleration of technological innovation under globalization is likely to increase the knowledge gap.

Given the public-good nature of knowledge, there is a need for national strategies to address this problem. To shrink the knowledge gap, the only choice is to create a comparative advantage through targeted public investment. The acquisition and dissemination of global knowledge, and the facilitation of this through investment in human capital and technology, are only part of the responsibilities of national governments.

Concluding remarks

The collapse of the centrally planned socialist economies and the difficulties encountered by the capitalist welfare states have revealed that if nation-states neglect the market mechanism, they may damage national welfare and even fail to maintain national economies. However this does not mean that we need only the market, but no longer the nation-state, or that national economies are no longer relevant units to people's welfare.[8]

Welfare states emerged because the market was unable to bring about distributional equity and ensure the adequate provision of public goods. Moreover, as demonstrated by some marginalized economies, the loss of some state functions led to the collapse of national economies and a severe deterioration of people's welfare. Even under the capitalist system the market mechanism cannot work if people do not trust the system.[9] The fact that the market mechanism works based on anonymous price signals with minimal information costs does not deny the importance of trust in the system. While the rules that constitute the institutional infrastructure are intended to coordinate between egoistic interests, we should note that egoistic motivation can result in even being altruistic. Indeed the fact that income redistribution and social security systems have been institutionalized in the contemporary world suggests that the system is driven not only by self-interest, but also by humanitarianism and idealism.

With the integration of the world economy the market mechanism is penetrating across borders, which in the absence of impediments to the market, would tend to equalize opportunities and help those who are poor in terms of capital and technology to catch up with those who are rich. This could result in a diminution of the functions of national governments and the role of nation-states. But since it takes time for capital, knowledge and technology to be built up and redistributed, uncertainties and asymmetric information would be unavoidable and their accumulation and allocation would be inadequate. Hence, there are good reasons for governments to continue to undertake these functions and/or to minimize the problems of uncertainty and incomplete information through risk sharing and information provision.

Globalization can also exacerbate market failures by magnifying uncertainties and incomplete information, as occurred during the Asian crisis in 1997. This is because technological innovation, a driving force of globalization, exerts external effects in terms of economies of scale and agglomeration. If these cumulative effects marginalize developing countries, national welfare will decline and the income gap will widen. The task of minimizing such negative externalities can best be handled by national governments working collectively.

It is well known that economic development requires not only capital and labour but also institutional infrastructure, and its establishment, maintenance and management have traditionally been the responsibility of national governments. The modern market system could not function if governments were not there to enforce property rights, contracts and other basic rules, and to punish non-compliance with them.

Notes

1. Another is the cost of transportation and communication.
2. Of course static comparative advantage is not the sole determinant of MNC location. For example in the case of FDI in developed countries, MNCs might be motivated by possible technology transfers from the host country. In the case of FDI in developing countries, MNCs might have an eye to the host countries' potential for growth and the long-term profits. Note, however, that in either case the expected long-term returns would have to outweigh any short-term losses from static comparative disadvantages.
3. Or at least at the later stage. Historical experience seems to suggest that capital input is a major driving force in the earlier stage of industrialization. Whether or not this is a general pattern in economic development is debatable.
4. One could suggest that there is a need to establish a robust credit and risk management culture, which would take time. Increased competition from foreign financial institutions might help to accelerate the process.
5. Although things changed in 1997, it is impossible to deny their success over the past 50 years or so.
6. Here the term *institutions* refers to the set of formal and informal rules that govern the behaviour of individuals and organizations, as well as their interactions in the development process. 'Institutional infrastructure', which supports these institutions, consists of informal behavioural norms, such as reduction of the transaction costs for coordination and trouble solving, and formal legal rules, such as the enforcement of contracts, protection of property rights, management of bankruptcy, maintenance of competitiveness and so on.
7. The World Bank (2000) estimates the extent of public sector governance by means of six indicators: (1) political freedom and transparency of political decision making, (2) political instability and violence, (3) government efficiency, (4) regulations, (5) judicial rules and (6) corruption. While such measures are not necessarily reliable, the results are interesting. Governance in East Asia is found to be intermediate among the developing economies. More generally, the institutional quality of governance positively correlates with the degree of economic development, that is, per capita income levels.
8. The rationales behind the mixed economies and welfare states of the post-Second World War capitalist world were harshly criticized by the proponents of liberalization policy, who had doubts about the effectiveness of Keynesian-type discretionary

policies. As one economist said, 'One century ago, international trade was completely free and they had never heard of welfare states' (Dornbusch, 1997). Moreover 'the concept of a state is so obsolete that a nation-state cannot be a legitimate unit of economic framework anymore' (ibid.). For others, state intervention in national economies marked the end of the good old days of the nineteenth century and gave birth to the spectre of the welfare state.

9. However, when extolling the superiority of the capitalist system, Krugman (1997) states that 'while the socialist system could not work unless people trusted in it, the capitalist system works even without the trust. In the long run, neither dreams nor idealism, but only people's egoism drives the system.'

References

Aoki, M. (2002) '*Seido no Daitenkan Sokushin o*' (Promote a mega-shift of institutions [in Japanese]), *Nihon Keizai Shinbun*, 4 January.

Barro, R. J. and X. Sara-i-Martin (1995) *Economic Growth* (New York: McGraw-Hill).

Bordo, M. D., B. Eichengreen, and J. Kim (1998) 'Was There Really an Earlier Period of International Financial Integration Comparable to Today?', *NBER Working Paper*, no. 6738 (Cambridge, Mass.: NBER).

Dornbusch, R. (1997) 'Jiyu Keizai, Kojin-shugi e Kaiki' (Back to a Free Economy and Individualism [in Japanese]), *Nihon Keizai Shinbun*, 9 September.

Haque, N. U. and S.-J. Kim (1995) '"Human Capital Flight": Impact of Migration on Income and Growth', *IMF Staff Papers* no. 42 (Washington, DC: IMF).

International Monetary Fund (IMF) (2001a) *International Capital Market* (Washington, DC: IMF).

International Monetary Fund (IMF) (2001b) *World Economic Outlook, October* (Washington, DC: IMF).

King, R. G. and R. Levine (1994) 'Capital Fundamentalism, Economic Development, and Economic Growth', *Carnegie-Rochester Conference Series on Public Policy*, no. 40 (New York: Elsevier), pp. 259–92.

Kohsaka, A. (1999) 'Macroeconomic Management under the Increasing Capital Market Integration in the Asia Pacific Region: Beyond the Tom Yam Effect', in S. Motamen-Samadian and C. Garrido (eds), *Emerging Markets: Past and Present Experiences, and Future Prospects*, (London: MacMillan).

Kohsaka, A. and K. Ohno (eds) (1996) *Structural Adjustment and Economic Reform* (Tokyo: Institute of Developing Economies).

Krugman, P. (1997) 'Rikoshin Sijo no Shori Michibuku' (Egoism Led to the Victory of the Market [in Japanese]), *Nihon Keizai Shinbun*, 3 September.

Stiglitz, J. E. (2002) *Globalization and its Discontents* (New York: W.W. Norton).

UNCTAD (various years) *World Investment Report* (New York: UNCTAD).

World Bank (1993) *The East Asian Miracle* (New York: Oxford University Press).

World Bank (various years) *World Development Report* (New York: Oxford University Press).

World Bank (2000) *East Asia: Recovery and Beyond* (Washington, DC: World Bank).

Part II

Development Strategies under Globalization

5
Globalization and Development: A Re-examination of Development Policy[1]

Kaushik Basu

Introduction

The nature of policy making in developing countries has been undergoing a sea change in recent times. This is due in part to the increasing maturity of the discipline of development economics and in part to the changing nature of the global economy. Development economics has advanced rapidly on both the theoretical and empirical fronts. Better interaction with main-stream economic theory, and the increasing availability of data sets that enable us to analyze aspects of the economy that were previously beyond scrutiny, have deeply influenced the study of development. As far as the real world goes, technological advancement and globalization have had a huge impact on the nature of policy making in developing countries and, more generally, policy making for development.

This chapter not only investigates the changing face of development policy, but also goes further by raising new analytical issues and urging action in areas that have thus far seen little policy action. The two main themes are labour market policies in a globalizing world and the scope for policy inter-vention to curb poverty and inequality in a world with increasing mobility of capital and professional labour.

The former has been the subject of very good analysis and heated debate in various fora, such as the International Labour Organization (ILO) and the World Trade Organization (WTO), so the aim here is to shed some new light with the help of modern theory. Although the problem of inequality and poverty in the context of globalization has been studied, there is still scope for good analysis. This chapter does some spade work on the subject.

The changing global scenario

This section discusses the global backdrop against which the subsequent analysis of development policy will be conducted.

Colonizing the future

Two remarkable developments from the point of view of real-world economics are the recent advances in information technology and globalization. The best historical equivalent to the rise of the information technology (IT) industry was the invention of the wheel in about 3500 BC in Mesopotamia where depictions of the wheel on clay have been discovered and dated at just after that time. While the wheel is at times useful as an end in itself – in fact there is evidence that soon after its invention there were ancillary inventions of toys and games in which the wheel was the central feature – its main value is that it raises the productivity of other activities. Likewise while computers and other IT innovations can serve as ends in themselves, their main advantage is that they facilitate other activities, be it trade, communication or the simulation of nuclear bombs. The IT industry is currently one of the most profitable industries in the world and will probably remain so for some time. But it is conceivable that eventually it will be just one more industry, its value to the world being that it has made virtually all other industries more efficient and profitable.

Globalization is a close concomitant of the IT industry. It has been facilitated by the cheap and easy modes of communication and trade made possible by the rise of the IT industry. The two main components of globalization are international trade and global capital flows. Both these have grown rapidly. Tables 5.1 and 5.2 provide an overview of the historical trends.

It is evident that the period between the two World Wars marked a retreat from globalization, but barring this period of aberration the movement has been forward. Exports as a percentage of GDP, taken as the average of all countries of the world, rose from 4.6 per cent in 1870 to 17.2 per cent in 1998, with a brief reversal between 1914 and 1950. The same is true of the value of foreign capital stock, both on its own and as a percentage of GDP.

Table 5.1 Merchandise exports as percentage of GDP, 1870–1995

	1870	1913	1950	1995
Western Europe	8.8	14.1	8.7	35.8
Asia	1.7	3.4	4.2	12.6
Latin America	9.7	9.0	6.0	9.7
Africa	5.8	20.0	15.1	14.8
World	4.6	7.9	5.5	17.2

Source: Maddison (2001).

Table 5.2 Value of foreign capital stock in developing countries, 1870–1998

	1870	1914	1950	1998
Total ($ billion in 1990 prices)	40.1	235.4	63.2	3030.7
Stock as percentage of GDP	8.6	32.4	4.4	21.7

Source: Maddison (2001).

Today, however, foreign capital stock as a percentage of GDP is below the level in 1914, but two factors make this less significant than it appears to be. From 1914 to 1998, world GDP experienced enormous growth so it is not surprising that the stock of foreign capital lagged behind in relative terms, despite its own immense growth. In fact the total stock of foreign capital in all countries in 1998 stood at an astonishing $3030 billion, which was far higher than ever before. Second, it seems reasonable to presume that, until the early twentieth century, most of the foreign capital flows were from the imperial powers to their respective colonies. In those days it was necessary to establish political control before sending one's money somewhere. Now that this is no longer necessary the world has become much more of a market place. Of course, investing countries still use subtle forms of political control and checks on recipient countries, but that is very different from the control of a colony. One of the main features of globalization is the ability to invest in distant countries with little direct control.

These trends have continued in recent years, as is illustrated in Table 5.3. In the 10-year period covered in the table, all regions saw a rise in capital

Table 5.3 Globalization indicators, 1989–99

	Trade in goods as a percentage of goods GDP[1]		Gross private capital flows[2] as a percentage of PPP GDP	
	1989	1999	1989	1999
Low-income countries	41.3	60.0	0.8	1.2
Middle-income countries	69.0	81.5	1.9	4.9
High-income countries	93.5	123.5	2.1	4.9
South Asia	25.6	38.1	0.3	0.6
Sub-Saharan Africa	78.1	95.6	2.1	4.9
Latin America and Caribbean	49.8	74.6	2.2	7.3

Notes: 1. Excludes services.
2. The sum of the capital that flowed into and out of the countries.
Source: World Bank (2001).

flows, the overall average rise being approximately 50 per cent. Trade in goods as a percentage of GDP also rose substantially in all regions.

Of course, not all regions have merged with the global markets and financial economy with equal rapidity. The fastest integration occurred in most of Asia and parts of Latin America (Kohsaka, 2002); Africa has also done well as a percentage of its own GDP. Also, the composition of capital has changed, with a sharper increase in foreign direct investment and portfolio investment than in bank credit and loans. For some countries, such as India, the dominant form of capital market integration has been the flow of foreign capital into the stock markets.

While political instability or war can reverse the trend, it seems reasonable to conclude that the process of globalization, after a period of vacillation caused by the shock of the two world wars, is firmly on course. Ideas, goods and money now flow almost instantaneously between distant countries and cities. One implication of this is that inventions spread rapidly, generating interest in faraway places and facilitating further inventions. A ten-year-old computer now looks ancient, and it seems hard to believe that 10 years ago e-mail did not exist.

Contrast this with innovations in the design of the wheel. Initially (that is, around 3500 BC) it was made of solid disks. It took 1500 years for human beings to realize that it would be more efficient to carve the disk into a ring stretched by spokes. This made it lighter and better able to absorb shocks. It then took another 1400 years to realize that roller bearings would minimize friction and enable the wheel to turn more easily. Not only did inventions occur at great intervals, but ideas took a very long time to spread from one region to another. The Mayans built some of the world's most magnificent stone pyramids but were unaware of the machinery or wheeled vehicles that would have made their work considerably easier.

All these processes went on for hundreds or even thousands of years. The pace has picked up astonishingly in the past few decades, thus changing the nature of the global game faster than most of us can comprehend, creating new opportunities and new tensions, and rapidly altering the efficacy of policy instruments.

In today's world, the struggle is no longer to colonize and control new lands but to 'colonize the future', that is, to lay claims on tomorrow's output (Basu, 2000a). Two factors have made this feasible: the ability to take out patents and copyrights and enforce them, and the widespread availability of stocks, shares and other financial assets. The colonizers of today try to secure a large number of patents and hold huge amounts of shares. When tomorrow comes and the output emerges from factories and offices, part of this output will already have claimants from today (those holding patents and those holding shares) and the remainder will be split between the providers of tomorrow's inputs – labour, raw materials and so on.

It is worth noting that this colonization of the future is not happening equitably across countries. In 1995, for instance, 235 440 patent applications were filed in the United States, whereas in some of the poorer countries fewer than 100 applications were filed. Hence, the global inequalities of today are likely to be reinforced tomorrow.

Erosion of global democracy

Another aspect of globalization and the rise of modern technology is that it has a tendency to erode global democracy. To understand this, observe that it is much easier today for one country to interfere in the affairs of another. In ancient times to influence the policy of another nation, the only option would be to muster an army or sail the high seas to attack. Today, not only have military actions become much more arms-length and effective,[2] but a variety of economic reprisals are possible with the click of a mouse. Of course, coordinating these economic actions is not always easy, since it may involve the participation of firms and corporations that in principle are free agents. Nevertheless, countries have successfully used the threat of cessation of trade or the withholding of capital flows to influence policy. For example, the US Helms–Burton Act has been used to apply pressure on Cuba not only by curbing US business and trade with that country but also by threatening to cut off business with countries that trade with and invest in it. For instance the Act has been used to dissuade Mexicans, Italians and Canadians from doing business with Cuba, which is something they would not have contemplated of their own accord.

Now, if we use a rudimentary definition of democracy, namely, a political system where ordinary citizens have the ability to influence the choice of leaders who influence their lives by exercising their vote, it should be immediately transparent that globalization has a tendency to erode democracy.

Even though it is not possible for people in one country to influence events in another through the democratic electoral process, the leaders of some countries have developed more and more instruments to influence the lives of people elsewhere in the world (a definitional implication of globalization), with a consequent diminution of global democracy (Basu, 2002a). This phenomenon has major political and economic implications and calls for thought and institutional innovation.

Globalization and marginalization

While, on the whole, globalization creates more opportunities than it destroys, it can have the negative effect of marginalizing some people. If this is left unchecked it could lead to political instability and social decay. Not only are marginalization and the consequent rise in poverty undesirable in themselves, but we now have the ability to deal with them effectively. We are at a point in history where it is possible to talk – without inviting the label of idealistic crank – of rooting out poverty from the world altogether. And unlike smallpox there will be no need to keep a small supply of the germs of poverty in stock to counter possible terrorist attacks.

To understand how globalization can lead to marginalization, consider a poor person in a Third World nation, say, India whose livelihood is off-shore fishing. If India were to modernize and become more integrated into the world economy, it might well be that technologically advanced fishing companies would go out to the high seas and bring in larger catches than ever before. The exportation of these catches would make India better off as a whole, but it could diminish the available stock of fish closer to the coast-line, resulting in smaller catches by the poor fisherman thereby leaving him worse off. This is an obvious 'resource route' which can result in some people getting marginalized and made worse off by the processes of technological advancement and globalization.

But there is another, more complex, route. Suppose now that the fisherman catches all his fish from a lake. He consumes some of the fish and sells the remainder on the market, which enables him to buy other essentials such as salt, sugar other food and clothing (no one in today's world is totally self-sufficient). At first sight, it may appear that the activities of the deep-sea fishing companies would have no effect on his standard of living, but this is actually unlikely. It is entirely possible that the larger hauls of ocean fish would cause the price of all fish to drop. Hence the fisherman would receive less money for his fish and could buy fewer essentials.[3] Hence he would become poorer even though the resources to which he had access remained unchanged. The extent of such 'market-route' marginalization could be very significant, but as economists and statisticians have shown little awareness of the phenomenon, no data is available.

Together, the market and resource routes could create very large constitu-encies of losers in the globalization process. Apart from its innate unfairness, this could cause large-scale disillusionment, dissent and ultimately political instability. It is arguable that some of the myriad forms of global dissent that we are seeing today, ranging from terrorism to roadside protests, have their roots in such marginalization. To describe this as a cause of today's global dissent is not to deny that there may be other causes. Economists and social scientists tend to concentrate overly on the proximate causes of global dissent, not realizing that unless the deeper underlying causes are recognized and dealt with we shall perennially be putting out little fires.

Markets can be very good instruments for generating greater productivity and efficiency but they do not have an in-built mechanism to ensure better distri-bution of the fruits of progress. Hence it is essential to establish institutions to improve the distribution of goods and services and to obliterate poverty.

With this global scenario as a backdrop I shall now consider some concrete themes in development policy. The focus will be not just on developing countries but also on the poorest sections of these countries, particularly in terms of the well-being of workers and inequality in general.

Labour market policy

Labour market policy is important both because it can influence the performance of the whole economy and because workers are typically the poorest constituents of the economy[4] and therefore deserve special attention. Moreover, this is the area in which globalization has changed the terms of debate more dramatically than anywhere else.

Labour markets have always been more closed than the market for goods and services. For reasons mired in politics and sociology, people have generally preferred to stay where they were born and raised and where they have their cultural roots, which means that the economic incentive for moving has to be substantial for those who decide to migrate. Moreover, nations have tended to erect barriers against immigration that are more formidable than those erected to curtail the importing of goods and services. Hence labour markets are one area in which countries have felt relatively free to have their own laws and regulations, designed according to their own tastes, politics and cultural prerogatives. Of course, through the import and export of goods, which are ultimately made by labourers, this freedom had its limits. But what has happened in recent times is that this freedom to craft one's own laws has been more severely curbed by the global mobility of capital. Even if workers from country x cannot move to the factories of country y, globally mobile capital means that the factories of country y can now come to the workers of country x.

This *de facto* labour mobility has two implications. First, when a developing country now drafts a new law for its workers, for instance to enhance some workplace right, it has to be sure that this will not drive capital away to another country. Hence countries' legislative freedom is much more limited in today's globalized world.[5] Second, this *de facto* labour mobility means that industrialized countries are now paying greater attention to working conditions and the labour market in developing countries. This is based on the fear, often misplaced, that the outward flow of capital will result in a loss of jobs in industrialized countries. Child labour is a matter of moral concern to most people, but opposition to it can be used as an instrument of protectionism. In effect, the blending of economics and politics is making the crafting of labour market policy a much contested and intricate matter. To illustrate these points I shall construct a simple model of statutory working hours.

Statutory limits on working hours and international labour standards

Statutory limits on working hours is an old topic. It was hotly debated in the United States in the nineteenth and twentieth centuries and in Britain during the industrial revolution, when it was routine for workers and even child labourers to work 14 hours a day. As early as 1825, skilled workers in Boston were unionizing and holding strikes to have their working day limited to ten hours. In 1842, the Ten Hour Republican Association distributed campaign leaflets for a statutory limit on working hours and the movement soon gained considerable momentum (Murphy, 1992).

The standard argument against a statutory limit proceeded by appealing to the Pareto principle. If a worker voluntarily accepts a work offer that entails 14 hours of work a day, then, while this may seem unbearably long to us, it must be the case that the money earned by the worker more than compensates him for the hard work. And since the employer makes the offer voluntarily, she must be gaining from this as well. It seems we have a Pareto-improving deal here, so why should we object, especially if the agents involved are adults and therefore able to judge what is in their own best interests? So widely accepted was this argument that, when the first Factories Act came into force in Britain in 1802, it was still impossible to set limits on working hours for adult males, who were supposed to know what was in their own best interests. So the Factories Act of 1802, displaying a rare gender bias that probably helped rather than hurt women, set a limit on the number of hours that women and children could work. The limit was 12 hours within the time range of 6 a.m. to 9 p.m. An upper limit of 12 hours today would be seen as enabling employers to extract an unreasonable amount of work from individuals, but in the early nineteenth century there were those who worried that the new interventionist Factories Act would encourage sloth in the working class and hurt Britain *vis-à-vis* its trading partners.

The general question of whether all voluntary contracts among adults should be allowed without government intervention has been a hotly debated subject, going back to at least John Stuart Mill's classic works of 1848 and 1856.[6] I shall here pursue a line that contests this by recognizing the possibility of multiple equilibria, which is an important feature of developing countries (Hoff and Stiglitz, 2001).

Consider a very poor country where many people's incomes are close to the subsistence level. In such an economy, workers' job decisions will reflect their concern for survival. A simple way to model this is to think of workers making their job decision in the way that workers do in developed countries but with an additional eye to subsistence or survival. If their incomes tend to fall below the subsistence, level they will work as much as is feasible to ensure that they stay above subsistence. This can be captured by specifying the workers' utility function as follows:

$$J(x, 1-e) = \begin{cases} x - u(e) & \text{if } x \geq s \\ x - u(1) & \text{if } (x < s) \end{cases} \tag{5.1}$$

where x is the amount of consumption by the workers, e is the amount of work done by him, and s is the subsistence level of consumption. As usual we shall assume that the cost of work, $u(e)$, increases with the amount of work and at an increasing rate. That is, $u'(e) > 0$ and $u''(e) > 0$. Effort, e, is supposed to be an element of $[0,1]$ and we normalize by setting $u(0) = 0$. That is, there is an upper limit on the amount of work that individuals can possibly do, and this is by definition equal to 1. Thus 1 represents a very large amount of work, say, 15 hours a day. According to Equation 5.1, until individual workers reach a consumption level of s (the subsistence consumption), consumption is their sole objective – note that $u(1)$ is a constant. They will work as hard as necessary to reach this target, but once they have done so the first line of the utility function takes over and they take an interest in increasing their consumption and their leisure time.

To work out an individual's supply function, suppose that w is the market wage rate and the price of the good being consumed is 1. For the moment, we shall ignore the subsistence factor (that is, pretend that $s = 0$) and work out the worker's supply. Since the person has no other source of income, x must be equal to ew. Making this substitution in the first line of Equation 5.1 and working out the first-order condition we get:

$$w = u'(e) \qquad (5.2)$$

If w rises, for Equation 5.2 to hold, e must rise as well. This follows from the assumption that $u''(e) > 0$. Hence Equation 5.2 describes an upward-sloping curve. Let us describe the inverse of (5.2) by $e = e(w)$. What we just proved is that $e'(w) > 0$. Now let us bring in the subsistence requirement, where $s > 0$. Define w^* to be such that $w^* e(w^*) = s$. Therefore for all $w \leq w^*$, $we(w) < s$. Now, solving the full maximization problem of the labourer, that is, with the subsistence constraint taken into account, for $w \geq w^*$ the supply is given by $e(w)$, but for all $w < w^*$ the supply is given by $\min\{1, s/w\}$. The particular form $\min\{1, s/w\}$ simply takes account of the fact that 1 is the technically feasible maximum amount of work. Summing up this in a single equation, we have the following labour supply function of the labourer, $E(w)$:

$$E(w) = \begin{cases} e(w), & \text{if } w \geq w^* \\ \min\{1, s/w\}, & \text{if } w < w^* \end{cases} \qquad (5.3)$$

This supply curve is illustrated in Figure 5.1 by the line $ABCD$. Since the supply curve has a backward-bending section, clearly there can be multiple labour market equilibria. To complete the story, suppose that there are m identical workers. In this case the aggregate supply curve of labour is an m-fold horizontal aggregation of an individual's supply curve. Without loss of generality, let $ABCD$ in Figure 5.1 represent such a supply curve.

Let us suppose that the country in question has n firms, each endowed with the production function $f(L)$, where L is the amount of labour used by

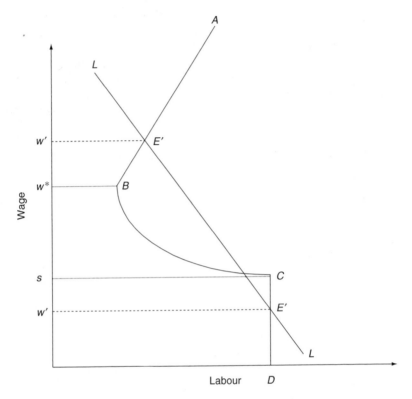

Figure 5.1   Labour market equilibrium

the firm and $f(L)$ is the output produced by it, and for all L, $f'(L) > 0$, and $f''(L) < 0$. Assuming that the price of the good is 1 and the wage is w, a firm will demand L units of labour, where $f'(L) = w$. Using d to denote the inverse of this function, a single firm's demand function for labour is $L = d(w)$. It is easy to check that this is a downward-sloping curve. Aggregating the demand curves of all n firms we have the market demand curve for labour. This is illustrated by the line LL in Figure 5.1. Equilibrium is defined in the usual way, as a wage rate at which aggregate demand equals aggregate supply:

$$mE(w) = nd(w)$$

In the case illustrated in Figure 5.1 there are three possible equilibria, of which the points marked by E' and E'' are the two stable ones. If the wage rate is low, at w', workers are forced to work many hours just to survive, and the increased supply of labour in turn keeps the wage low. If the wage is high, at w'', workers are happy to work less and this 'limited' supply reinforces the wage high.

Clearly, workers are better off at the high wage equilibrium, that is, at E''. Since all agents are price takers, both equilibria will be Pareto efficient. This is illustrated formally, in the context of child labour, by Basu (2002b). So the difference between the two equilibria is that at E'' workers are better off and profit earners are worse off; and vice versa at E', in a way akin to what Swinnerton and Rogers (1999) have illustrated in the context of child labour.

Suppose now that the economy is stuck at the equilibrium E'. Since workers usually constitute the poorest class in developing countries there is reason for the government to try to move the economy to the superior equilibrium, which in this economy is easy to achieve. The government simply has to announce a statutory limit on the number of hours that a worker can work. This will shift the CD segment of the supply curve to the left. If this shift is sufficient there will be only one remaining point of intersection between the supply and demand curves, namely E''. Hence the wage will rise to w'' and the market will settle into that equilibrium.

In this model, the statutory equilibrium law has a very interesting feature. Once it has been imposed for a while it ceases to be necessary, and it can be removed without the economy reverting back to the old equilibrium. Basu and Van (1998) refer to such a legal intervention as 'benign intervention'. It is a law that is meant to deflect the economy from one equilibrium to another pre-existing equilibrium. The law does not hold the economy where the market could not have held it, rather it simply helps to select from the various positions where the market could potentially hold it. Moreover, once the new equilibrium is established the law plays no further role. Since multiple equilibria are germane to developing economies, benign legal intervention has a large role to play in development economics.[7]

Before moving on to the subject of globalization, let us briefly digress to the subject of free contracting and Pareto improvements. It is a staple of economics that, if two consenting adults agree to a contract or an exchange, which has no negative fall-outs on any uninvolved third party, then the contract or exchange results in a Pareto improvement. Hence, economists typically believe that government and politicians should not intervene in such contracts and exchanges. Laws such as rent control legislation are often frowned upon by economists precisely for this reason. If a person is willing to take up a tenancy that requires him or her to pay a low rent but to vacate the dwelling at a day's notice, and if the landlord wants to have such a tenant for the rent agreed upon, there seems to be no obvious reason why the government should disallow such a contract since it will lead to a Pareto improvement. This, however, is a matter of considerable contention and misunderstanding, the debate going back at least to the writings of John Stuart Mill in the early 1800s.

There are three ways that one can justify a legal ban on certain kinds of voluntary contract among adults while continuing to adhere to the Pareto criterion.[8] The first is to argue that there is a difference between single acts of exchange or contract and a class of such acts. In particular, it may be the case that each such act can be justified on Paretian grounds but a class of such acts cannot be justified. Parfit (1984) laid the philosophical foundations of this argument and I have tried to formalize this in Basu (2003; see also Genicot, 2002).

The second argument is based on the recognition that human beings are often irrational, and systematically so, as the new literature on behavioural economics has made obvious to economists (others already knew it). If people are irrational when making choices over time, it is possible for some to be systematic losers in certain kinds of market transaction, such as when taking credit. If in today's society a weak person is deprived of his property by someone stronger him, this is not considered acceptable. But if someone makes a borrower part with her or his property because the latter has failed to repay a loan taken out on terms that reflected the borrower's irrationality and miscalculation we do not raise an eyebrow. The reason for this is the presumption, deeply embedded in traditional economics, that no one miscalculates, no one is irrational. But once we recognize that people are often irrational we can legislate against certain transactions, for instance by putting an interest rate ceiling on credit agreements. It is true that this could prevent some efficiency-raising transactions between smart borrowers and lenders, but it could also prevent some irrational borrowers from being duped. Good policy making entails intelligently balancing the potential gains and losses.

The third argument based on the proposition that some economies are characterized by multiple equilibria, where each equilibrium can be Pareto optimal. In such a situation, if we are in the vicinity of one equilibrium and we disallow a particular transaction, we may shift the economy to a Pareto suboptimal outcome. But if all transactions in a certain class of transactions are disallowed, we may move to a new Pareto optimal outcome. Hence the new outcome is not Pareto-dominated by the old equilibrium. The model constructed above belongs to this third category. If individual workers and a firm are prohibited from entering a contract in which each individual is required to work, say, 14 hours a day, this will be Pareto suboptimal. However, if no worker is allowed to work more than a certain number of hours per day, say 10, it is entirely possible that all workers will be better off by such legislation.[9] Hence we cannot use the Pareto criterion to rule against such legislation. This argument was not available to those who debated statutory limits on working hours in the nineteenth century, or even in the early twentieth century. It is only the advance of economic theory that has enabled us properly to understand the role and consequences of such legislation.

We shall now analyse how globalization can render certain benign laws ineffective. In general, under globalization the labour market legislation adopted by a country can lose much of its force due to the fact that capital is able to escape to another country. This also applies within a country if that country has a federal structure. In the United States there was once a considerable degree of interstate competition in terms of relaxing or not enforcing labour laws in order to attract or retain capital (see Kelley, 1905), and this eventually prompted the nationwide imposition of the Fair Labor Standards Act in 1938 (see Bhagwati, 1995; and Engerman, 2002, for a lucid account of the history of labour standards). India, given its large size and growing regional freedom in terms of the law, including labour laws (Besley and Burgess, 2002), can learn lessons from this experience.

To understand the problem that globalization creates in terms of development policy, suppose now that there are many countries, say t, just like the one described above. So what was described in Figure 5.1 refers to country 1 and there are identical countries, 2, 3, . . . , t. Let us suppose that each country is caught in the 'bad' equilibrium, namely at E'. In each country there are n firms. But now let us suppose that these firms are mobile across countries. Each can pick up its capital and move to another country should the need arise. To keep the analysis general, suppose that a firm has to incur a fixed cost of C to shift its operations to another country.[10]

If $C = \infty$ we have the case of a closed economy, and if $C = 0$ we have a fully globalized world in which capital can move costlessly between economies. C can be a product of nature and governmental nurture. Some transactions' cost of movement are in the nature of economic life. Certain kinds of capital are typically sunk, and they cannot be uprooted and moved without loss; and even when they can be moved or sold off, transportation costs or advertisement and selling costs may have to be incurred. In addition to such natural costs, the government can enact laws and impose taxes that make it costly for capital to move. Hence C can take different values depending on the policy followed, which may in turn be the product of the attitude towards globalization. In reality, C is probably never zero or infinite, but polar cases can shed light on and help us understand the kinds of response we can expect from the market. I have already discussed the case of $C = \infty$, so now turn to $C = 0$.

Suppose that all the economies of the world are caught in the 'bad' equilibrium and therefore wages are equal to w' in each country. Now suppose that the government of a single country wants to nudge its economy towards the better equilibrium. In the case of $C = \infty$, as we have already seen, it could simply impose a statutory limit on working hours – say, 10 hours a day. If the limit is severe enough there will be only one point of intersection between the demand and supply curves for labour. Such a case is illustrated in Figure 5.2. Each worker is allowed to work for a maximum of D'/m hours, where D' is as described in Figure 5.2. Then the new supply curve for labour is $A'A''BC'D'$, and if C is so high that no firms leave the country the goal of raising labour standard will be achieved. If, however, C is very low – say, the extreme case of $C = 0$ as soon as the new law comes into effect and the wage

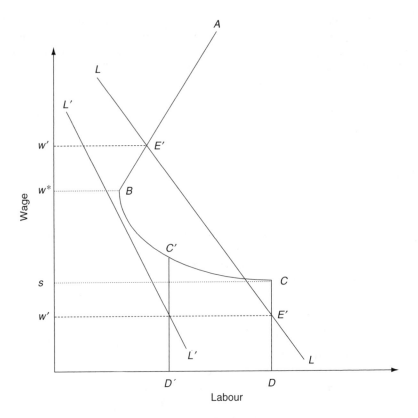

Figure 5.2 Labour market equilibrium, small nation case

rises, firms will begin to pack up their capital and leave for greener pastures. This will cause the demand curve for labour to move leftwards, which will continue as long as wages elsewhere are lower. Clearly, some of the aims of the government intervention will be defeated. The extent of this will depend on market parameters and how large the country is in comparison with the rest of the world, since as firms move out of this country to other countries, wages elsewhere will rise.

In the extreme case of this country being so small that the flight of firms does not raise wages in the rest of the world, wages here must fall to *w'* (Figure 5.2). So the new law to improve labour standards in country 1 causes firms to leave and the demand for labour keeps falling in that country until it reaches the position of *L'L'*, wages fall to *w'* and nothing of value is achieved by the country. In reality C>0, so we would not expect such extreme response, but the theoretical result is nevertheless suggestive. It also explains why the issue of international labour standards is so politically charged and highly contested.

The reason why the demand for international standards has arisen is obvious from this model. When capital is free to move between a set of countries, each country's power to impose unilateral labour standards tends to be impaired. One way of restoring this power is for the cluster of relevant nations to coordinate their labour market policies, which is exactly what international labour standards is all about.[11]

Before moving on to consider actual policy questions it is important to offer some words of caution about the use of this model. Clearly the model applies to similarly placed countries and we have considered an extreme version of this – a set of identical countries. The model cannot be applied to a set of countries at very different levels of industrialization. The sort of work carried out by children in Ethiopia will be something that no worker in the United States or Japan would have to do. Hence there will be very little movement of firms between Ethiopia and these countries and the banning of child labour in Ethiopia is unlikely to impact seriously on them. The reason why this is important to caution against is that the misunderstanding of this is one of the major factors that has given rise to the chorus for international labour standards in developed nations and created a platform for Northern protectionism.

Labour market policy in a globalized world

When thinking about labour market policy it is worth reminding ourselves that legislative intervention is not the only way to ensure workers' wellbeing and rights. Ultimately the biggest guarantor of labour standards and wellbeing is labor demand. If the demand for labor is sufficiently high so that employers have to compete with one another to obtain workers, the workers will be able to get themselves decent wages and have their basic rights ensured. Hence open trade channels that boost demand for labour in developing countries is good policy. Developed nations can do more to boost workers' welfare by opening their doors to products from the Third World than they can by campaigning for 'social clauses' and chanting slogans. However, at times the market cannot do much to help workers' interests. This can happen when there are multiple equilibria or when the moral status of a set of actions happens to be different from the moral status of individual acts. For certain kinds of labour standard, such as the requirements not to engage in sexual harassment or expose workers to excessive hazards, legislative action and government intervention may be needed (Basu, 2003).

While in these matters countries could once enact laws unilaterally, the scope for such action has diminished with globalization. One can also find examples of this within large countries. As mentioned earlier, the United States experienced ruinous interstate competition until 1938, when the enactment of the Fair Labor Standards Act brought all states under a common labour code. In 1904, for instance, the glass industry of New Jersey declared that if it were prevented from the night-time employment of children under the age of 16 it would shift to Delaware or West Virginia, which imposed no such restrictions. In India, individual states have often competed over labour market policy, which has often led to flights of capital away from states that attempted to implement pro-poor labour market policies (Basu, 2002c; Besley and Burgess, 2002). Besley and Burgess classify the amendments made by Indian states to the Industrial Disputes Act of 1947 as pro-poor, neutral or antipoor. They show that states with more pro-poor amendments have ended up discouraging investment, often hurting the very constituency they meant to help. One lesson of this is that a pro-poor policy may cease to be so when capital is mobile, as is the case in India.

Returning to the subject of international labour policy, as we saw in the previous section there is a case for concerted international action. However, this does not mean that international labour standards should be enacted and enforced in the way that they are currently being enforced. Ideally they should be formulated, designed and executed by developing countries. The current suggestion that they be designed and enforced by the WTO fails on this score. Despite the fact that the WTO operates on the principle of one-country one-vote and, whenever possible, on consensus, much has been written about the 'greenroom effect' and behind-the-scene attempts by rich countries to set the agenda in advance. As long as power is vested disproportionately in the hands of the industrialized nations, the risk of trade sanctions being used for protectionist purposes cannot be ruled out, nor can the risk of international labour standards being used as an instrument for Northern protection (Bhagwati, 1995; Bhagwati and Hudec, 1996).

Hence, for now, the matter of labour standards is best left to the International Labour Organization (ILO), which is unlikely to interfere with trade. The main method used by the ILO is to draft a convention and then to encourage countries to sign it – in this case signing means a commitment on the part of a government to enforce the terms of the convention. Convention 138, for instance, entails a commitment not to allow children below the age of 15 to do regular work. A similar effort has been made by the United Nations. Its 'Global Compact' is a voluntary agreement to uphold minimum labour standards, but unlike the ILO's conventions the signatories are not countries but corporations and multinational companies. Corporations that sign the Global Compact are essentially committing themselves to abjure certain labour market practices that are deemed harmful to workers. Unlike in the case of the WTO – which, if it were to introduce a social clause in its agreements, would use trade sanctions and other forms of punishment as retribution for countries that violated the specified standards – the ILO and the UN work on the basis of self-enforcement by the signatories and rely on the power of publicity and social disapproval.

Global inequality and poverty

Another area where there is a growing need for the global coordination of policies is the mitigation of inequality and poverty. As noted above, globalization has a tendency to marginalize sections of the population. Hence, it has created a concomitant need for policies to control inequality. Ironically, however, globalization often makes it hard for countries to control inequality and poverty unilaterally.

Analysts have claimed that inequality is higher today than in medieval times. This is hard to substantiate because there is little historical data on inequality and because the products we consume today are very different from what our forebears consumed. Genghis Khan may have been very rich but he had no way of taking a holiday in Hawaii or visiting the French Riviera for a quick weekend break. If he had a debilitating headache he would not have been able to swallow an aspirin and get straight back to the business of conquering others. How, then, can Genghis Khan's wealth be compared with that of a billionaire today? While it would take the best of cliometrics and historical research, not to mention intelligent guesses, to amass intertemporal inequality data and a lot of abstract theorizing to make sense of it, what we can assert on the basis of cursory research is that (1) the plight of the very poor has remained more or less the way it was during the time of Genghis Khan, (2) inequality today, irrespective of whether or not it is greater than in the past, is astronomically high[12] and regional inequality, by all accounts, is higher than ever before, and (3) inequality and poverty are unnecessary today as we have the technology required to provide all human beings with food, housing, basic health facilities and most other necessities of life.

The reason for the first assertion is simply the knowledge that the very poor today, as in the past, live barely above the subsistence level, that is, they are barely alive. This is because death truncates income distribution at the bottom end. It did so thousands of years ago and it continues to do so today in large parts of Sub-Saharan Africa and some parts of Asia and Latin America. Evidence on regional inequality emerged quite clearly from Angus Maddison's (1979, 2001) research on economic progress over the last 1000 years. Tables 5.4 and 5.5 summarize some of the relevant data.

In the year 1000 AD, while within regions there would have been grave inequalities, since all regions had kings and subalterns, across regions there was immense homogeneity, with per capita income standing at just above $400 dollars. The reason for this could be a Malthusian one. With very little in the way of technology, each region supported the size of population that food production allowed. By 1998, disparity had soared, with the income ratio between the richest and poorest regions being 19 to 1.

Another interesting feature of regional disparity is that the disparity within regions has grown over time. From Table 5.4 it is clear that a certain

Table 5.4 Per capita GDP by region, 1000–1998 (1990 dollars)

	1000	*1820*	*1950*	*1998*
Western Europe	400	1232	4594	17921
Japan	425	669	1926	26146
Asia (excl. Japan)	450	575	635	2936
Latin America	400	665	2554	5795
Africa	416	418	852	1368
Interregional spread	1.1:1	3:1	15:1	19:1

Source: Maddison (2001).

Table 5.5 Per capita GDP, Asian countries, 1820–1998 (1990 dollars)

	1820	*1950*	*1998*
China	600	439	3117
India	533	619	1746
Japan	669	1926	26146
South Korea	–	770	12152
Vietnam	546	658	1677

Source: Maddison (2001).

amount of global inequality had already emerged by 1820, when the inter-regional per capita income spread was 3 to 1. However, if we take a region such as Asia (Table 5.5), we find that at that time the disparity within the region was not very high (a spread of 1.3 to 1). By 1998 huge inequalities had emerged, so Asia is now much more heterogeneous than it was in 1820.

In India, regional inequality has been on the rise since at least the 1960s (see for example Rao *et al.*, 1999), and one suspects that this process goes quite deep and probably indicates a rise in overall inequality.

Finally, if we compare countries for which we have recent data, we find that inequality is still on the rise. For instance the income ratio of the richest 10 per cent of the world to the poorest 10 per cent has rose very sharply from 52 to 1 in 1988 to 64 to 1 in 1993. During this same period the Gini coefficient of world income distribution, based on household survey data from 91 countries, deteriorated from 62.8 to 66.0 (Milanovic, 1996; Thorbecke and Chutatong, 2002).

While all this does not tell us unequivocally whether interpersonal inequality is greater or lesser today as part of a secular trend, it does suggest that global inequality is growing. Moreover, because the world as a whole is now a much richer place. It is this that makes today's poverty, even if it were comparable to the poverty of a hundred or two hundred years ago, so intolerable. It is shocking that there are regions in the world where

25 per cent of children aged 10 to 14 are still toiling away as full-time labourers.[13]

If we could skim off a little from the richest segment of the population and make this available to the poorest there would be no acute poverty in the world. The rich might not even feel the burden, but the poor would certainly feel the benefit. It is possible that many of the rich would be willing to participate in such a project if there were sure ways of directing the funds to the poorest and ensuring that they received adequate medical facilities, food, clothing and housing.

The problem of global inequality and poverty is not so much an intellectual problem as a problem of determination and commitment, of finding ways to transfer basic necessities, which are now available in abundance, to the needy. This problem relates closely to some of the issues considered earlier in this chapter. Consider, for instance, the subjects of international labour standards and environmental standards. These would not have been such major issues if it were not for the fact that the nations of the world have such dramatically different living standards. Hence a level of labour wellbeing that may appear tolerable to Ethiopians would seem downright degrading to the Swiss, and the level of pollution that Mexicans are required to endure would be totally unacceptable to the Japanese. If there were less global inequality there would also be less variation in labour and environmental standards across nations. Hence some of the controversies touched on above would be mitigated automatically if we had a more equitable world.

The degree of inequality between, say, the poorest in Burundi and the richest in Switzerland would be considered unacceptable if it were to occur within the same country. If the poorest people of Burundi were to reside in the United States, the latter would find it impossible to ignore their plight or dismiss it as the fault of the Burundians themselves. This is where the subject of global democracy, developed earlier in this chapter, comes into play. If global democracy were sufficiently developed, then in the world as a whole the inequalities that exist today would be questioned, debated and no doubt considered intolerable.

There is another sense in which globalization and inequality are intimately related. In today's globalized world, even if a country wants to reduce the extent of inequality in its territory it may not be able to do so, because of the ability of professional workers and capital to cross boundaries. Let us formalize this idea a little. Suppose there are two identical countries, 1 and 2. In each country, in the absence of government intervention, there is a high-productivity person (in short, rich) with an income of x (> 0) and a low-productivity person (poor) with an income of 0. Now suppose that the government introduces an income tax, with tax rate t, that is used to transfer money from the rich person to the poor person. In other words a fraction, t, of the rich person's income is transferred to the poor person. It seems reasonable to argue that the rich person's incentive to work will be affected by the tax. Hence let us assume that the rich person's income, given a tax rate of t, is given by $x(t)$, where

$$x(t) = x - 16t \qquad (5.4)$$

Of course, an expression such as this can only be true within some bounds of t. Instead of complicating the algebra with a formal specification of bounds, we shall simply be careful to remain within reasonable limits when we consider the examples below.

Since the poor person receives what is collected from the rich person as an income subsidy, the poor person's marginal income is unaffected by his or her labour, so I shall assume that the poor person's level of work is unchanged by the subsidy. Hence after the tax system is put in place the rich person's income is $(1-t)x(t)$ and the poor person's income is $tx(t)$. Let us suppose that each country's social welfare, W, is positively related to its per capita income, m, and negatively related to the income gap, g, between the richest person and the poorest. Since all these variables depend on t, assuming that there is no international migration we can derive these terms as:

$$m(t) = [x(t)]/2 \qquad (5.5)$$

and

$$g(t) = x(t)(1 - t) - x(t)t \qquad (5.6)$$

As this is meant to be a simple illustrative exercise let us assume that social welfare, W, consists of four times the per capita income minus the income gap. Hence

$$W(t) = 4m(t) - g(t) = (1 + 2t)x(t). \qquad (5.7)$$

Assuming from here on that $x=16$, substituting Equation 5.4 into the Equation 5.7 and maximizing it, it is easy to check that the optimal value of t is 1/4 and $W(1/4)=18$. Check also that $W(0)=16$.

So in this model we have a clear policy prescription. If each country could be sure that its tax policy would not cause an out or in migration, then it would fix the tax rate at 25 per cent. This would cause social welfare to rise to 18 from a base line of 16, which occurs when there is no tax.

Now let us bring in the global aspect of the problem. We shall assume that people will want to work in whichever country offers them the higher income, that if both countries offer the same income they will prefer to remain in their own country, and (this only for simplicity) that both countries only allow high-productivity persons to migrate to their country. In other words, the only people who are able to migrate are high-productivity people. Since both countries are innately identical, taken together the above assumptions mean that high-productivity people will migrate from their own country if and only if the other country charges a lower tax rate.

With these assumptions it is clear that the global optimal occurs when each country sets t at ¼. Both countries then achieve a welfare level of 18. Let us now suppose that country 1 sets t at ¼ and country 2 sets it at zero. The latter's welfare level is then given by 26 2/3. To see how this is calculated, note that country 2 will now have two rich people and one poor, because of migration. So its per capita income will be $[2(16)+0]/3$ and the income gap will be 16. Applying the welfare function to this we get 26 2/3.

If, on the other hand, country 1 sets t at zero and country 2 it at more than zero sets (for instance $t=¼$) then all productive workers will leave country 2 and its welfare will be given by zero. Clearly it would then be better off to lower t to zero. In short, if we view this as a game between countries, setting t at zero is the dominant strategy for both countries, although both would be better off if they could set t at ¼. In other words, what we have is a classic prisoners' dilemma. The payoff matrix Figure 5.3 – in which for simplicity we assume that each country has to choose between setting t_i at 0 or ¼, where the subscript i refers to the country in question and the payoffs are the welfare levels of the two countries – sums up this model. It is obvious that no matter what the other country does, it is better for both of them not to tax the rich and to leave income distribution untouched, even though both would be better off if they taxed the rich and transferred some money to the poor.

The model just described, though highly simplistic, drives home the need for global cooperation if countries are interested in improving their income distribution. Globalization means that independent countries do not have quite the independence that countries had in earlier times in terms of exercising their individual policy prerogatives.

While we talk about the need for global coordination of labour market policies, environmental policies and trade norms, we seldom talk of global coordination when it comes to discussing countries' policies for achieving

	Country 2	
Country 1	$t_2 = 0$	$t_2 = ¼$
$t_1 = 0$	16, 16	26 2/3, 0
$t_1 = ¼$	0, 26 2/3	18, 18

Figure 5.3 The international inequality game

greater equity. This chapter, however, has indicated that some of the same problems arise here. The fact that capital and professional worker, migrate from one country to another in response to economic incentives has created a need for international coordination.

There is, however, a need to sound two words of caution. First, the model must not be taken as justification for closing borders against the movement of people or capital. The advantages of the free movement of resources, physical and human, in and out of countries are immense, and the pressure should be kept up on governments to keep the corridors open rather than set up barriers. Second, in the above model there is no conflict between poverty and inequality – the policy that curbs inequality also curtails poverty. But that does not always happen in reality. Some policies can curb poverty only by increasing inequality. At times countries can be so overzealous in controlling inequality that they are unmindful of the fact that this may cause poverty to increase.

What should be done if such a conflict arises? I have taken the view elsewhere and would endorse it again, that poverty alleviation should be the priority objective. So if there is a conflict between poverty removal and inequality mitigation, we should go for poverty removal. However there are many situations in which the alleviation of inequality and of poverty are compatible objectives and may even be complementary.

With regard to the objective of reducing poverty, one way of encouraging countries to do so would be to present their economic performance not in terms of their overall per capita incomes, as is the common practice, but according to the per capita incomes of the poorest 20 per cent of each country, or what could be called its 'quintile income'.[14] The objective of raising quintile incomes would be a good way of combining poverty alleviation with growth. The focus on quintile income would make for a natural Rawlsian focus on the weakest sections of the population. At the same time, a focus on the *relatively* poor, rather than on those below an exogenously defined poverty line, means that one would eventually have to be interested in everybody. The target of raising poor people above an exogenously given poverty line can be reached, but the aim of raising the living standard of the poorest 20 per cent of a society can never be fulfilled totally, because there will always be a category of the poorest 20 per cent of a population. In a perfectly equitable society, for instance, the objective of raising quintile income would coincide with the objective of raising per capita income. This is the strength of the quintile income target proposed here.

One could legitimately ask whether a focus on quintile income, rather than the more common per capita income, would make that much of a difference. The cross-country view of these measures in Table 5.6 shows the substantial difference between the two. As can be seen, there is not only a large difference in absolute terms (in the 1990s the bottom 20 per cent of people in Peru had a per capita income of less than $1000, whereas the figure for the country as a whole was more than $4000 dollars; most people in Sierra Leone were poor, but those in the quintile income group were unbelievably poor), but also reference to the quintile measure changes the rankings of countries quite sharply. For example, the United States drops from first place in per capita terms to a position under Norway, Japan and Sweden. Likewise Bolivia, which ranks higher than India, drops to below India when the quintile measure is used.

Of course, the quintile income measure is less inclusive than, say, the human development Index, compiled by the UNDP, which takes account of life expectancy and literacy as well as income, but it has the advantage of a sharper focus. It is not claimed here that other measures of standards of living do not matter; rather we merely stress that when looking at a country's economic (or, more narrowly, income) performance we should focus our attention on the bottom end of income distribution.

Despite the advantages of, and the moral case for, focusing on quintile incomes, there is a considerable problem with lack of data. In Table 5.6 the data on the share of income that the bottom 20 per cent of each country commanded were collected in different years (shown in parentheses), which reflects the fact that such data are compiled only occasionally. Moreover, it is arguable that the poorest 20 per cent people have a very different consumption pattern from the average person. Hence, ideally, we should use index numbers that are specific to this class when computing their per capita

Table 5.6   Per capita incomes and quintile incomes, selected countries

	Per capita GNP, 1999 (US dollars at PPP)	Percentage share of income of bottom quintile (survey years in parenthesis)	Per capita income of poorest 20% (or quintile income), 1999 (US dollars at PPP)
Sierra Leone	414	1.1 (1989)	23
India	2149	8.1 (1997)	870
Bolivia	2193	5.6 (1990)	614
China	3291	5.9 (1998)	971
Peru	4387	4.4 (1996)	965
Thailand	5599	6.4 (1998)	1792
Mexico	7719	3.6 (1995)	1389
Malaysia	7963	4.5 (1995)	1792
Korea	14 637	7.5 (1993)	5489
Sweden	20 824	9.6 (1992)	9996
France	21 897	7.2 (1995)	7883
Japan	24 041	10.6 (1993)	12 742
Norway	26 522	9.7 (1995)	12 863
United States	30 600	5.2 (1997)	7956

Source: Compiled from World Bank (2001).

incomes. Clearly these are data that we will have to strive to collect if we are seriously interested in focusing on the poor.

To reiterate what was said above, concern for poverty alleviation should take priority over concern for income inequality. Inequality is something we should strive to minimize, but not by jeopardizing improvement of the income of those in the lower quintile group. To understand this, consider the policy question of whether to extend intellectual property rights over a long duration, say 15 years. If this were judged to be against the lower-quintile income-maximization criterion, then we would have to work out precisely what such a policy was likely to do to the poorest 20 per cent. It is, for instance, entirely conceivable that it would make a few people very wealthy, namely those who patent commercially useful ideas. This should not be considered a reason for or against extending the rights to intellectual property, but if such a policy could somehow help to raise the living standard of the poorest people, then it should be considered worthwhile.

Similar issues arise in respect of tax policy. If an overly aggressive tax system were used to divert money from the rich to the poor, it is arguable that this could damage richer people's incentives to such an extent that the poor would end up being hurt when all effects were taken into account, despite the income subsidy they received. This is because their incomes could drop so much (because there was not enough capital to work with or because firms would shut down, causing a drop in demand for labour) that despite the subsidy they would be below the pre-policy intervention level. In such a case the tax would obviously be counter productive. Note that tax policy is not being evaluated here in terms of general efficiency, as mainstream economics normally does, but in terms of a kind of truncated efficiency where efficiency is judged by its effect on the poorest.

A large number of policies, however, have no obvious effect on the poorest people, and from these we should choose the ones that could minimize inequality. And since the effectiveness of many such policies will crucially depend on what is being practised in other countries, we return to the subject of the global coordination of equity policies. In practical terms this will require a lot of institutional spade work. As mentioned earlier, for discussions of intercountry trade policy we have the WTO, and for crafting intercountry labour market policy we have the ILO, but there is no forum for coordinating the effort to alleviate poverty and inequality. These issues have been written about and discussed by the World Bank, but in adequate attention has been paid to the intercountry dimension of this problem, which is an increasingly significant omission in a globalizing world.

Conclusion

This chapter has addressed the changing nature of development economics, and in particular the changes brought about by the process of globalization.

The focus has been on curtailment of the freedom of individual countries to draft policy. In the ancient world, where the cost of crossing borders and the uncertainties awaiting in distant lands caused most countries to isolate themselves, national governments could pursue the policies they wanted with impunity and with little concern for what other countries were doing. This is no longer the case, and goods, capital and people are flowing in and out of countries at unprecedented levels and at a much lower cost than ever before.

This chapter has argued that one consequence of globalization is the erosion of global democracy. Because powerful nations and the activities of MNCs can have huge effects on the well-being of people in other countries, a retreat of democracy is a natural concomitant of globalization. This has led to the increasing marginalization of some groups and contributed to global political instability. One way of controlling this problem would be to strengthen the democratic working of international organizations, giving much more voice to poorer countries than they currently have.

As an illustration of one area in which globalization has had a major impact on the nature and effectiveness of development policy, this chapter has considered the subject of international labour standards. Models have been constructed to show the need to coordinate policies among developing countries, which will require a democratic forum to help with the coordination. The chapter went on to argue that global inequality is reaching an intolerable level, and once again this is an area where policies will have to be coordinated across countries if they are to be effective. To this end there is a need for international organizations to take the initiative.

Advances in development economics, the availability of large data sets and the growing sophistication of economic theory have enabled us to understand economic underdevelopment and global poverty much better than ever before. The challenge is to combine this understanding with political will in order to do away with poverty, which is unacceptable and unnecessary in this generally prosperous world.

Notes

1. This chapter was presented as a paper at the conference on Development Strategies towards the 21st Century', organized by IDE-JETRO and held in Tokyo on 29–30 January 2002. It has benefited from the comments of Takashi Kurosaki, Koji Nishikimi, Jeff Nugent and Hiroshi Sato. The paper also provided the background material for the keynote address to the conference on Labour Markets and Poverty in South Africa in Johannesburg on 22 October 2002, and for a plenary lecture at the South and Southeast Asia Regional Meeting of the Econometric Society in Lahore on 28 December 2002.
2. Dreze (2000), drawing on the research of Sivard (1996), reports that the ratio of civilian casualties to military casualties in armed conflicts rose from 1:1 to 5:1 between the beginning and end of the twentieth century.

3. This argument of course hinges on there being more technological advancement in the fishing sector than in other sectors, but this causes only a minimal loss of generality. As long as there is not perfectly balanced innovation among all sectors, some sectors will see more technological advances than others. One such sector could be 'fishing'.

4. In making this remark I am aware that there are other, more acutely dispossessed people in society. There are the jobless and the homeless, and within households there may be women and girls who are intolerably poor. Needless to say, we need policy instruments to reach out to them. But here, I am not trying to be comprehensive but to consider some major illustrative examples involving the poor in places where globalization is changing the nature of development policy. And it seems reasonable to focus on the case of the working class in poor nations.

5. This is also noted by Kimura (2002), who rightly points out that the competition is not just about wages and workers' compensation but also about the productivity of workers, their education, language skills and so on.

6. See Mill (1970, 1971). For more contemporary references see Trebilcock (1993), Neeman (1999), Kanbur (2001), Satz (2001) and Basu (2002b). The model constructed here is similar to those in Raynauld and Vidal (1998) and Singh (2002).

7. Once we recognize that social norms are an ingredient of human choice, the role of benign legislation becomes even more important, since a law can help shape human preferences and norms; and once these have been formed – even if the law were to be removed – behaviour might well remain unaltered.

8. It could be argued that the Pareto criterion should not be treated as a sacred cow, and that if we eschew the Pareto criterion we can develop justifications for intervention. Such an argument has been advanced by Sen (1970), Kanbur (2001) and others. Kanbur actually looks into a variety of Paretian and non-Paretian justifications for intervening in what he describes as 'obnoxious markets'. Here we shall remain within the Paretian framework.

9. While this sounds obvious, it involves some tricky problems concerning the number of agents involved in an economy. Conventional economics makes very strong assumptions about this, and the only reason why such assumptions are accepted by economists is that they are so used to them (Basu, 2002c).

10. A similar analysis pertaining to child labour was conducted by Basu (1999).

11. While the consequences of such coordinated action have not been studied empirically, a recent empirical study of which countries are likely to ratify labour market conventions sheds interesting light on what prompts countries to ratify standards (Chau and Kanbur, 2001). There seems to be evidence of a peer-group effect – that is, if the other countries in a country's 'peer group' ratify a convention it is more likely that the latter country will ratify it.

12. Based on *Fortune* magazine data and world development indicators, it seems that in 1998 the 50 richest Hollywood personalities earned as much as the entire population of Burundi (11 million), and that the rise in the value of stocks owned by Bill Gates of Microsoft was equal to the combined income of the entire 60 million people of Ethiopia. Turning to more serious data, the income ratio between the richest 10 per cent of the world and the poorest 10 per cent was 64:1 in 1993 (Thorbecke and Chutatong, 2002, based on Milanovic, 1996).

13. According to the Census of England and Wales of 1861, 36.9 per cent of boys and 20.5 per cent of girls aged 10–14 were regular labourers.

14. The normative basis of using quintile incomes to rank countries and evaluate economic policy is discussed by Michael Lipton, Paul Streeten and myself in Meier and Stiglitz (2001).

Reference

Basu, K. (1999) 'Child Labor: Cause, Consequence and Cure with Remarks on International Labor Standards', *Journal of Economic Literature*, vol. 37, pp. 1083–119.

Basu, K. (2000a) 'Whither India? The Prospect of Prosperity', in R. Thapar (ed.), *India: Another Millennium* (New Delhi: Penguin).

Basu, K. (2000b) *Prelude to Political Economy: A Study of the Social and Political Foundations of Economics*, (New York: Oxford University Press).

Basu, K. (2002a) 'The Retreat of Global Democracy', *Indicators*, vol. 1, pp. 77–87.

Basu, K. (2002b) 'A Note on Multiple General Equilibria with Child Labor', *Economics Letters*, vol. 74, pp. 301–8.

Basu, K. (2002c) 'Labor Laws and Labor Welfare, in the Context of the Indian Experience', mimeo: Cornell University.

Basu, K. (2003) 'The Economics and Law of Sexual Harassment in the Workplace', *Journal of Economic Perspectives*, vol. 17, pp. 141–57.

Basu, K. and P. H. Van (1998) 'The Economics of Child Labor', *American Economic Review*, vol. 88, pp. 412–27.

Besley, T. and R. Burgess (2002) 'Can Labor Regulation Hinder Economic Performance? Evidence from India', mimeo, London School of Economics.

Bhagwati, J. (1995) 'Trade Liberalization and "Fair Trade" Demands: Addressing the Environmental and Labor Standards Issues', *World Economy*, vol. 18, pp. 745–59.

Bhagwati, J. and R. Hudec (1996) *Fair Trade and Harmonization*, vols. 1 and 2 (Cambridge, Mass.: MIT Press).

Chau, N. and R. Kanbur (2001) 'The Adoption of International Labor Standards Conventions: Who, When and Why?', mimeo, Cornell University, Ithaca, NY.

Dreze, J. (2000) 'Militarism, Development and Democracy', *Economic and Political Weekly*, vol. 37, pp. 1171–83.

Engerman, S. (2002) 'The History and Political Economy of International Labor Standards', in K. Basu, H. Horn, L. Roman and J. Shapiro (eds), *International Labor Standards: Issues, Theories and Policy Options* (Oxford: Blackwell).

Genicot, G. (2002) 'Bonded Labor and Serfdom: A Paradox of Voluntary Choice', *Journal of Development Economics*, vol. 67, pp. 101–28.

Hoff, K. and Stiglitz, J. E. (2001), 'Modern Economic Theory and Development', in G. M. Meier and J. E. Stiglitz (eds), *Frontiers of Development Economics* (Oxford: Oxford University Press.).

Kanbur, R. (2001) 'On Obnoxious Markets', mimeo, Cornell University, Ithaca, NY.

Kelley, F. (1905) *Some Ethical Gains through Legislation* (London: Macmillan).

Kimura, F. (2002) 'Development Strategies for Economics under Globalization: Southeast Asia as a New Development Model', mimeo, Keio University, Japan.

Kohsaka, A. (2002) 'National Economies under Globalization: A Quest for New Development Strategies', mimeo, Osaka University, Japan.

Maddison, A. (1979) 'Per Capita Output in the Long Run', *Kyklos*, vol. 32, pp. 412–29.

Maddison, A. (2001) *The World Economy: A Millennial Prospective* (Paris: OECD).

Meier, G. and J. Stiglitz (2001) *Frontiers of Development Economics: The Future in Perspective* (Oxford and New York: Oxford University Press).

Milanovic, B. (1996) 'True World Income Distribution, 1988 and 1993: First Calculation Based on Household Surveys Alone', mimeo, World Bank, Washington, DC.

Mill, J. S. (1970) *Principles of Political Economy* (Harmondsworth: Penguin).

Mill, J. S. (1971) *On Liberty*, reproduced in Mill, *Utilitarianism, Liberty and Representative Government* (London: Dent and Sons).

Murphy, T. A. (1992) *Ten Hours' Labor: Religion, Reform, and Gender in Early New England* (Ithaca, NY: Cornell University Press).

Neeman, Z. (1999) 'The Freedom to Contract and the Free Rider Problem', *Journal of Law Economics and Organization*, vol. 15, pp. 685–703.

Parfit, D. (1984) *Reasons and Persons* (Oxford: Clarendon Press).

Rao, M. S., R. T. Govinda and K. P. Kalirajan (1999) 'Convergence of Incomes across Indian States: A Divergent View', *Economic and Political Weekly*, vol. 34, pp. 769–78.

Raynauld, A. and J.-P. Vidal (1998) *Labor Standards and International Competitiveness: A Comparative Analysis of Developing and Industrialized Countries* (Northampton, Mass.: Edward Elgar).

Satz, D. (2001) 'Why Shouldn't Some Things be for Sale', mimeo, Stanford University, CA.

Sen, A. (1970) 'The Impossibility of a Paretian Liberal', *Journal of Political Economy*, vol. 78, pp. 152–7.

Singh, N. (2002) 'The Impact of International Labor Standards: A Survey of Economic Theory', in K. Basu, H. Horn, L. Roman and J. Shapiro (eds), *International Labor Standards: Issues, Theories and Policy Options* (Oxford: Blackwell).

Sivard, R. (1996) *World Military and Social Expenditures 1996* (Washington, DC: World Priorities).

Swinnerton, K. and C. A. Rogers (1999) 'The Economics of Child Labor: Comment', *American Economic Review*, vol. 89, pp. 1382–5.

Thorbecke, E. and C. Chutatong (2002) 'Economic Inequality and Its Socio-economic Impact', mimeo, Cornell University, Ithaca, NY.

Trebilcock, M. (1993) *The Limits of Freedom of Contract* (Cambridge, Mass.: Harvard University Press).

World Bank (2001) *World Development Report 2000–01: Attacking Poverty* (Oxford and New York: Oxford University Press).

6
New Development Strategies under Globalization: Foreign Direct Investment and International Commercial Policy in Southeast Asia

Fukunari Kimura

Introduction

With the rapid progress of globalization there has been increasing demand for a fundamentally different policy framework for industrial development in less developed countries (LDCs). Today LDCs are facing a vastly changed economic environment. Corporate activities have rapidly globalized and channels of international transactions have become ever more diversified. Enforcement power has been given to the international policy discipline imposed by the World Trade Organization (WTO) and participation in the formation of free trade agreement (FTA) networks has become a sort of obsession. In the 1950s and 1960s developing countries such as Japan, Korea and Taiwan existed in a much quieter world and took a lot of time to foster their firms and industries. Today's LDCs cannot afford to be slow in building up the foundations of economic development. The key issue when formulating development strategies is how to catch up with the wave of globalization.

Since the latter half of the 1980s the Southeast Asian (SEA) countries[1] have provided important examples when considering a new development model for LDCs in the era of globalization. These countries began to accept massive amounts of FDI when their phase in domestic firms were barely mature, and their manufacturing sectors, with foreign affiliates at their core, led the rapid economic growth. An important turning point came in the mid 1980s. Before that time, these countries were cautious about accepting excessive amounts of FDI, as many LDCs still are, and foreign companies were only allowed to enter selected sectors in specified forms. In the latter half of the 1980s and the early 1990s the SEA countries switched their policies and began to host almost all kinds of FDI using facilitating measures. This led to the formation on an unprecedented scale of international production/distribution networks to take advantage of fragmentation and agglomeration.

The development pattern of the SEA countries is quite different in many aspects from that of earlier developers such as Japan and Korea, where industrialization started with import substitution by domestic firms. The pattern is also different from that of China, where there are certain links between domestic firms and foreign affiliates. The role of FDI is different from that in Latin America and other parts of the world in terms of the number of countries involved in the international production/distribution network. Market forces are of course important, but the policy framework is far from the simple *laissez faire* that would be advocated by the so-called neoclassical development school.

Today the SEA countries are facing new challenges. China is emerging as a great attractor of FDI, and competition over location advantages is becoming intense. The difficulties include stubborn technological gaps between domestic firms and foreign affiliates, a lack of human capital and highly distortive investment incentives aimed at keeping footloose foreign affiliates within territories. The key issues now are how to remove inefficiencies in import-substituting industries and how to invigorate international production/distribution networks, and the new role of international commercial policy, including FTAs, is being discussed.

This chapter investigates how far and in what sense the SEA countries can be regarded as forerunners in utilizing global factors in their development, and discusses the relevance of their experiences to other LDCs. The following section presents an overview of the development strategies that have been applied by the SEA countries in the past. The third section examines the logic and structure of the traditional import-substituting FDI policy. The fourth section explains the economic logic behind the formation of international production/distribution networks and emphasizes the importance of government policies. The fifth section interprets current issues on industrial development in the SEA countries in the context of this chapter, and the final section briefly discusses the relevance of our argument for LDCs in other parts of the world.

Southeast Asia as a model

As we look back on the industrialization path of SEA countries, particularly Malaysia, Thailand, the Philippines and Indonesia, we find that the basic structure and changes in their trade and FDI-related policies are as summarized Table 6.1.

The manufacturing sectors in these countries consist of both import-substituting industries and export-oriented industries, and the two have been subjected to different policy packages. The development economics literature tends to classify development strategies into two categories: import

Table 6.1 Dual-track approach in development strategies: the case of the SEA countries

	Phase 1 (1970s to mid 1980s)	Phase 2 (mid 1980s to 1998)	Phase 3 (1998 to present)
Import-substituting industries	Acceptance of FDI for import substitution	Acceptance of FDI for import substitution	Reorganization of protected sectors required. More competition needed
Export-oriented industries	Selective acceptance of FDI in export-processing zones	Emphasis on forming agglomeration. Formation of international production/distribution network	Further activation of international production/distribution network required
Development strategies re hosting FDI	Acceptance in selective sectors with capital share restriction and performance requirements	'Accept everybody' policy. Duty drawback system. Various FDI facilitating measures	Structural adjustment. Utilization of FTAs as a booster
External factors	Globalization of corporate activities. Reduction of service link cost		Asian currency crisis. China shock. FTA boom

substitution and export orientation. However throughout the development process the SEA countries have maintained two types of industry with deliberate policy packages. This is the so-called 'dual-track approach'. Another fact that should be noted is that the hosting of FDI has been an essential element of their development strategies, and that their industrialization has proceeded essentially with foreign companies at the core. The significance of foreign companies in the overall picture of their development strategies is qualitatively different from that in Japan and Korea in the 1950s and 1960s.

In addition, development strategies related to the hosting of FDI in the SEA countries have changed drastically over time. From the 1970s to the mid 1980s the SEA countries introduced FDI selectively, mainly in import-substituting industries. Export-oriented FDI was also invited, but competing domestic industries were carefully protected by policies that limited the activities of export-oriented FDI, for example, to geographically segregated export processing zones.

After the mid 1980s, however, these countries switched their FDI hosting policies from selective acceptance to almost an 'accept everybody' policy. While maintaining trade protection for import substituting industries, they began to invite as many foreign companies as they could and to establish industrial clusters. The extensive introduction of duty drawback systems and various FDI facilitation measures more than offset the bias against exports. This important policy change allowed these countries effectively to utilize the wave of corporate globalization and to capture the benefits of fragmentation and agglomeration. They were also able to establish efficient international production/distribution networks. Figure 6.1 shows the explosive increases in intraregional trade in machinery parts and components.

The SEA countries are now facing new challenges. Some of these are the result of the Asian currency crisis, which revealed various structural problems, but a more fundamental issue is the growing competition from China over location advantages for multinational enterprises (MNEs). To invigorate their international production/distribution networks they must restructure their inefficient import-substituting industries. They must also reduce their service-link costs and formulate a critical mass of agglomeration. The formation of an FTA network in East Asia is one possible way of accelerating the required structural adjustments.

The SEA countries have been pioneers in effectively utilizing the forces of globalization in the context of development strategies. Their initial conditions were similar to those of many other LDCs in terms of, among other things, a narrow domestic market, immature human capital and weak domestic firms. Despite these handicaps they have achieved sustained economic growth and impressive industrialization. The development strategies they have applied are worth investigating in detail.

(a) Export value of machinery parts and components (unit: US$100 million)

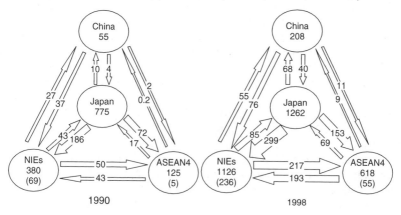

1990

1998

(b) Share of machinery parts and components exports in total machinery exports

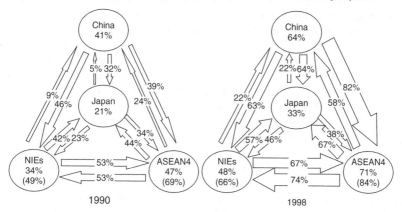

1990

1998

Figure 6.1 The expansion of intraregional trade in intermediate goods among the East Asian countries: Machinery parts and components, 1990–98

Notes: 1. For the figures 1990, 1991 data are used for the Philippines and 1992 data for China and Hong Kong. For the figures 1998, 1996 data are used for Taiwan and 1997 data for Thailand. 2. The numbers below the names of countries/regions are in (a) the values of exports to the world, and in (b) they are shares of exports to the East Asian countries. 3. The numbers in parentheses for NIEs and ASEAN4 indicate the values of interregional exports (a) and the shares of interregional exports (b).

Data sources: METI (2001); Kimura and Ando (2003).

FDI for import substitution

We shall first examine the logical structure of policy packages for hosting import-substituting FDI, and discuss their blessings and drawbacks.

Development economics textbooks have long preached the need to protect infant industries, but they have provided few instructions for LDCs that host FDI. Infant industry protection enables immature industries to expand their production by temporarily providing some protection in forms such as import tariffs, and tries to make the industries internationally competitive by creating dynamic economies of scale.

Figure 6.2 illustrates the welfare effects of such protection policies, using a partial equilibrium framework. In 2000, for instance, the domestic supply curve of this hypothetical country was so high that production could start without protection. Once the protection was provided the product was produced, and learning-by-doing effects were gained, shifting the domestic supply curve downward. By 2010 it may no longer need any protection, and may even start exporting. There are three criteria that can be used to judge whether an infant industry protection policy is economically justifiable. The first is Mill's criterion, which states that the industry in question should have a good prospect of being able to stand alone without protection in the future. The second is Bastable's criterion, which it states that the sum of the present value of the future benefits generated by protection must be larger than the cost of protection. The third criterion involves checking whether externalities exist; if they do not, government intervention in the market cannot be justified.

The traditional argument in favour of infant industry protection was clearly aimed to promote domestic firms. The selective trade protection policies applied in Northeast Asian countries in the past followed this tradition. However, the SEA countries have adopted very different development strategies. One of the key factors they have considered is the globalization of corporate activities. Particularly when the technological gap with foreign companies is large, FDI can be a powerful tool to boost industrialization.

A key departure from the traditional argument for protecting infant industries comes from an interpretation of the domestic supply curve shown in Figure 6.2. The traditional argument implicitly assumes that the main cause of the higher domestic supply curve is the low technological and managerial capabilities of domestic firms. When production starts under proper protection, the argument goes, domestic firms will improve their productivity through dynamic economies of scale, leading to a lower domestic supply curve. In the case of import-substituting FDI, on the other hand, there should not be any handicap in technology or managerial ability at the firm level because MNEs' firm-specific assets must be competitive. The issues, then, are why LDCs still have a higher domestic supply curve even with FDI, and how LDCs can lower the curve after starting production.

An advantage of introducing FDI for import substitution is that it requires lower protection than that which would be needed to foster domestic firms directly. However, because of the existence of negative factors of production in LDCs, it cannot be assumed that MNEs can operate within them in an

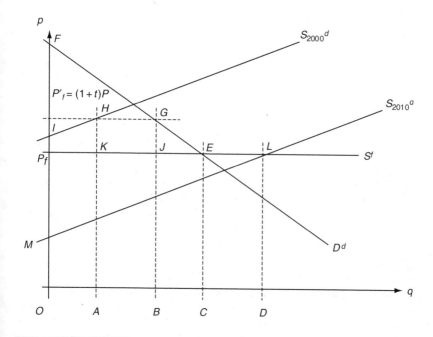

Figure 6.2   Welfare effects of infant industry protection
S_{2000}^d: domestic supply curve in 2000 S^f: foreign supply curve
S_{2010}^d: projected domestic supply curve in 2010 D^d: domestic demand curve

	Without tariff (2000, 2010)	with tariff (2000)	Downward shift in domestic supply curve due to protection (2010)
Domestic production	0	OA	OD
Domestic consumption	OC	OB	OC
Export minus import	-OC	-AB	CD
Consumer surplus	FEP_f	FGP'_f	FEP_f
Producer surplus	0	$P'_f HI$	$P_f LM$
Tariff revenues	0	HGJK	0
Change in welfare because of protection	-	$-IHKP_f - GEJ$	$P_f LM$

internationally competitive manner. If this is the case, the government must help foreign companies to capture the domestic market by setting trade barriers or other incentives to compensate for the local disadvantages.

A primary reason for the low productivity or higher domestic supply curve is inferior macro/sectoral economic conditions and social capabilities, which are mostly external to individual corporations. These include a lack of human capability, poor economic infrastructure and an inferior policy environment.

Another reason is the small size of the domestic market. A small market makes it difficult for firms to rise above the minimal scale of efficiency. Therefore, high and prolonged trade barriers will be required to encourage MNEs to invest. In addition the small market makes vigorous competition among MNEs unlikely, possibly leading to politico-economic pressure for the continuous provision of preferential status. Furthermore, the higher the trade barriers the slower the expansion of the domestic market will be. Thus a small domestic market is a curse in many ways. Actually, countries with a large domestic market have many advantages in this regard. If the domestic market is large enough, MNEs may be willing to invest even without any policy incentive in the hope of capturing the forerunner's advantage. The problem is that most LDCs, with the notable exception of China and India, do not have sufficiently large markets.

A third factor is related to industrial organization and policy packages, in terms of managing the whole value chain of production and distribution. One major disadvantage of operating in LDCs is the lack of local suppliers of parts and components. In the case of parts and components for which there is no immediate prospect of domestic production, the government must set trade barriers as low as possible to reduce the cost of inviting downstream assemblers from abroad. However, complete knockdown operations generate almost no technological spillovers and may force the country to give up a development path leading to greater industrialization. Nor is the domestic production of parts and components necessarily easy. In many cases, the government must provide additional trade protection to local or FDI producers, thus pushing up production costs.

Once foreign affiliates are stuck in this high domestic supply curve, what can be done to lower the curve? MNEs must have some prospect of productivity growth in their own plants, and the host government may expect too much from it. We should not forget that other factors are involved shifting the supply curve, including improvement of the macro/sectoral economic conditions and social capability, growth of the domestic market and the formation of parts and components supply networks. Taking these factors into account, Bastable's test should be used to check whether it is worth providing policy incentives to attract import-substitution FDI.

In the past, strategies that made use of import-substituting FDI were popular, but in recent years there has been greater recognition of the difficulty of designing and implementing proper policy packages. It is not claimed here that proper policy design is impossible. In the case of mobile phones in China, cars in Thailand and steel products in Vietnam, for example, import-substituting FDI seems to have worked to some extent. In addition, long-term efforts to foster import-substituting industries may provide a secure basis for further development. However we must recognize that the designing a proper policy package is not always an easy task.

A current question in the SEA countries is how to reorganize their import-substituting industries. The cost of protection is enormous, and the results are not always favourable. The possible inconsistency of this with hosting export-oriented FDI is also an issue that cannot be ignored.

International production/distribution networks under globalization

The SEA countries have long used the dual track approach to foster both import-substituting and export-oriented industries. However, the balance and relationship between the two tracks have changed over time. Before the mid 1980s the introduction of foreign companies was selective, and FDI in export-oriented industries was welcomed cautiously, with the proviso that it would not damage infant domestic firms. The activities of MNEs were sometimes limited to export-processing zones and other segregated areas.

When the SEA countries were hit by an economic slump in the mid 1980s, various problems with their industrial structures were revealed. The economic difficulty marked a turning point, with the SEA countries switching to aggressive FDI policies, although the timing of this differed slightly from country to country. They loosened their foreign entry restrictions with regard to choice of industries and shares of foreign capital, and began to improve the economic environment for foreign companies by constructing basic economic infrastructure and providing tax incentives. The various measures to facilitate FDI were particularly effective in encouraging FDI by small and medium-sized foreign enterprises (SMEs). They tried to build up a critical mass of industrial clusters, demonstrating efficient upstream–downstream interfirm relationships, and to link them to international production/distribution networks.

The international production/distribution networks established in the 1990s in East Asia were almost unprecedented in terms of the sophistication of the vertical production/distribution division of labour across countries. To grasp the pattern of production and trade we must add a few new elements to traditional international trade theory. The theory of comparative advantage, based on relative production costs in autarky (a situation with no trade), is still valid in various circumstances; technological gaps and factor price differences can to some extent explain the location patterns of industries. However, in the era of globalization we must incorporate three new lines of thought into our analytical framework.

The first line of thought is fragmentation theory. This is a powerful tool for analyzing FDI to LDCs and the formation of international production/distribution networks.[2] Traditional international trade theory primarily explains industry location patterns. However, in East Asia we often see

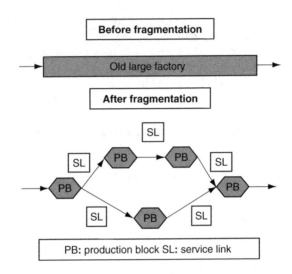

Figure 6.3 Fragmentation: an illustration

product–process location patterns. A typical example is the semiconductor-related electronics industry. This industry as a whole is obviously capital intensive or human capital intensive, but its production activities are finely segmented and located in various places. Fragmentation theory neatly presents the logic behind such location patterns.

Deardorff (2001) defines fragmentation as 'the splitting of a product process into two to more steps that can be undertaken in different locations but that lead to the same final product'. There are various patterns of fragmentation, one of which is illustrated in Figure 6.3. For example, there may initially be a large factory in Japan that carries out all production activities, from upstream to downstream. When it comes to individual production blocks, however, some may require close supervision by technicians while others are purely labour-intensive. If the production blocks can be located separately in Japan, Malaysia and China, for example, it may be possible to reduce the total production cost.

Fragmentation becomes economical when the cost of the service links (SLs) connecting the production blocks is low enough. SL costs include transport costs, telecommunication costs and various coordination costs between the various production blocks. SL costs are heavily dependent on the nature of the technology in each industry. For example a full-scale iron mill cannot be economically fragmented because of its energy efficiency. However, globalization reduces overall SL costs and enables firms in many industries to fragment further in order to reduce total production costs. Because SLs tend to carry strong external economies of scale, globalization may accelerate concentration and fragmentation simultaneously, polarizing countries into some that enjoy the fruits of globalization and others that do not. International trade theory has long used the concept of transport costs. What is new to fragmentation theory is the reinterpretation of transport costs as SL costs between production blocks, and reformulation of the behaviour of MNEs in the framework of traditional trade theory based on comparative advantage.

The second line of thought is agglomeration theory. This is an extension of international trade theory with external economies of scale, which involves the introduction of the concept of 'space' from city planning and other fields.[3] Although we cannot say that the micro foundation of spatial agglomeration has been fully established, the importance of agglomeration as a source of location advantage has been increasingly recognized in both the empirical and the theoretical literature. Traditional comparative advantage theory defines comparative advantage on the basis of relative production costs between two locations in a state of autarky. However, economies of scale or agglomeration effects do not necessarily depend on the initial conditions under autarky; in an extreme case a country might start experiencing agglomeration purely by chance. In this sense, the sources of the gains from trade in the new international trade theory are logically different from those under the traditional theory of comparative advantage, and the nature of the new theory generates the possibility of multiple equilibria and a new role for government. As illustrated in Figure 6.4, a small agglomeration seed can attract further economic activities, and thus, or at least theoretically, a tiny amount of government intervention in the market can generate agglomeration.

Among the factors that generate location advantages for MNE investment, agglomeration is one of the most crucial, particularly in LDCs. Governments in East Asia are obviously conscious of the potential role of government in bringing about agglomeration. There are several types of agglomeration or industrial cluster. One is 'horizontal', where SMEs that conduct similar activities are geographically concentrated in specific places, such as Oota Ward in Tokyo, Higashi-Osaka City in Osaka and Tsubame City in Niigata. Another type has an upside-down pyramidal structure with a large assembler at the bottom, such as Toyota City in Aichi and Hitachi City in Ibaraki. In existing examples of East Asian agglomeration, vertical links along the value chain have been important, although there are usually multiple assemblers.

Figure 6.4   Agglomeration: an illustration

The cluster of producers of photocopiers and printers in Guangdong, the agglomeration of Taiwanese computer producers in Dongguan and the cluster of car producers in the eastern seaboard of Thailand are such agglomerations. Assemblers take advantage of both fragmentation and agglomeration. For standardized parts and components, the inventory costs are not particularly high, so they look for the cheapest suppliers by utilizing network information. Customized parts and components, for which information exchanges with suppliers are important, enjoy the benefits of agglomeration.

The third line of thought is the theory of the firm. Firms base their decisions on the location of activities, as well as on their own corporate structures, their interfirm relationships and the firm-specific assets they possess. Figure 6.5 provides an example of a firm's decisions on location and internalization. A single firm usually does not carry out all processes from upstream to downstream. It sets the upstream boundary by purchasing materials or parts from other firms, and determines the downstream boundary by selling its products to other firms or consumers. Such boundary-setting decisions are called 'internalization decisions'. In addition, the firm cuts its

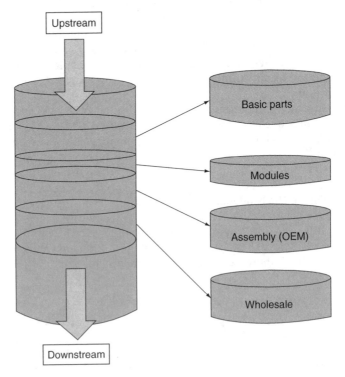

Figure 6.5   Location and internalization

internalized activities into thin slices and places these slices at appropriate locations. These are called 'location decisions'. The firm makes both types of decision at the same time, taking into consideration its firm-specific assets such as technology and managerial know-how. Figure 6.5 illustrates upstream–downstream internalization, but internalization can have other dimensions. For example decisions may be made across different functional activities, such as financial management, personnel management, R&D activities, parts procurement, sales activities and so on.

The internalization pattern in Figure 6.5 is somewhat complicated. The firm delegates the assembly process to other firms using OEM (original equipment manufacturing) contracts. In East Asia, various internalization patterns with innovative interfirm relationships have emerged from efforts to concentrate on core competencies. Such efforts have been particularly salient in the machinery, textiles and garment industries. International trade theory has not yet fully digested all the elements of the ownership and internalization advantages presented by Dunning's OLI theory.[4]

The SEA countries have effectively utilized the global economic forces that are present in these three new lines of thought and have attained rapid economic growth. What were the policy packages that attracted export-oriented foreign firms and enabled these countries to join connect international production/distribution networks?

Because the SEA countries lacked mature domestic firms they chose to accept as much FDI as possible in order rapidly to establish a critical mass of agglomeration. How did they attract FDI? The answer is simple: they tried to enhance the location advantages for foreign companies to produce internationally competitive products for export by making their location the best (or second best, for hedging purposes) in the world. Given the fact that traditional sources of comparative advantage, namely high-quality labour and an advanced technological level, could not be established in the near future, they made a substantial effort to facilitate the pre- and postinvestment activities of foreign firms and to provide the basis for agglomeration.

Government policies were again crucial in providing a competitive supply of parts and components. Fostering domestic parts and components suppliers is very important but it must be accomplished with economic efficiency. When domestic firms are immature they have to invite in foreign parts suppliers and use them to create an agglomeration. For intermediate inputs that cannot be produced domestically, or at least not for a while, the government must facilitate imports by removing trade barriers or providing a duty drawback system on the imported parts and components that are used to produce goods for export. With regard to parts and components for electronic machinery, the SEA countries introduced substantial tariff cuts, particularly in the mid 1990s, under the initiative of APEC. In addition, the duty drawback system was used extensively in cases where trade protection was maintained. Partly thanks to the drawback system, customs duty import ratios are generally low in the SEA countries (Figure 6.6). Although there is still substantial trade protection for import-substituting industries, the export-oriented affiliates of foreign firms pay little in tariffs.

The SEA countries also made a significant effort to establish good economic infrastructure. Transportation, telecommunications, energy and water supply, and industrial estate services were drastically improved, with a portion of the public investment being financed by Japanese official development assistance. The countries also entered agreements tie-ups with major trading companies and other private agencies for the construction and operation of industrial parks.

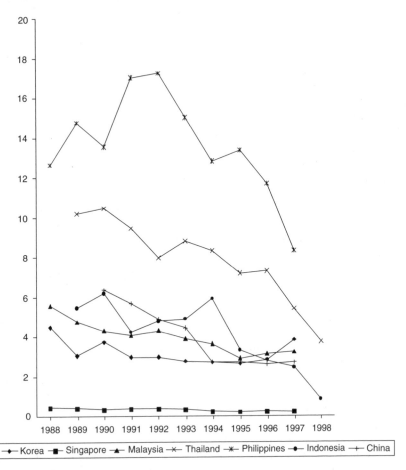

Figure 6.6 Customs duty as a percentage of import value, East Asian countries, 1988–98 (per cent)

Sources: IMF (1999); *International Financial Statistics Year book* (IMF, various years).

In the past, LDC governments often tried to manage their industrial organization by applying a complicated policy combination of entry regulations for FDI and performance requirements, together with investment incentives. However, these policy mixes were often contradictory and led to economic inefficiency. From a number of bitter experiences, they have learned that – or at least for export-oriented FDI – it is important to introduce before and after entry regulations/incentives that are as simple as possible, and to place great emphasis on policy stability and transparency. It is better not to select particular firms or industries, but rather to welcome all foreign companies that are willing to invest and set up an industrial cluster of a certain size as soon as practicable.

The current agenda

Today the SEA countries are facing new challenges. They have been successful in attracting foreign companies and have been able to achieve a certain degree of agglomeration. However, their domestic firms are still largely immature, and they have not been able fully to penetrate the international production/ distribution networks. Meanwhile, the large and competitive China has stepped into the scene. For the SEA countries, which depend heavily on foreign companies, competition with China for location advantages has become a serious issue.

Trade theorists sometimes make logical statements while intentionally neglecting the existence of FDI. For example, Krugman (1994) has criticized Thurow's book *Head to Head* (1992) by claiming that competition between countries is fundamentally different from that between firms. It is true that in the standard setting, use of an international trade model will yield the conclusion that foreign technological progress enhances the home country's welfare unless the negative terms of trade effect is too large. However, we should not forget the set of conditions we impose. In particular we assume that (1) no international mobility of productive factors is allowed and (2) the exchange rate is adjusted to balance the trade account. If we loosen condition (1), productive factors such as capital will move from a country with low (capital) productivity to one with high productivity. At this point the competition does become 'head to head'. Furthermore, in an extreme case almost all mobile factors will move to one particular country and other countries will suffer a great blow to their location advantages. There is good reason for the SEA countries to feel threatened by the emergence of a strong Chinese economy: keeping foreign affiliates in their territories is truly crucial for them.

China's advantage ultimately resides in its abundant human resources, including not only unskilled but also skilled workers and, more importantly, entrepreneurs. Entrepreneurship is the bedrock of domestic firms, some of which are fairly competitive. Firms with different nationalities, including Chinese, have formed an active agglomeration, offering many possibilities for interfirm relationships. The potentially large domestic market in China is also a major attraction. Poor economic infrastructure and a bad policy environment were once weak points, but they are quickly being improved. The SEA countries were forerunners in hosting FDI, but China has clearly caught up with them in the competition to attract foreign companies.

The weaknesses of the SEA countries are essentially the opposite of China's strengths: scarce human resources, immature domestic firms and small markets. The development of human resources must be given particularly high priority in government policy, although it is a rather long-term objective. The short-term agenda should be to strengthen international production/distribution networks and to foster larger industrial clusters. There are many measures that the governments can take in this regard.

The recent FTA boom has the potential to boost structural reforms if it is properly used. When the SEA countries formed the ASEAN Free Trade Area (AFTA), one of the main motives was to attract a continuous flow of FDI in the face of China's receipt of massive inflows. However, AFTA was initially used simply as a sort of announcement vehicle, and fully fledged trade liberalization was not implemented in the 1990s. The SEA countries now realize that concrete action must be taken within AFTA and other negotiated arrangements.

There are two faces to free trade arrangements. One is the reorganization of import-substituting industries. This is a traditional function of regional trade arrangements. A number of protected import-substituting industries in the SEA countries failed to attain the expected growth, and the cost of protecting has gradually become untenable. In addition we cannot neglect the negative effects of protection on export-oriented industries. The removal of tariffs and other trade barriers in FTA commitments triggers a competitive restructuring of import-substituting industries. Actually, the ASEAN market is not that small: it has a population of 600 million and an aggregate GDP of $500 billion, compared with China's population of 1.3 billion and a GDP of $1 trillion.[5] The first question, then, is whether or not AFTA will be effectively implemented. The SEA countries must show the will to conduct essential restructuring in their import-substituting industries, including car production. The implementation procedure, including methods of issuing certificates of origin, should also be improved in order to bring about seamless free trade.

Another possible use of free trade arrangements is to provide a package of trade/FDI facilitation measures in order to improve international production/distribution networks. FTA is a policy tool with tariff concessions at its core, but many other things can be placed under its umbrella. Despite the development of international production/distribution networks, the business environment in East Asia is still far from seamless. In Southeast Asia in particular there is considerable room for improvement. Facilitation measures for trade and FDI could include the improvement of customs procedures and related infrastructure, the convergence or harmonization of SPS (Agreement on the Application of Sanitary and Phytosanitary Measures)- or TBT (Agreement on Technical Barriers to Trade)-related regulations, institutional building for intellectual property rights and the harmonization of environmental standards. Some of these could be a part of a free trade arrangement, and others might be dealt with by subsidiary agreements. Although it is rather unconventional to place stress on such functions in the context of free trade agreement, this would suit the characteristics of East Asian economies under globalization.

Since the Asian currency crisis, many commentators have expressed concern about the weakening integrity of ASEAN. Indonesia was the major political leader of ASEAN before the crisis, but suffered from domestic problems in the subsequent years. Singapore and Thailand seem to be impatient about the slow movers in ASEAN and are taking steps towards bilateral agreements. Free trade networks in East Asia are likely to be led by such agreements, but the integrity of ASEAN must be maintained because it is the source of political stability in the region.

Lessons for LDCs in other regions

Southeast Asia has been a major world growth centre for 20 years and has made substantial improvements in national welfare. While the SEA countries were lucky to capture the wave of globalization at the right time, LDCs in other regions can still learn a lot from these countries because many have similar initial conditions, such as small economies, immature human resources and infant domestic firms.

One important lesson is that the 'accept everybody' policy makes sense for small LDCs. In the era of globalization the key to successful industrialization is to form an agglomeration of a certain size and to connect it to international production/distribution networks. The quickest way to generate an agglomeration is to host a critical mass of FDI enterprises. Because international competition over location advantages is intensifying, selective acceptance of FDI would give a bad impression to prospective foreign investors.

Another lesson is the importance of measures to facilitate FDI. Immediately after the outbreak of the Asian currency crisis the Thai government was afraid there would be a drastic decrease in inward FDI, so it made a serious effort to improve the one-stop services of the Board of Investment in order to encourage new influxes. As a result, the amount of FDI received by Thailand in 1998 was the highest ever, though the increase came partly from mergers and acquisitions. Such services are particularly important in luring foreign SMEs, which become major players in local procurement networks.

The very difficult but crucial role of government in the long term is to enhance human resources. Without this, LDCs cannot escape from their heavy dependence on foreign companies and make the necessary economic transitions at the right time. The SEA countries have not yet perfected this task.

Notes

1. In this chapter, 'Southeast Asian countries' refers to the original members of ASEAN (Association of South-East Asian Nations) namely Singapore, Malaysia, Thailand, the Philippines and Indonesia.
2. For fragmentation theory see Jones and Kierzkowski (1990), Deardorff (2001) and Cheng and Kierzkowski (2001).
3. For agglomeration theory see Krugman (1991, 1995) and Fujita *et al.* (1999).
4. See Dunning (1993, p. 81 ff.) Kimura (2000a, 2001c) analyzes the micro data of Japanese manufacturing firms and concludes that corporate structure and interfirm relationships are chosen along with the location of activities.
5. Statistics from World Bank (2002), pp. 232–3.

References

Cheng, L. K. and H. Kierzkowski (2001) *Global Production and Trade in East Asia* (Boston, Mass.: Kluwer).
Deardorff, A. V. (2001) 'Fragmentation in Simple Trade Models', *North American Journal of Economics and Finance*, vol. 12, pp. 121–37.
Dunning, J. H. (1993) *Multinational Enterprises and the Global Economy* (Wokingham: Addison-Wesley).
Fujita, M., P. Krugman and A. J. Venables (1999) *The Spatial Economy: Cities, Regions, and International Trade* (Cambridge, Mass.: MIT Press).
International Monetary Fund (IMF) (various years) *International Financial Statistics Yearbook* (Washington, DC: IMF).
International Monetary Fund (IMF) (1999) *Government Finance Statistical Yearbook* (Washington, DC: IMF).
Jones, R. W. and H. Kierzkowski (1990) 'The Role of Services in Production and International Trade: A Theoretical Framework', in R. W. Jones and A. O. Krueger (eds), *The Political Economy of International Trade: Essays in Honor of Robert E. Baldwin* (Oxford: Basil Blackwell).
Kimura, F. (2000) 'Location and Internalization Decisions: Sector Switching in Japanese Outward Foreign Direct Investment', in T. Ito and A. O. Krueger (eds), *The Role of Foreign Direct Investment in East Asian Economic Development* (Chicago, Ill.: University of Chicago Press).
Kimura, F. (2001) 'Fragmentation, Internalization, and Interfirm Linkages: Evidence from the Micro Data of Japanese Manufacturing Firms', in L. K. Cheng and H. Kierzkowski (eds), *Global Production and Trade in East Asia* (Boston, Mass.: Kluwer).
Kimura, F. and M. Ando (2003) 'Fragmentation and Agglomeration Matter: Japanese Multinationals in Latin America and East Asia', *North American Journal of Economics and Finance* vol. 14, issue 3, pp. 287–317.
Krugman, P. (1991) 'Increasing Returns and Economic Geography', *Journal of Political Economy*, vol. 99, pp. 183–99.
Krugman, P. (1994) 'Competitiveness: A Dangerous Obsession', *Foreign Affairs*, vol. 73, pp. 28–44.

Krugman, P. (1995) *Development, Geography, and Economic Theory* (Cambridge Mass.: MIT Press).

Ministry of Economy, Trade and Industry (METI) (2001) *White Paper on International Trade 2001* (Tokyo: Ministry of Finance Printing Office).

Thurow, L. C. (1992) *Head to Head: The Coming Economic Battle among Japan, Europe, and America* (New York: Morrow).

World Bank (2002) *World Development Report 2002: Building Institutions for Markets* (Oxford: Oxford University Press).

7
Development Strategy and the Role of Government Policies: Reconsidering the East Asian Experience

Koichi Ohno

Introduction

Until recently, government intervention in the process of economic development was not seen in a positive light in debates on the successful industrialization experience of East Asia. Rather, under the growing dominance of neoclassical development economics the role of markets was emphasized. However, the naïve neoclassical explanation is now being questioned as a result of more careful analyses of the East Asian experience, together with the lack of success with structural adjustment programmes in developing countries in other regions and with marketization schemes in the former centrally planned economies. Many commentators have reconsidered the part played by government in economic development and spoken positively of the rationality of government intervention in markets.

Even the World Bank (1993) has concluded that the government can substitute for the market in some cases. Moreover, some writers (for example Aoki *et al.*, 1995) emphasize the part played by governments in facilitating or complementing private-sector coordination in the process of creating market systems in developing countries, proposing a 'market-enhancing view'. On the other hand, the recent currency crisis in East Asia has complicated the debate on development experiences. While some attribute the crisis to failures in short-term macroeconomic management, others claim that the development-state regimes in these countries were the main cause of the crisis.

Against this background, this chapter considers the way in which we should understand the process of economic development in immature market economies, and what policies are necessary and desirable for developing countries in their transition to market economies. The following issues will be dealt with: the roles of the market and government in the process of economic development, with particular reference to the East Asian experience, industrial development in Korea and Taiwan in the 1960s and 1970s, and the parts played by government and the rationality of these in the light of recent economic theories.

Market structures in developing economies

Arguments continue, from various points of view, on what constitute desirable development strategies and development policies for developing countries. However, there is agreement that developing countries should conduct as much trade and investment liberalization as possible and promote industries that are able to compete in the world market. There remain, however, many questions, such as what influence the governments of developing countries should bring to bear in the process of liberalized policy execution and what policy measures are necessary in the adjustment process. What are seen as desirable development strategies and development policies will vary according to how we understand the market structures of developing countries and under what assumptions we begin our analysis.

Defining 'market'

Today, market liberalization and the deregulation of domestic markets are being pushed under the banner of 'globalization' in both advanced and developing countries. According to the textbook argument, when the conditions of perfect competition are met the market equilibrium solution is optimal. Policy intervention by the government always results in inefficiency because the adjustment function of the market is obstructed. In the extreme, proponents of this view assert that the most suitable outcomes will emerge from competition even in the case of institutions and organizations.

According to this framework, development policies that involve market intervention are not desirable. If this is the case, then it can be concluded that liberalization and deregulation are both necessary and sufficient conditions for economic development, and that the parts played by the government should be limited to market-neutral activities such as maintaining the basic conditions and providing social safety nets (this is the basis of 'market fundamentalism').

It is likely that anywhere where economic transactions are performed there will exist market dealings in which prices are used as signals to adjust between supply and demand. This applies not only to advanced industrial countries but also to developing countries and transitional economies. Conceptually, it is difficult to find any other resource allocation system that is as efficient as the market system. The existence of market dealings in developing countries, however, does not necessarily imply the existence of a market system (that is, a modern market-economy system), as is assumed by general equilibrium theory. It would not be realistic to assume that networks of domestic regional markets, market sectors (goods, labour, capital, financial, and so on), industries and firms have developed as they have in industrialized countries. We therefore need to be careful about defining the word 'market'.

Immature market systems in developing countries

Development economics has traditionally been concerned with creating the conditions for economic take-off in developing economies. In the early days the emphasis was on the initial conditions in and the economic structure of less developed countries. For example, Lewis (1954) explained the 'dual economy', where traditional rural markets coexisted with modern urban markets. Until recently, when greater recognition was given to the importance of the international trade regime in economic development, the dominant arguments about development strategy took place in the framework of traditional trade theory and its assumption of homogeneity. In many cases, concern about the salient features of developing economies tended to be abstracted from the analysis.

More recently, commentators have begun to advocate a greater focus on the development of the economic system (the market system, organizations and institutions) and economic performance. Aoki *et al.* (1995) have taken a new look at the roles of market and government and proposed a 'market enhancing view' that recognizes the importance of government in fostering efficient market systems in developing countries. Ishikawa (1990) has stressed the importance of considering the problem of immature markets in developing countries.

To establish efficient market systems, as Aoki *et al.* (1995) have suggested, there must be efficient linkages and networks between the various markets: input–output linkages, sectoral and factor markets, and regional markets. Here we shall focus on the linkage between regional markets and formulate a framework for discussing how the integration of regional markets affects the economic performance of the country as a whole.

The free trade regime and distribution problems

The problems of economic development remain even if the various assumptions about perfect competition hold true and the optimum equilibrium of a completely unified world market is realized. In other words, while an efficient division of labour in the world market can be brought about by free trade the problem of economic gaps between countries, which reflect their initial conditions, cannot be resolved in the short term. In the case of the EU, which has abolished national barriers against intra-EU economic transactions, the existence of gaps between the advanced northern industrial countries and the southern agricultural ones is still an ongoing problem.

The problem of economic inequality among regions within domestic economies, where there are far smaller barriers to transactions and factor movements than is the case in the international market, has also remained unsolved. Even in Japan, where economic inequality between domestic regions is considered to be small, it has been deemed necessary to introduce policy measures to reduce regional gaps in production, employment and wage levels.

In essence, it can be said that as the liberalization of trade and investment advances, the problem of economic development becomes that of narrowing the gap between developing and advanced regions in the integrated world economy. In this sense, market-fundamentalist assertions about development strategies do not offer a solution to the main problem of economic development.

Global competition and strategies for industrialization

The East Asian economies have been involved in the global competition among multinational enterprises (MNEs) since the mid 1980s, when barriers to trade and investment began to fall, technology progressed and it became easier to manage the complexities of cross-border transactions. The explosion of foreign direct investment (FDI) flows to the region since the mid 1980s highlights the fact that MNEs have been propelled onto centre stage in the formulation of countries' development strategies.

The national economies in the region have been steadily internationalized since the early 1970s as cross-border flows of money, information, trade and investment have grown more quickly than GDP. Such trends have served to render obsolete the common assumption that the external economy is quite separate from the domestic economy and can be safely ignored when formulating domestic policy.

However, as the global bandwagon gathered momentum from the 1980s another began to roll in the opposite direction. There have been many attempts to put the issue of national competitiveness at the centre of domestic policy agendas, not only in East Asia but also in developed countries. Possible sources of national advantage have been given serious attention in many countries. The East Asian countries, and particularly the members of ASEAN, have designed solidarity pacts with political, business and union interests to increase the attractiveness of their countries as a place for new investment. The formation of AFTA can be seen as a competitive collaboration among the ASEAN countries to attract FDI into the region, exploiting diverse comparative advantages under a free trade system. The aim is to stimulate MNEs to operate an international division of labour in their networks. Another motivation for the creation of AFTA was concern about FDI shifting away from the region to China.

It must be pointed out, however, that merely liberalizing trade and investment is not a sufficient strategy for creating national advantage in order to attract FDI. The potential for involvement in the globalization process remains constrained by the need for immobile resources rooted in national advantage. Therefore, the basic objective of industrial policy is to create a dynamic and diversified industrial sector that can contribute to the sustainable expansion of the economy. The World Bank also defines industrial policy from a dynamic viewpoint – as a government effort to alter the industrial structure to promote productivity-based growth – and points out that productivity-based growth can be achieved by means of learning, technological innovation and catching up with international best practices.

The notion of learning and innovation rests on the hypothesis that exposing individuals to new phenomena, new ideas and new things results in learning. At the same time, the 'new' should not be too new – it should be sufficiently close to the familiar to be recognizable, but novel enough to provoke new understanding and new insights. Learning applies to a variety of activities, most obviously production but also consumption and lifestyles in general. In developing economies, where the variety of manufacturing activities is very limited, extending the scope of protected manufacturing activities is intended to provide opportunities for this learning process. In this sense, the practice of import-substitution manufacturing in developing countries may be a prerequisite for successful export expansion.

Industrial growth in Korea and Taiwan

Patterns of industrial development

In the 1960s and 1970s, the Republic of Korea and Taiwan made remarkable economic progress, bolstered by rapid industrial development. This rapid industrialization has been dubbed 'export-led industrialization' and 'outward-looking industrialization'. Even today, Korea and Taiwan are often held up as successful examples of and are recommended as models for industrial development in developing countries.

Most studies of export-led industrialization have focused on two measures when accounting for the achievements of these countries. First, in the early 1960s their restricted trade regimes were liberalized and they moved from import substitution to export promotion. Second, under the liberalized trade regime the countries' comparative advantage in labour was utilized to increase their exports of labour-intensive manufactured products, supported by growing world trade.

These explanations are both clear-cut and in line with traditional trade theory. The effectiveness of the policy switch in improving the two countries' export performance has been empirically verified, but answers are still needed for how the increase in exports financed overall industrialization, and there are still many questions to answer on the roles of government.

Careful consideration of the industrial development process in these countries exposes some anomalies in the export-led industrialization explanations in the literature: (1) not only labour-intensive manufacturing industries but also certain capital-intensive ones expanded rapidly in the 1960s and1970s; (2) the direct contribution of exports to total supply in the manufacturing sector was limited – the increase in the domestic supply of intermediate products was even more important; and (3) export-promotion policies and import-substitution policies, which are often considered to be mutually exclusive, in fact coexisted throughout the period in question.

Dual industrial growth

Ohno and Imaoka (1987) have examined the various features of industrial development in Korea and Taiwan after the 1960s. They divided the manufacturing sectors of the two countries into 24 industrial categories and then calculated and compared various indices of the industries. Two of these indices – the capital–labour ratio and the intermediate output ratio – of each industry in the manufacturing sector were given fuller consideration. The capital–labour ratio indicates the comparative advantage of industries in terms of factor intensity, and the intermediate output ratio reflects the backward-linkage effects of industries.

In Table 7.1, the manufacturing sectors in each country are classified by factor intensity and intermediate output ratio into four groups of industries: (A) capital-intensive and intermediate products, (B) capital-intensive and final products, (C) labour-intensive and intermediate products, and (D) labour-intensive and final products. The table shows the average annual growth rates of production in the four groups of industries. In the case of Korea, production in group A increased relatively rapidly in the periods

Table 7.1 Growth rates of four groups of industries in Korea and Taiwan (per cent)

Group	1960–70	1970–77	1960–77
Korea			
A	33.14	18.52	26.91
B	15.24	15.88	15.51
C	24.91	18.80	22.35
D	9.70	20.01	13.84
E	17.41	18.77	17.95
Taiwan	*1961–70*	*1970–81*	*1961–81*
A	17.4	11.4	15.6
B	5.2	6.2	5.4
C	24.1	16.7	23.6
D	23.4	14.3	18.3
E	17.7	13.3	17.5

Notes: A = capital-intensive and intermediate products; B = capital-intensive and final products; C = labour-intensive and intermediate products; D = labour-intensive and final products; E = average of manufacturing sector.
Source: Ohno and Imaoka (1987) p. 312.

1960–70 and 1970–77. The average growth rate for group A was 26.9 per cent in 1960–77, while the manufacturing sector as a whole increased by just 18 per cent in the same period. Thus group A can be regarded as a significant growth pole in the manufacturing sector. Production in groups C and D also increased by solid rates, and these categories can also be considered as significant growth poles. The industries in group C performed well in both periods: 24.9 per cent in the 1960s and 18.8 per cent in the 1970s. The sluggishness of group D in the earlier period probably reflects the fact that Korea's export promotion policies were not particularly effective prior to the late 1960s, even though the trade policy regime shifted in the first half of the decade. Thus most of the growth in Korea's manufacturing sector occurred in two industrial groups: labour-intensive and capital-intensive industries expanded simultaneously in a pattern of dual industrial growth. This deserves consideration as a potential model for industrialization in developing countries.

In Taiwan, the pattern was somewhat different. As Table 7.1 shows, production by the labour-intensive industries in groups C and D expanded rapidly. In fact, group C had the highest average growth rate throughout the period. Although the growth rates for the capital-intensive industries in groups A and B were relatively low, group A's production increased as rapidly as that of group D.

Patterns of specialization

As demonstrated by the ratio of exports to imports in the manufacturing industries, most of the labour-intensive industries enjoyed an increase in their net export ratios. In these industries the specialization of trade and production, through either import substitution or export promotion, progressed in both countries. There does not seem to have been any progress in trade specialization in group A, which was another growth pole. For example in the case of chemicals, petroleum and coal products, and of non-ferrous metals, both the import ratios and the net import ratios increased in Korea. In Taiwan, they increased for some industries in group A, including chemicals, petroleum and coal products, and paper and printing.

The lack of change in the trade structure of these industries can be explained by the fact that the increase in demand for their products was so rapid that it raised the import ratios in spite of the increase in domestic production. The coefficients of specialization for Korea and Taiwan are defined as the production shares of the manufacturing industries in both countries, divided by the corresponding shares in Japan for the year 1975. These coefficients indicate the degree of specialization in domestic production in comparison with Japan.

In Korea, there was significant progress in specialization in group A, together with the machinery and electric machinery industries. Specialization in the group A industries in Taiwan also increased, but much more slowly than in Korea. These findings accord with the previous evaluation of dual industrial growth in the two countries.

Interfactor relationships

We shall now consider the relationship between factor intensity, the intermediate output ratio, the export and import ratios and the annual growth rate of manufacturing in the two countries, together with the rank correlation coefficients between these factors.

The inverse correlation between the export ratio and the capital–labour ratio means that in both countries, industries with high export ratios were likely to be those with a high labour intensity. While there is evidence of a positive correlation between export ratio and growth rate in Taiwan, there was no such correlation in Korea. This suggests that certain features of industrial development differed between Taiwan and Korea. However, there was a positive correlation between export ratio and growth rate in both countries. This means that production growth rates were high in industries with large opportunities for import substitution. In addition, the industries with high intermediate ratios were more capital-intensive in both countries.

Finally, it is worth noting the findings on two of the indices considered in this section – the capital–labour ratio and the intermediate output ratio. A look at the development of the manufacturing sector in terms of factor intensity shows that the expansion of the sector was not achieved solely by means of production increases in labour-intensive industries. Most industries with high export ratios were indeed labour-intensive, seemingly bearing out the principle of comparative advantage for labour-abundant countries. However, in contradiction to this principle, capital-intensive industries also achieved significant growth rates.

The effect of exports on domestic production is usually measured in terms of direct and indirect effects. The direct effect relates to the volume of exports supplied by domestic industries, and the indirect effect to the intermediate demand induced by exports. In both Korea and Taiwan the ratio of exports to total manufacturing sector demand was below 25 per cent during the 1960s and 1970s. The remaining 75 per cent was accounted for by domestic final demand and intermediate demand. Although the intermediate demand for the products of the industries in question was not wholly met by domestic firms, and therefore some imports would have been needed, it had the effect of increasing production by domestic industries and creating investment opportunities.

Mechanisms of dual industrial growth

How did Korea attain success with dual industrial growth? What factors made it possible? Three points are central to answering these questions: the coexistence of alternative strategies, the allocation of investment capital, and economies of scale.

Bearing these points in mind, the mechanism of dual industrial growth in Korea in the 1960s and 1970s can be summarized as follows. First, it is wrong to assume that industrial development took place under a free trade regime. In actuality the regime was characterized by the coexistence of the alternative strategies of export promotion and import substitution. Second, under this regime, labour-intensive industries increased their production and exports with the support of export-promotion policies. Third, because of the growing demand for intermediate goods induced by exports, capital-intensive industries producing intermediate products were able to expand. This was boosted by protection under import-substitution policies and large inflows of foreign capital that were sufficient to allow economies of scale (Figure 7.1).

Coexistence of alternative policies

In discussions of development strategy, export-promotion and import-substitution policies have generally been treated as mutually exclusive alternatives. While import substitution is designed to protect the domestic market, even at the cost of distorting resource allocations, export promotion liberalizes the trade regime to capture world markets and is suggestive of a free trade regime.

For both Korea and Taiwan it is said that the governments strove to shift from a protectionist regime aimed at import substitution and utilizing import quotas, tariffs and subsidies, to a more liberal one aimed at correcting price distortions and promoting exports. However, in Korea imports were

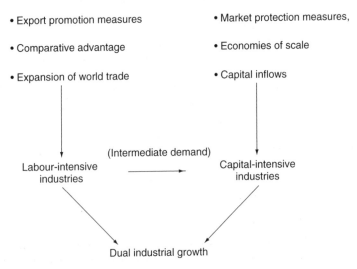

Figure 7.1   Framework for dual industrial growth
Source: Ohno and Imaoka (1987 p. 318).

only nominally liberalized and the domestic market was rather heavily protected until the late 1970s. Under this protective trade regime, labour-intensive industries required the assistance of export-promotion measures to compete in world markets. Various export incentives were introduced. For instance, imports of intermediate and capital inputs for export goods were given preferential treatment in respect of import quotas and tariffs. The government even granted loans to firms in proportion to their export volumes.

Thus from the mid 1960s to the late 1970s, the Korean economy was managed with a policy that consisted of both export-promotion and import-substitution measures. It should be noted that this dual policy regime was not equivalent to free trade. While export-promotion measures offset the cost of import protection for the producers of export goods, import-substitution measures remained in effect for the domestic market as a whole.

Remarks

In light of Korea's experience of dual industrial growth, two points should be emphasized in discussions of industrial development strategies. First, while the development of capital-intensive industries during the period of export expansion has often been criticized as an adverse and inefficient result of excessive protectionist policies, it should be reappraised from a dynamic point of view if the experiences of industrial development in Korea and Taiwan are considered to have been successful. Second, it should be noted that in the process of dual industrial growth, export-promotion and import-substitution measures coexisted. We should carefully examine the effects of this dual policy on overall industrial development.

Changes in Korea's trade structure

From the latter half of the 1960s Korea's rapid progress in industrialization led to astonishing economic development, and the rapid growth in exports and imports made the Korean economy part of the international system. The increasing share of exports and imports among manufacturers also greatly changed the trade structure.

Korea's industrial development is often described as taking advantage of the country's relatively ample labour endowment, and as focusing on expanding the exportation of labour-intensive manufactures. Backing this description is the well-known Heckscher–Ohlin theorem on the international division of labour: a country with a relatively ample supply of labour (compared with capital) has a comparative advantage in industries that use labour intensively, and is able to use export promotion policies in a free trade system to promote progress in industrialization. If this thinking were correct, industrial progress in Korea would have been limited to the labour-intensive manufacturing sector and the trade structure would have been labour intensive.

However, as mentioned in the previous section, Korea's capital-intensive industries were also developed under government protection from the early 1960s, and the subsequent expansion of import-substitution industries was equivalent to that of the labour-intensive industries. Against this background, Ohno (1988) conducted an empirical study of Korea's trade structure and the changes in it during the period of industrial progress.

The well-known Leontief index (an integrated index of factor intensity embodied in trade) indicates the effects of a country's trade and industry structure, such as the size of the coefficient of factor input for each industry, the export–import configuration and the effects ensuing from the intermediate demand structure (Leontief, 1954). The changes in Korea's trade and industry structure, as shown by factor intensity, were decomposed into the effects of: (1) export promotion, (2) import substitution, (3) changes in the capital coefficient and labour coefficient and (4) structural changes in the input–output matrix, by industry and rate of contribution for each cause. For purposes of comparison, the same measurements were calculated for Japan. Table 7.2 shows the results for changes in the factor intensity of trade. The Leontief index (F) for Korea exceeded 1 in the years 1970, 1975, 1980 and 1983. If we interpret this as an index of factor endowment, we can conclude that Korea had already become a capital-abundant country by 1970.

Breaking down the decline in the index during 1970–75, we find that the factor intensities embodied in exports (F_e) and imports (F_m) increased together. However, because the increase in F_m was much more rapid the aggregate trade structure became more labour intensive. The quantity of labour embodied in per unit of trade declined from 1.33 to 0.95 for exports and from 1.47 to 0.98 for imports, while the quantity of capital increased from 2.06 to 2.25 for imports and declined from 2.33 to 2.27 for exports. In other words Korea's trade structure during this period was one of labour

Table 7.2   Factor intensity of trade in Korea, 1970–80

	1970	1975	1980	Rate of change (%)	
				1970–75	*1975–80*
F_e	1.7502	2.4054	2.8465	37.44	18.34
F^k	2.3312	2.2731	1.8511	−2.49	−18.57
F_e^l	1.3320	0.9450	0.6503	−29.05	−31.19
F_m	1.3961	2.3041	2.5724	65.04	11.64
F_m^k	2.0616	2.2482	1.8033	9.05	−19.79
F_m^l	1.4767	0.9757	0.7010	−33.93	−28.15
F	1.2537	1.0440	1.1066	−16.73	5.99

Notes: F_e^k, F_e^l = capital and labour embodied in exports; $F_e = F_e^k / F_e^l$; F_m^k, F_m^l = capital and labour embodied in exports; $F_m = F_m^k / F_m^l$.
Source: Ohno (1988, p. 371).

abundance. Although aggregate labour productivity increased, the trade structure became more labour intensive in relative terms.

In contrast, the Leontief index increased during 1975–80. This is because there was a rise in the factor intensities embodied in both imports and exports, but the intensity of exports rose faster. The major causal factor was that although the required quantities of capital and labour were declining in per unit terms for both imports and exports, there was a much more dramatic drop in the quantity of labour needed per unit of exports. Hence the major change in the trade structure during this period was a capital intensification of exports.

The proportion of capital and labour embodied in exports climbed from 1.75 in 1970 to 2.41 in 1975 and 2.85 in 1980, and the proportion embodied in imports rose from 1.39 to 2.30 and 2.57 over the same period. The backdrop to this trend was the heightening of aggregate capital intensity. The labour intensification of the trade structure during 1970–75 and capital intensification during 1975–80 were brought about by relative differences in the changing factor intensities embodied in exports and imports.

In summary, as shown by factor intensity in the industrial development process, during the 1970s the trade structure in Korea became more capital intensive, especially in the manufacturing sector. Thus it would be inappropriate to describe industrialization during this period as specialization in labour-intensive industries. The coexistence of import substitution in the capital-intensive industries and export expansion in the labour-intensive industries constituted a dual industrialization strategy, with labour intensification dominating in 1970–75 and capital intensification dominating in 1975–83. The labour intensification in 1970–75 was mainly caused by a decline in agriculture, forestry and fishery imports.

A very interesting point emerges when the statistics are looked at on an industry-by-industry basis: the capital intensity of each industry and the capital intensity of aggregate trade did not always match. In other words the expansion of exports by labour-intensive industries did not necessarily result in increased labour intensity in the trade structure. During the 1970s and early 1980s, many firms in the Korean manufacturing sector were moving ahead with export promotion and import substitution, while the changes in nearly all industries created a more capital-intensive trade structure.

Dual industrial development and trade policy

Learning effects

The effectiveness of trade liberalization is usually emphasized when explaining the achievements of Korea and Taiwan. It is argued that the most important factor in their success was their policy switch from a restricted strategy based on import substitution to a more liberal one designed to promote exports. In fact, after the policy switch in the 1960s, exports of manufactured products increased in both countries, and their rapid industrial development started in the same period.

Most theoretical explanations of the mechanisms of export-led industrialization are less than satisfactory, as mentioned previously. Within the framework of traditional trade theory, it is argued that under a liberalized trade scheme a country uses its comparative advantage in labour to increase exports of labour-intensive manufactured products, and that the efficient allocation of resources facilitates rapid industrial development. However, this traditional framework is essentially static and is inadequate for analyzing the process of economic development in and changes in the industrial structure of Korea. It also leaves two questions unanswered: how did the policy switch promote overall industrial development in a dynamic way, and by what process was this development promoted? Four points have to be considered in relation to these questions.

First, many studies have focused on the demerits of protective measures. It is necessary, however, to examine the implications of Korea's import-substitution policy in the period before the policy switch. Likewise the timing of the switch must be discussed.

Second, the policy switch was not as substantial as is commonly claimed. The switch is said to have occurred in the early 1960s, but in fact the economy was only nominally liberalized and the domestic market remained rather heavily protected until the late 1970s. To consider the factors behind the success of export-led development, we should closely examine the real features of policies and their effects on the process of structural adjustment after the transformation.

Third, export expansion after the switch did not proceed under conditions of free trade. In addition to the remaining import-protection measures, various export incentives continued to exist. Thus the transformation should be understood as a shift of government focus from fostering import-substituting industries to promoting export industries, and not as a move from protectionism to free trade.

Fourth, it is essential to shed light on the dynamic process of overall industrial development. According to the static framework of traditional trade theory, when labour-intensive industries expand as a result of a policy switch, capital-intensive industries must decline in response. However, in Korea some capital-intensive industries – such as iron and steel, shipbuilding, and chemicals – expanded even after the switch and became internationally competitive. Thus the dynamic aspects of industrial development should be analyzed carefully when considering export-led growth.

In light of the above, Ohno (1989) examined the effects of export-promotion policy on an economy in which the government was simultaneously fostering import-substitution industries, and discussed the rationale for a dual industrial strategy. For this purpose he introduced a two-period, three-sector model of learning effects, with reference to the analysis of 'Dutch disease'. He discussed the equilibrium of the model and examined the effects of an export-promotion policy on the economy of a developing country in which the government had attempted to promote industrialization through an import-substitution policy.

In the model, the government had been fostering an infant industry (in which there were learning effects) by providing a production subsidy and protecting the domestic market. The optimal level of subsidy for the infant industry was determined in order to maximize social welfare in two periods. At the same time, the government had introduced an export promotion policy.

Ohno examined the question of how to set the optimal subsidy when exports are expanding. Two cases were considered, depending on the relative magnitude of learning effects and intertemporal substitution effects in the infant industry. When the learning effects exceeded the substitution effect, an increase in exports reduced the level of the optimal subsidy. In this case, the export promotion policy should have been used in tandem with a reduction in the subsidy. Conversely, an increase in the subsidy would have been necessary if the substitution effect had been larger.

The above conclusion may contribute to the discussion on the efficacy of policy switches in the context of export-led industrialization. When the learning effects in import-substituting industries are sufficiently large, export promotion and liberalization of the domestic market should be conducted simultaneously. Conversely, when the learning effects are small, a higher level of protection is called for. It is worth noting that market liberalization is supported in the case of larger learning effects, which intuitively calls for higher protection.

Trade policy and economic geography

Many researchers have estimated the positive effects that trade liberalization has on the economic growth on individual countries and the world economy as a whole. Most writers on regional economic arrangements such as the European Union (EU) and the North American Free Trade Agreement (NAFTA) argue that removing barriers to international border transactions leads to the more efficient allocation of resources through markets, and therefore to the optimal solution.

According to Krugman and Venables (1990), the effect of trade liberalization is determined by three factors: the extent of economies of scale, the cost of concentrating production (such as a rise in the wage level) and the trade barriers that remain after liberalization (for example transportation costs). They conclude that if trade barriers reach a level near zero due to trade liberalization, manufacturing firms in developing countries will shift to advanced nations. Conversely, manufacturing firms will remain in developing countries if trade barriers remain relatively high after liberalization.

Trade liberalization and economic growth

In the context of economic development, we should consider the effects of market integration on technological change. If a country has segregated regional markets there is no technological spillover between regions and the efforts made in one region to advance its technology are conducted independently of the efforts of other regions. This means that identical technologies may be developed separately in each region, leading to redundancy in research and development. On the other hand, if the market is completely integrated anyone in the country can access the technology of any region and there is no redundancy. In the latter case, it is likely that the integration of domestic regional markets will lead to higher rates of technological development and economic growth for the country as a whole.

There are conflicting arguments about the effects of trade restrictions on technological development. Using a growth model with endogenous technological change, Romer (1990) found that restrictions on trade between countries serve to reduce worldwide economic growth. However, Grossman and Helpman (1990) found that under some conditions, trade restrictions can improve worldwide growth.

Rivera-Batiz and Romer (1991) point out that the contradiction between these two findings is due to different specifications of trading partners. While Romer (1990) looked at identical trading partners, Grossman and Helpman (1990) looked at trading partners with different technologies. Rivera-Batiz and Romer (1991) argue that trade restrictions have three effects on economic growth: an integration effect, an allocation effect and a redundancy effect. Here we shall discuss the effects that the integration of regional markets has on the economic performance of a country, using the framework from Rivera-Batiz and Romer's model.

Suppose there are two sectors in each region of a country: a manufacturing sector, Y, and an R&D sector, A. In the manufacturing sector all tangible goods, such as consumption goods and physical capital, are produced using capital (K_y), labour (L_y), human capital (H_y) and technology or stock of knowledge (A). In the R&D sector, new knowledge is produced using K_a, L_a, H_a and A. The production functions of these sectors can be written as:

$$Y = F(H_y, L_y, K_y, A),$$

and

$$g(A) = R(H_a, L_a, K_a, A),$$

where $g(A)$ denotes an increase in the stock of A.

Now suppose that the country consists of two identical regions. If the two regions are completely segregated and Z_y and Z_a are the vectors of inputs in manufacturing and R&D respectively, the manufacturing output of the country is the sum of the outputs of the two regions: $2Y = 2F(Z_y)$. If the two regions are completely integrated, the total output of the country can be expressed as $F(2Z_y)$. If the production function exhibits increasing returns, the total output of the country could increase: $F(2Z_y) > 2F(Z_y)$.

In the R&D sectors the total output of the country is between $R(Z_a)$ and $2R(Z_a)$ in the case of segregated regions. Since R&D is conducted separately by the two regions, new developments may be duplicated. If the two regions are integrated this redundancy can be avoided. Moreover, if the production function, $R(Z_a)$, exhibits increasing returns, the total research output of the country increases: $R(2Z_a) > 2R(Z_a)$.

Hence the degree of integration of regional markets can affect the economic performance of a country through three channels: the integration effect in manufacturing, the integration effect in the R&D sector and the redundancy effect in the R&D sector. This suggests that integration benefits the economic growth of the country. However, the influence of the fourth effect, which Rivera-Batiz and Romer called the allocation effect, is ambiguous.

Suppose that a transportation cost (the magnitude of trade barriers, including tariffs and distance) of t per manufactured good is incurred in trade between two regions. The relationship between the level of t and the growth rate of the country is not monotonic. If the initial level of t is very low, the relationship between t and the growth rate is negative: a high level of t leads to a lower growth rate. On the other hand, if the initial level of t is high, the relation is positive.

Transportation costs can affect the economy in two ways. First, the higher import price of capital goods from region A to region B reduces the demand for imported capital goods, leading to a decline in the price of capital goods in the region. Therefore the price (or the rent) of new knowledge will be depressed, potentially causing a shift of human capital from the R&D sector to the manufacturing sector and lowering the growth rate of the country. On the other hand, the decrease in capital imports can result in the marginal productivity of human capital in the manufacturing sector being low, leading to a shift of human capital from the manufacturing sector to the R&D sector. The net effect depends on the relative magnitude of the two effects, and the allocation effect of transport cost becomes non-monotonic.

When two regions in a country have quite different technological levels, the allocation effect can be so large that it dominates the three positive effects. In this case, Grossman and Helpman's (1990) conclusion holds. In the case of identical regions, the allocation effect is small and the lower transportation cost could correspond to higher growth for the country, as shown by Romer (1990).

In summary, Romer's model assumes trade between two countries whose economic structure is the same, and therefore his conclusion should be interpreted as illustrating a case of trade between advanced nations. On the other hand Grossman and Helpman's model assumes two countries where the technical levels are different, and therefore can be said to be suitable for considering the situation in developing countries. Their conclusion is that the resource allocation effect from trade liberalization will be large and the growth rate may fall. This suggests that the implementation of a trade intervention policy in a developing country will raise the economic growth rate. The industry protected in such a way must be one with a relatively low intensity of skill (human resources).

Concluding remarks

First, with regard to the relative importance of the roles played by the market and by government policy during the process of economic development, while it is true that there has been no case of economic development being accomplished without the development of a market system, it is equally true that there have been no examples of successful development without government policies.

Second, industrial development in Korea after the 1960s was characterized by dual industrial growth. Two growth poles – labour-intensive industries, and capital-intensive producers of intermediate products – contributed to Korea's rapid industrial growth. (This pattern, however, was not evident in Taiwan.) It should be noted that in the process of dual industrial growth, export-promotion and import-substitution measures were implemented together. The effects of these dual measures on overall industrial development warrant further examination.

Third, there may be theoretical rationales for policy intervention during the development process in terms of learning effects, factors of economic geography and endogenous growth. However, the conclusions drawn in this chapter depend on the characteristics (parameters) of individual countries and industries. It cannot be said that there has been adequate theoretical clarification of the effect of government initiatives on economic development.

Finally, in the East Asian countries economic liberalization took place gradually in a process of trial and error. Flexible policy measures were carried out according to the situation in each country – the various countries did not necessarily succeed by following a simple liberalization manual. When discussing the desirability of policy interventions, more careful consideration should be given to the diverse initial conditions (including historical and social conditions) in developing countries. This remains a task for the future.

References

Aoki, M., H. Kim and M. Okuno-Fujiwara (1995) *The Role of Government in East Asian Economic Development* (Oxford: Oxford University Press).

Bai, M. K. and C. Kim (1985) 'Industrial Development and Structural Changes in Labor Market: Korea and Southeast Asia', Joint Research Program Series 46 (Tokyo: Institute of Developing Economies).

Chenery, H. B. and L. Taylor (1968) 'Development Patterns among Countries and Over Time', *Review of Economics and Statistics*, vol. 50, no. 4, pp. 391–416.

de Melo, J. and A. Panagariya (1993) *New Dimensions in Regional Integration* (Cambridge: Cambridge University Press).

Findlay, R. (1995) *Factor Proportions, Trade, and Growth* (Cambridge, Mass.: MIT Press).

Frank, C. R., K. S. Kim and L. E. Westphal, (1975) *South Korea: Foreign Trade Regimes and Economic Development* (New York: Columbia University Press).

Grossman, G. and E. Helpman (1990) 'Comparative Advantage and Long Run Growth', *American Economic Review*, vol. 80, pp. 796–815.

Imaoka. H., K. Ohno and H. Yokoyama (eds) (1985) *Chushinkoku no kougyou hatten* (*Industrial Development in Middle-Income Countries* [in Japanese]), Kenkyu Sousho no. 337 (Tokyo: Institute of Developing Economies).

Inada. K., S. Sekiguchi and Y. Shoda (1972) *Keizai hatten no mekanizumu* (*Mechanisms of Economic Development* [in Japanese]) (Tokyo : Sobunsha).

Ishikawa, S. (1990) *Kaihatsu keizaigaku no kihon mondai* (*Basic Problems in Development Economics* [in Japanese]) (Tokyo: Iwanami Shoten).

Krugman, P. (1995) *Development, Geography, and Economic Theory* (Cambridge, Mass.: MIT Press).

Krugman, P. and A. J. Venables (1990) 'Integration and the Competitiveness of Peripheral Industry', in C. Bliss and J. B. Macedo (eds), *Unity with Diversity in the European Economy* (Cambridge: Cambridge University Press).

Kubo, Y. (1987) 'Seigenteki rodo kyoukyu to fukusengata kogyo hatten' (Dual industrial growth with a limited supply of labour [in Japanese]), *Ajia keizai*, vol. 28, no. 10, pp. 19–29.

Leamer, E. (1984) *Sources of International Comparative Advantage: Theory and Evidence* (Cambridge, Mass.: MIT Press).

Lewis, W. A. (1954) 'Economic Development with Unlimited Supply of Labor', Manchester School of Economics and Social Studies, vol. 22, no. 3, pp. 139–191.

Leontief, W. W. (1954) 'Domestic Production and Foreign Trade: The American Capital Position Re-examined', *Economia Internazionale*, vol. 7, pp. 3–32.

Maruksen, J. R., J. R. Melvin, W. H. Kaempfer, and K. E. Maskus (1995) *International Trade: Theory and Evidence* (New York: McGraw-Hill).

Michaely, M. (1986) 'The Timing and Sequencing of a Trade Liberalization Policy', in A. M. Ohoksi and D. Papageorgiou (eds), *Economic Liberalization in Developing Countries* (Oxford: Basil Blackwell).

Mundell, A. (1957) 'Transport Costs in International Trade Theory', *Canadian Journal of Economics*, vol. 23, pp. 331–48.

Neary, J. P. and S. V. Wijnbergen (eds) (1986) *Natural Resources and the Macroeconomy* (Oxford: Basil Blackwell).

Ohno, K. (1988) 'Changes in Trade Structure and Factor Intensity: A Case Study of The Republic of Korea', *The Developing Economies*, vol. 26, no. 4, pp. 367–85.

Ohno, K. (1989) 'A Note on the Dual-Industrial Growth and Learning Effects', *The Developing Economies*, vol. 27, no. 4, pp. 350–58.

Ohno, K. (ed.) (1993) *Regional Integration and Its Impacts on Developing Countries* (Tokyo: Institute of Developing Economies).

Ohno, K. and H. Imaoka (1987) 'The Experience of Dual-Industrial Growth: Korea and Taiwan', *The Developing Economies*, vol. 25, no. 4, pp. 310–24.

Rivera-Batiz, A. and P. M. Romer (1991) 'International Trade with Endogenous Technological Change', *European Economic Review*, vol. 35, pp. 971–1001.

Romer, P. M. (1990) 'Endogenous Technological Change', *Journal of Political Economy*, vol. 98, pp. 71–101.

Syrquin, M. and S. Urata (1986) 'Sources of Change in Factor Intensity of Trade', *Journal of Development Economics*, vol. 24, no. 2, pp. 225–37.

World Bank (1993) *The East Asian Miracle: Economic Growth and Public Policy* (New York: Oxford University Press).

Part III

Policy Reforms and the Asian Financial Crisis

8
Political and Institutional Lessons from the Asian Financial Crisis

Stephan Haggard

Introduction

The debate on the Asian financial crisis followed a curious path in the United States. Paul Krugman (1998) wrote an early theoretical analysis that emphasized the role of moral hazard and 'crony capitalism'. This theme was reflected in a number of journalistic accounts and US policy pronouncements. But Krugman changed his mind (in 1999). He and other analysts gradually moved away from the political economy of the crisis and towards one of three different foci: the macroeconomic and exchange rate policies that left countries vulnerable to shocks; the vulnerabilities associated with high corporate leveraging and weak financial sectors; and the international dimensions of the crisis. This last cluster of issues included the costs of capital account liberalization, the role of contagion and a particularly heated debate on whether the IMF had eased or exacerbated the crisis (Stiglitz, 2002).

Yet country studies of the onset and initial management of the crisis – although told from a variety of different theoretical standpoints (Jomo, 1998; Pempel, 1999; Haggard, 2000; MacIntyre, 2002) – repeatedly found that political factors played a crucial part in the onset and management of the crisis. Moreover, many of the reforms proposed by the international financial institutions clearly reflected political concerns, particularly about the nature of business–government relations and their effects in terms of moral hazard, rent seeking and outright corruption.

This chapter reflects on three political and institutional issues raised by the crisis. The first is how government decision making during times of economic vulnerability or crisis influences economic outcomes, particularly by generating uncertainty. Uncertainties associated with democratic rule, including coalition politics in Thailand and the electoral cycle in Korea, contributed to the onset and depth of the crisis in those two countries. In Thailand, these problems were deep-seated, and remained so even after the constitutional revision of 1997. In Indonesia, the design of new democratic institutions also poses daunting, even insurmountable, challenges not only to economic management but also to coherent policies of any sort.

In Thailand and Korea, democracy allowed new governments to take office and initiate reform with electoral and legislative support. In authoritarian systems, by contrast, changes of government are rarely smooth. In semi-democratic Malaysia, internal divisions within the political leadership associated with succession politics generated policy uncertainty in 1997–98. But Mahathir's control over the party allowed him to reassert his authority, reduce politically generated uncertainty and pursue an unorthodox response to the crisis. Indonesia, by contrast, had few institutionalized mechanisms for managing either succession or opposition. Doubts about Soeharto's longevity and political challenges meant that the very fate of the regime, and the complex property rights associated with it, came into doubt. Indonesia's unstable authoritarian regime contributed directly to the worst economic performance in the region.

The second issue has to do with the nature of business–government relations in East Asia, which was long considered a contributing factor in the region's growth. But it is now clear that such relationships also have the potential to generate moral hazard, lax regulation and outright corruption. The question is how to combine the benefits of close business–government interaction with checks on private power. One supposed virtue of liberalizing markets and increasing competition is to provide such a check by limiting the opportunities for rent-seeking. However, the crisis has shown that this expectation is misguided because business interests are capable of capturing liberalizing reforms in ways that increase risk as well; financial sector reforms demonstrate this clearly.

Institutional reforms are required to control private power, including the strengthening of regulatory capabilities and reforms of corporate governance that assure multiple channels for monitoring corporate behaviour. However, these reforms are themselves dependent on broader political reforms – in some cases even constitutional ones – that make business–government relations more transparent and check private influence on government decision making.

The third question is how governments will manage the social consequences of globalization. With some interesting exceptions, such as Singapore's Central Provident Fund, the social welfare bargain in East Asia rested primarily on high growth and upward mobility, with very limited formal mechanisms of social insurance. In the wake of the crisis, countries institutionalized more formal social safety nets but legacies of the previous social welfare bargain and East Asia's growth strategy placed political limits on a new social contract. A new approach requires a return to some basic tenets of the 'East Asian model', especially continuing investment in human capital.

When examining these three issues, this chapter will focus primarily on six administrations that were responsible for the early management of the crisis in four countries. Four of these were democratic ones, two in Korea's presidential system (Kim Young Sam and Kim Dae Jung), two in Thailand's parliamentary system (Chavalit and Chuan). Malaysia's government under Mahathir is best described as a semidemocratic, dominant-party parliamentary system. The Soeharto regime, by contrast, was clearly authoritarian. Some reference will also be made to the transitional Habibie government, the new democratic administrations of Wahid and Megawati in Indonesia and the Thaksin government in Thailand.

Decision making during the crisis: the generation of political uncertainty

When countries exhibit signs of economic vulnerability, the reactions of market and non-market actors – international financial institutions, ratings agencies, financial analysts, banks and institutional investors – are based on expectations of how governments will respond. These agents will be concerned, first, with the capacity of governments to act in a decisive and coherent fashion and, second, with what they actually expect governments to do – the question of intent. One source of political uncertainty lies in the decision-making process, where a trade-off can arise between decisiveness and credibility.[1] This trade-off is related to the nature of institutional checks and balances in the decision-making process, or more specifically the number and preferences of different veto gates.[2]

A decision-making system with few checks on executive authority – a single or just a few veto gates – has the advantage of being decisive. Indeed, decisiveness is one of the purported advantages of authoritarian rule. But precisely because policy can be changed easily, it may not be credible and can become erratic. By contrast, a system with multiple veto gates has the advantage of checks and balances that force deliberation and bargaining. It will be slow-moving and less decisive, and at the extreme it may generate outright stalemate. Such an outcome may be desirable if the policy *status quo* is favourable, but it can be highly costly during crises when there is strong pressure for policy change.

In Thailand, the problem of institutionally generated uncertainty was quite profound (Hicken, 1999; MacIntyre, 1999a, 2001). All of the democratically elected governments prior to the crisis – the Chatichai, Chuan, Banharn and Chavalit governments – rested on shaky multiparty coalitions. These coalitions were made up of internally weak and fragmented parties that provided opportunities for private interests to gain access to the policymaking process and made that process extraordinarily contentious. Party leaders constructed parliamentary majorities from a pool of approximately a dozen parties, and coalitions typically consisted of six or more parties. Cabinet instability was a chronic problem. The prime minister was vulnerable to policy blackmail by coalition partners, and in some cases individual ministers threatened to defect in pursuit of better deals in another alliance configuration. In turn, the parties relied heavily on national or provincial businessmen with strong personal as well as political interests in financial and other economic policies.

The Chavalit government was made up of a six-party coalition that included many of the parties in the previous government. Although the relatively independent and competent central bank succeeded in staving off two speculative attacks on the baht prior to its collapse in July 1997, the government failed to make fiscal policy adjustments or change the fixed exchange rate regime. The problems of coalition politics were made most apparent by the government's inability to manage the mounting problems in the financial sector, particularly with regard to finance companies. The government put off devising a plan to address their weaknesses and continued to provide a number of them with costly liquid support.

These problems were visible prior to the collapse of the baht and were taken by several influential Western market analysts as signs of the government's weakness. The inability of the cabinet to take a coherent policy stance contributed directly to the resignation of the finance minister two weeks before the final assault on the baht in July.

But the crisis did not immediately spark a more coherent approach. The review of the finance companies did not occur in a timely fashion, and in mid October the second finance minister resigned.[3] In the face of rising public protest, Chavalit also resigned.

Korea appeared to be much better positioned to respond to the crisis than Thailand. It had a presidential system in which the president enjoyed a range of legislative powers, and Kim Young Sam also enjoyed a legislative majority. But the government faced institutional constraints that were due in large part to the presidential elections scheduled for December.

Korea has a 'no re-election' rule for its presidents. As economic performance deteriorated during the course of 1997 the ruling party fragmented. One faction of the party broke away and contested the presidential election, contributing to the party's ultimate defeat at the hands of Kim Dae Jung. Equally if not more important was the fact that neither the ruling party's presidential candidate nor its legislators had a strong incentive to cooperate with a weak president. In effect the last year of Kim Young Sam's rule was characterized by a divided, do-nothing government.

These political problems affected economic policy making in two crucial areas: the management of major corporate bankruptcies and the passage of important financial reform legislation. The failure of large firms began in January 1997 with Hanbo, but the most damaging corporate collapse was that of the Kia group. Kia's management exploited the elections and the government's weakness to mount a major campaign in the summer of 1997 for government support in dealing with its creditors. By late October – prior to the onset of the crisis – the Korean banking system had been damaged by a highly politicized process that left the ultimate disposition of Kia in limbo for months.

Financial reform had been a stated priority of the government since January 1997, but the actual legislation to implement it was stalled by disagreements within the ruling party. When the crisis broke, financial reform was one of the conditions of the first IMF programme. But neither the ruling party's presidential candidate nor the opposition cooperated with the government to get the controversial legislation passed.

In both Thailand and Korea, the crisis generated disaffection with the incumbents and led to changes in government. In Thailand, the fall of the Chavalit government led to the formation of a new government led by the Democrats under Chuan. While the Democrats also had to form a multiparty coalition that included parties from the previous government, the crisis allowed them to maintain control over the key economic portfolios. The new government was able to take decisive action on several fronts, most notably the swift closure of virtually all the suspended finance companies and the strengthening of the agencies responsible for managing the disposition of bad assets.

The new government was not altogether immune from the constraints that had plagued its predecessor. The legislative process required legislation to be reviewed by the senate, which was populated by businessmen with a direct stake in important reform legislation. Divisions both within the coalition and within the Democrats in the cabinet delayed the introduction of a number of important reform measures for over a year, including new laws governing foreign investment and bankruptcy. In late 2002, important legislation that remained pending included a financial institutions Act, a central bank reform and further amendments to the bankruptcy procedure.

The Thaksin government, which came to office in 2001, enjoyed a more solid electoral majority, despite its decision to form an oversized coalition. Interestingly the government also took a much more centralized approach to asset management than had been the case in the past.

The importance of strong government is nowhere more apparent than in Korea's response to the crisis. Kim Dae Jung exploited an important legislative window between his election and inauguration. With the support of his predecessor (whose party still controlled the national assembly), the government was able to pass a number of important reforms, including the package of financial bills that had languished under Kim Young Sam and a range of reforms of corporate governance. While the Kim Dae Jung government faced its own constraints, it is widely agreed that Korea moved with greater alacrity in addressing the crisis than its Southeast Asian counterparts, and that its more rapid rebound was due at least in part to this political decisiveness (see Haggard, 2000, ch. 2, for a more detailed exposition).

Malaysia's political system is notoriously difficult to classify. The dominant party and the ruling coalition were clearly subject to some electoral constraints. But when the crisis struck in mid 1997, the dominant party did not face substantial challenges from its coalition partners, the opposition or the public as the elections were not due until 2000. Moreover, Prime Minister Mahathir had shown his willingness to use both legal and legally questionable means to limit the scope of opposition activity.

Mahathir did face challenges within his party, however, and these had an influence on the course of policy. From the outset of the crisis, Mahathir's heterodox views, intimation of capital controls and attacks on 'speculators' and hedge funds created profound uncertainties and contributed to the rapid decline of the ringgit in the second half of the year. Efforts to bail out politically favoured companies added to the uncertainty. In December, Mahathir reversed course by delegating authority to Deputy Prime Minister Anwar, who introduced an 'IMF programme without the IMF'.

But at the same time, Mahathir set up a parallel decision-making structure in the form of a National Economic Action Council, which served to undermine Anwar's authority. For the next six months, policy seesawed between Anwar's more orthodox views and those of his reflationist opponents.

These disagreements were related to the question of succession. Anwar's position as deputy prime minister suggested that he would ultimately take over leadership of the party, and after the fall of Soeharto in May, Anwar stepped up his campaign against Mahathir. But the prime minister rallied the party, sidelined Anwar and ultimately had him arrested and convicted of corruption. As this political drama was unfolding, Mahathir also dismissed the governor of the central bank, took over the finance portfolio and moved policy in a more expansionary direction. The imposition of capital controls was the final act in a set of policy and political conflicts that had been unfolding for over a year.

The opposition proved incapable of responding effectively to Mahathir's coup within the party. In snap elections in November 1999, Mahathir managed to maintain his leadership position and his substantial legislative majority, while distancing himself from some of the more egregious cases of cronyism the crisis had revealed. Malaysia's Danaharta asset management company enjoyed broad legal powers and made substantial progress in restructuring most of the assets under its control.

It is important to recall that the highly centralized Indonesian government initially responded to the crisis in ways that signalled Soeharto's strong commitment to adjustment. The government responded quickly to the crisis by freeing the rupiah rather than subjecting the country to a costly defence and initiated a number of reforms, some of which appeared to go against the interests of cronies and family. But within months, Soeharto reversed these initiatives, reviving costly investment projects and providing damaging liquid support to a number of crony banks following a mismanaged bank closure in November.

In December, Soeharto failed to participate in an important international meeting and rumours circulated that he was in poor health (it was later revealed that he had had a stroke). In democracies such rumours can be unsettling, but in a system as highly centralized as that of Indonesia, where the succession procedure was highly uncertain, they threatened not only the regime but also the entire set of property rights that went with it. Even before Soeharto's controversial budget was read in January, it was clear that Indonesia was experiencing much greater difficulties than other countries in the region. Soeharto's imposition of Habibie as his vice presidential choice, and thus his anointed successor, deepened the sense of alarm, as did the growing opposition to the regime, which peaked in the violence of mid May and ultimately resulted in Soeharto being ousted. The transitional nature of the Habibie government made it less than ideally suited to under-take restructuring in an aggressive fashion. His democratic successors fared no better. Both the Wahid and the Megawati government, albeit to different degrees, suffered from afflictions that were visible in the Thai system, namely highly fractious and divided coalition cabinets.

This cursory review of the performance of these four countries is relevant to the long-standing debate on the economic and policy performance of authoritarian and democratic regimes. The leaders of Malaysia and Indonesia exploited their powers to isolate technocratic advisors and pursue erratic policies that served to increase market uncertainty. Indonesia also suffered from the more profound uncertainty associated with the absence of mechanisms to manage opposition and the problem of succession. Mahathir's more institutionalized system, by contrast, had mechanisms for both. In 2002, Mahathir's announcement that he intented to retire had no apparent effect on economic performance.

Democracies have the advantage of possessing procedures to replace failing incumbents. However, not all democracies are equal and the problems of fragmentation can be quite debilitating. This is now highly visible in Indonesia (MacIntyre, 1999b). Because of decades of dictatorship, Indonesia's new constitution is designed to check the power of the president. The president is chosen by an assembly made up largely of members of parliament; moreover the assembly has the power to depose the president. As in Thailand, the choice of a proportional representation system means that the party system is highly fragmented. Both Wahid and Megawati had strong incentives to placate legislative interests through cabinet positions, over which Wahid in particular exercised only minimal control. The lesson here is: if decisive leadership has its drawbacks, so too do democratic systems that severely limit executive authority.

Managing business–government relations

Political economists in the United States have been quite divided over the influence of business–government relations on policy and growth. The standard neoclassical political economy approach emphasizes the risks associated with rent seeking and corruption.[4] But as Maxfield and Schneider (1997, p. 13) argue, 'trust between business and government elites can reduce transaction and monitoring costs, diminish uncertainty, lengthen time horizons and...increase investment'. Even the World Bank (1993) has offered cautious support for consultative institutions to link the public and private sectors.

These two contrasting positions can be reconciled by focusing on political institutions in East Asia and the extent to which they have permitted or limited private rent seeking, moral hazard and corruption. Johnson (1982, 1999) was the first to argue that a 'strong' or 'developmental' state was important, a state that, in the first instance, enjoyed a certain degree of political independence or autonomy from private interests. Such autonomy was necessary to 'discipline' firms (Amsden, 1989) and guarantee that industrial policy tools did not result in the misallocation of resources that was so common in the developing world.

The concentration of decision-making power in leading economic agencies and competent, meritocratic bureaucracies played a key role in this picture. By socializing government officials towards common goals, meritocratic bureaucracies limited the opportunities for rent seeking (Evans, 1995). A certain centralization of bureaucratic authority and the granting of discretion to bureaucrats also served to increase the decisiveness and coherence of policy.

Finally, the governments of the region were able to limit rent seeking by controlling the way in which business was organized and interacted with the government. In some countries, such as Korea, the government directly established and effectively ran sectoral business associations. In others, 'deliberation councils', made up of government, business and other representatives, guaranteed broad representation and a degree of transparency that limited the opportunities for private dealing (Campos and Root, 1996).

This model of the developmental state – based on political independence from the private sector, centralized and independent bureaucracies, and government-controlled business organization – had at least two shortcomings. The first was the geographic scope of its applicability. The approach was developed with reference to Japan and was extended with relative ease to Korea and to a lesser extent Taiwan. With the possible exception of Singapore, however, the East Asian countries lacked not only the industrial policies of the first newly industrializing countries but also the political conditions required to conduct such policies efficiently.

The second shortcoming of the model was that it tended to downplay the costs associated with close business–government relations if these restrictive political conditions were not met (see for example MacIntyre, 1994, and Kim, 1997, on Korea; Gomez and Jomo, 1997, on Malaysia; Phongpaichit and Piriyarangsan, 1994, on Thailand; and Robison, 1986, on Indonesia, among many others). The economic critique of industrial policy is well known and need not be rehearsed here; rather the focus will be on the political risks of close business–government ties.

The first of these risks was the high concentration of private economic power. In Japan this power was initially curbed by the American occupation, but it later resurfaced in the LDP–business alliance. These ties clearly imposed a major constraint on the capacity of the government to undertake needed reforms throughout the 1990s. In both Korea and Taiwan, the extent of business concentration was initially much less and in any case the strong governments (under Park Chung Hee and the KMT respectively) acted as a counterweight to private power. Over time, however, government support served to increase concentration (most evidently in the case of the Korean *chaebols*), or did not nothing to curb it, as in Thailand's *laissez faire* stance towards the highly concentrated and collusive banking sector. Size did not necessarily translate directly into political influence; in Indonesia the ethnic vulnerability of the Indonesian–Chinese conglomerates actually made size a liability. However, there can be little question that 'big business' – in the form of diversified conglomerates – came to exert substantial political and policy influence in developing Asia.

A second, closely related, problem was the way in which government support for the private sector generated moral hazard. Some Western analysts have argued that the source of moral hazard could be found in industrial policies of various sorts. In most countries, however, such policies had either been reduced (Korea) or were too small to be consequential to the ensuing crisis (Thailand, Malaysia and Indonesia).

The problem was not industrial policy as traditionally conceived, but the deep involvement of the government in the financial sector. In Korea, Malaysia and particularly Indonesia, government involvement in the financial sector created the danger that banks and firms would be protected against excessive risk taking or (much the same thing) would be allowed to walk away from their debt. The governments of Indonesia and particularly Malaysia also made strong financial commitments to programmes for the advancement of indigenous Indonesians and Malaysians, the *peribumi* and *bumiputera* respectively. Whatever the merits of such ethnic redistribution programmes, they also carried the risk that governments would have an ongoing interest in the success of their beneficiaries.

Corruption and cronyism were other sources of moral hazard that have received substantial attention in popular Western accounts of the crisis. However, the connection between corruption and the crisis is not straightforward. After all the countries in the region had grown rapidly for decades despite at least some degree of corruption.

The corruption problem is frequently misunderstood: it is not limited to the distortions it causes to the economy but extends to its effects on the credibility of economic policy making. In Korea, the Hanbo scandal further weakened the lame duck president. In Malaysia, the government's efforts to support politically connected firms prompted questions about the integrity of the corporate restructuring process. In Thailand, the government exhibited costly forbearance towards ailing financial companies with close ties to the government. In Indonesia, the responsiveness of the Soeharto government to the demands of cronies and close family members raised serious doubts about the government's commitment to reform and led to highly costly bailouts in the crucial months of October and November 1997.

If corruption could do all that, how had the region managed to grow so rapidly? First, it is important to emphasize that East Asia's growth was far from crisis-free. Korea, for example, saw government-led investment booms followed by crises, most notably in the early 1970s and again after the heavy and chemical industry drive in the 1980s. Second, it is not necessarily the case that corruption was constant. Although assessments of corruption are always difficult, it appears that corruption increased in Indonesia, Malaysia and Thailand during the 1990s.

Opening such economies to capital movements made them more vulnerable to the problems of moral hazard, corruption and lack of transparency in business–government relations than they would otherwise have been. When growth was high, foreign investors were perfectly willing to tolerate (and even contribute to) these problems. But when growth slowed the non-transparent nature of business–government relations generated substantial uncertainties. Would some firms enjoy special treatment? Would contracts be honoured? What financial condition were banks and firms actually in?

However, not all of the region's problems stemmed from rent seeking as traditionally conceived; another source of risk was the mismanagement of liberalization, particularly in the financial sector. The dangers involved in opening the capital account while maintaining a fixed exchange rate have attracted most scrutiny in accounts of the crisis, but an equally important problem was the lack of proper prudential regulation of the banking system (Caprio, 1998). In all cases, this stemmed in part from the weakness of the relevant statute and the sheer lack of administrative capacity; governments had not devoted adequate attention to the development of a modern regulatory framework. However, problems also arose from regulatory for-bearance: politically generated laxity towards the government's financial and corporate oversight role or outright corruption of the independence of regulators. These problems were visible in the licensing of Korea's merchant banks and a variety of weaknesses in Korean corporate governance, in the expansion of finance companies in Thailand, and most egregiously in the opening of the banking sector in Indonesia, which created the opportunity for industrial groups to acquire banks, with all of the attendant problems of related-party lending that ensued.

In sum, the region's vulnerability stemmed not simply from discrete policy failures but also from deeper political problems: private power had grown, government involvement in the financial sector had generated moral hazard, and corruption, while not directly responsible for the crisis, made it more difficult to manage. Liberalization was not in and of itself a solution to these problems and could itself be 'captured'. More direct means of oversight – whether by regulatory agencies, public interest groups, financial analysts or stockholders – were required. To what extent are these problems now being addressed?

Changing business–government relations

The restructuring of business–government relations reduces to two core issues. The first is the ability of the government to impose losses on the managers and shareholders of failing banks and firms. Banks and firms that experience severe distress have a strong interest in delaying the recognition of losses, even if such a delay compounds the social costs and increases uncertainty. Of course, there is no virtue in bankrupting potentially viable firms, and the existence of wholesale distress requires emergency measures. But in periods of distress, all companies have an interest in claiming that they are viable. To limit the public costs of such crises, governments must have the political and administrative ability to distinguish among the competing claims for financial support and forbearance.

The second issue is the capacity and willingness of the government to impose regulatory oversight. For financial entities these include a well-known set of prudential regulations, the most basic of which are capital adequacy requirements. The regulation of corporate governance is also an issue of increasing significance in the face of more open capital markets. Shinn (2001) has provided a useful typology of governance institutions that is applicable to financial entities as well:

- *Information institutions* include accounting rules, audit procedures, standard setting and third-party analysis.
- *Oversight institutions* include the rules governing boards of directors.
- *Control institutions* give minority shareholders guarantees that check expropriation risk.
- *Managerial institutions* are the rules that govern the hiring, salaries and firing of senior managers to guarantee that shareholder value will be maximized and expropriation risk minimized.

The introduction of these regulatory and corporate governance changes is politically difficult for a simple reason: in many Asian countries they constitute a frontal assault on prerogatives that the owners and managers of major business groups have long enjoyed.

Comparisons of the strategies used by the East Asian countries are complicated by the fact that their initial conditions and the magnitude of their problems varied. Nonetheless, some stylized facts suggest some fairly clear differences among the seriously affected countries. After the delays under Kim Young Sam, Korea appears to have been the most decisive in addressing the problems in the financial sector and instituting changes in the rules of corporate governance, although problems with some of the largest firms remained. Indonesia clearly made the least progress in addressing these issues. Malaysia did better than Thailand, although its financial difficulties were much less severe (see Claessens *et al.* 1999). These differences reflected in no small measure differences in the nature of business–government relations.

The crisis initially focused attention on problems in the financial sector. Governments had to decide which banks and non-bank financial institutions were unviable and should be closed, develop a rehabilitation plan for the remainder, dispose of non-performing loans and recapitalize the banks.

In Korea, the Kim Young Sam government gave support to the banking system after the corporate failures of 1997 and nationalized two major banks, but without a clear strategy for rehabilitating the sector. Following Kim Dae Jung's election, the government quickly established a powerful new regulatory agency to manage the crisis and set aside funds to carve out non-performing loans and recapitalize the banking system. All banks were made subject to a thorough review, on the basis of which five were shut down and merged with others under government direction. A large number of non-bank financial institutions were also shut down, although many weak ones were left open and in 2000 the government had to initiate a second, quite costly round of financial restructuring. All the East Asian governments were slow to dispose of their acquired assets, but the Korean government moved more aggressively than those of Indonesia, Malaysia and Thailand. In early 2002 it announced a plan to sell off its controlling stake in the banking sector over three years.

Malaysia's banking problems were less serious than those of the other countries, but the government responded fairly aggressively to them through a combination of recapitalization and a government-directed merger plan announced in early 2000. The features of the Malaysian approach, which were distinctive, centred on long-standing issues of ethnicity: the bailout of state banks that financed *bumiputera* investments and a controversy over whether the merger plan would have the effect of weakening the Chinese presence in the banking sector.

Financial restructuring moved much more slowly in Thailand and Indonesia, and in late 2002 this was still imposing a constraint on those countries' full recovery. The Thai government (under Chavalit) continued to support weak institutions, particularly finance companies. Although some were suspended and a resolution agency (the Financial Restructuring Agency) was set up, the government lacked a clear strategy for managing the distressed companies. After the change of government in November 1997, the Chuan government moved quickly to close a number of finance companies and disposed of their core assets over the next 18 months. But it did not recapitalize the banks or purchase non-performing loans from them directly; rather it tried to induce banks to recapitalize on their own by enforcing capital adequacy and loan loss provisions. This strategy failed because a number of major banks proved unwilling or unable to raise new capital, and the government was finally forced to announce a plan in August 1998 that committed substantial resources to bank recapitalization. The conditions for participation were tough, and precisely for that reason few banks participated and the government was forced to manage the crisis through regulatory forbearance and acceptance of a continuing and high level of non-performing loans in the system. At the end of 2001 such loans still accounted for 30 per cent of total bank portfolios, but eventually they started to fall.

Indonesia responded decisively to its banking crisis, but the initial closing of 16 banks was badly handled and only served to complicate the government's problems. The government also continued to support a number of politically connected banks, with disastrous consequences. The reform efforts were further undermined by deepening political uncertainty about the regime's survival. The Habibie government initiated a strategy for recapitalizing the banking sector and sought to recover debts to the government. But implementation was subject to delay and gave rise to charges of political interference. Some banks with negative capital were allowed to survive. The problem of the politically important state-owned banks was not addressed in an aggressive fashion, permitting some restructuring to take place that was of highly dubious quality. Indonesia clearly made the least progress of the four countries in addressing the problems in its banking sector.

A second set of issues surrounds the corporate restructuring process, including the reform of corporate governance. As with banks, corporations may have an interest in delaying financial and operational restructuring, and may even collude with banks to do so at public expense. The government can solve this problem in one of two ways, each of which requires some political capacity. First, it can rigorously enforce capital adequacy and loan loss provisions while providing incentives for banks to engage in out-of-court settlements; this is the so-called London Rules approach.

The alternative strategy is for the government to play a more active role in the process. This may range from coordinating intracreditor and creditor–debtor relations and monitoring and enforcing agreements, to using various instruments to enforce financial and operational restructuring objectives, such as the extent of leveraging, the nature of business portfolios and corporate governance. The London Rules approach does this implicitly through the banking system; the government-led approach is likely to make it more explicit.

The incentives for corporate restructuring are powerfully affected by foreclosure and bankruptcy laws. If foreclosure and bankruptcy laws or their implementation are weak – typically in being overly favourable to debtors – firms have an incentive to delay debt and operational restructuring and even repayment (giving rise to what in Thailand have been called 'strategic non-performing loans'). Reform of the bankruptcy process and clear enforcement of bankruptcy and foreclosure laws are important not only for managing actual firm failures, but also for providing incentives to creditors and debtors to reach out-of-court settlements.

In East Asia, out-of-court settlements dominated, but these were dependent on the individual countries' bankruptcy procedures, which were stronger in Korea and Malaysia when the crisis hit. Bankruptcy reform was delayed in Thailand, and despite Indonesia's reforms its bankruptcy processes remained weak. Major differences separated Korea from the other cases (Haggard *et al.*, 2003). Despite nominal embrace of the London Rules, the president negotiated directly with the big five banks over their restructuring plans and the Financial Supervisory Commission played a strong role in pushing corporate debt restructuring. The most dramatic development with regard to the large firms was the financial and corporate restructuring of Daewoo – allowing a major *chaebol* group to fail sent a powerful signal of government intent. Moreover, the concept of corporate restructuring included wide-ranging reforms of corporate governance, ultimately enforced through the government's control of the banking system. Early in the Kim Dae Jung administration, the government undertook reforms in virtually all the areas of corporate governance outlined above, including the improvement of accounting standards, increasing the independence of boards and permitting hostile takeovers.

In Thailand and Indonesia, debt restructuring was much slower and had much weaker links, if any, to the reform of corporate governance. The forbearance shown towards the financial sector in Thailand was matched by debt 'restructurings' that largely took the form of rescheduling, with little use of new bankruptcy procedures. In Indonesia, the rescheduling of both onshore and offshore debt moved slowly; by May 2002 only about 50 per cent of domestic and foreign debt under the control of the two major agencies had been restructured and a sizable percentage of total outstanding debt remained outside these processes altogether. Bankruptcy courts faced a myriad of political as well as institutional constraints.

In Malaysia, the government established a restructuring agency that had quite ambitious goals for the operational restructuring of enterprises. Progress in both asset sales and restructuring was initially slow and any reform of corporate governance was voluntary. Despite a statute that approached international standards, several high-profile Malaysian cases suggested transactions that involved conflicts between the interests of the company and its major shareholders, if not outright corruption. By late 2002, however, the Danaharta asset management company had succeeded in resolving the vast majority of assets under its control.

Assuming that the broad differences outlined above had some basis in fact – and more would be required to establish that claim – what accounted for these differences? It seems that a successful strategy for managing the private sector involves three distinct components: the market; regulatory oversight, including by means of direct negotiations with firms; and encouraging countervailing private actors with incentives to monitor firms.

The governments in the region have substantially liberalized the rules that govern foreign investment, including allowing foreign firms to participate actively in the market for corporate control through mergers and acquisitions, including hostile ones. Trade liberalization is also gradually changing the competitive landscape across the region and will continue to do so in the future.

The second component of the strategy for managing the private sector is more directive and involves regulation and more explicitly negotiated *quid pro quos* with the largest banks and firms and their representative organizations. With reference to the financial sector, the core of the political bargain involves recognition of the need to develop franchise value and provide incentives for banks to develop reputational capital. This might require some forbearance in the short run with regard to reaching international capital adequacy requirements or regulating entry. (Of course the public has already made a huge downpayment in the form of recapitalization and the purchase of non-performing assets.) But in return, the financial community should be exposed to more rigorous prudential regulation and to greater competition. The latter can be achieved by permitting the entry of foreign banks, developing capital markets and reducing reliance on bank financing.

With regard to corporate restructuring, government support for the restructuring of corporate debt, including the granting of 'haircuts', can be exchanged for a commitment to the principles of good corporate governance and operational restructuring, using the government's short-term advantage as a bank shareholder as a lever. Finally, governments can also assist in the development of other agents with an interest in corporate accountability, including shareholders' movements and more aggressive monitoring of firms by pension funds, mutual funds, financial analysts, think tanks and the media.

The core question with all of these reforms centres on implementation and enforcement, and the problems associated with this are not simply ones of administrative capacity – they also involve avoiding the problem of capture of the regulatory process, particularly in respect of the core agencies for financial regulation and the oversight of monopolistic and collusive practices.

The formal independence of these entities is important. In Korea, the Kim Dae Jung administration transferred most but not all regulatory and supervisory responsibilities from the Bank of Korea and the Ministry of Finance and Economy to the new Financial Supervisory Commission. In Malaysia, Danaharta was granted a broad mandate. In the short term, such agencies can help to reduce the problems caused by multiple veto gates and private sector resistance. However, it is important not to confuse cause and effect. The differential capabilities of the Financial Supervisory Service in Korea and the Indonesian Bank Restructuring Authority in Indonesia are not simply administrative; indeed the latter has a strong reputation for the quality of its management. Rather the weaknesses have been political.

Ultimately, the regulation of the private sector requires support from political coalitions that are willing to check private power and hold themselves accountable for their relationships with private actors. This appears to be the most distinctive feature of the new Korean government compared with others in the region: it is headed by an outsider who lacks the links his predecessors had with the private sector (Haggard *et al.*, 2003).

In a number of countries in the region, political reforms of the government itself may be necessary to achieve the goal of accountability. Information is clearly the cornerstone of accountability at both the corporate and the government level. A first step of great importance is to increase the transparency of relations between politicians and their financial supporters. How tightly campaign contributions can or should be regulated remains a topic of substantial debate in advanced industrial countries, but again the principle of transparency and the provision of information is a first step. If such contributions were transparent, voters would at least have the ability to reach judgements about the political commitment of their legislators and vote accordingly.

Other institutions of accountability can also help to solve information problems by monitoring the government, including public interest associations and the media, although the latter have themselves been captured and dominated by business interests in a number of countries in the region.

But such institutions will not be sufficient to achieve healthy business–government relations unless they are buttressed by fundamental constitutional provisions that clarify the boundaries of the public and private spheres and limit the opportunities for rent seeking. These include institutions for punishing malfeasance, such as independent corruption agencies and ultimately the courts.

A new social contract?

The social fallout from the crisis, as manifested in a sharp decline in asset values, falling real wages and rising unemployment, forced an immediate response from the governments in the region. The pace of recovery determined the speed with which the subsequent increase in poverty was reversed. In Thailand and Indonesia, the countries hit hardest by the crisis, poverty remained above the 1996 levels into 2002. However, the more important policy question in the long term is whether the crisis affected the nature of the social contract in the region.

There has been substantial discussion of the political economy of the European welfare state, but much less analysis of the nature of social bargains in the developing world (on Asia, see Goodman *et al.*, 1998). For new democracies, the possibilities in this area will depend heavily on the implicit social contract and development strategies inherited from prior authoritarian periods. For example, while welfare reform in Eastern Europe has involved some inevitable shrinkage of public commitments and an expansion of private insurance and service provision, in East Asia the governments' stronger fiscal position and limited social contract provide the space to move in the opposite direction.

Prior to the crisis, countries in East and Southeast Asia did have a strategy of social protection, though a highly implicit one. Its components were as follows:

- The healthy rates of per capita GDP growth were broadly shared through rapid employment growth, increasing participation in the formal labour force (especially by women before marriage) and increasing returns on capital to small businesses and farmers.
- There was high investment in human development, including in areas that benefited the poor the most, including high private and public investment in education and basic curative and preventive health care.
- Balanced growth strategies emphasized labour-intensive manufacturing and addressed rural poverty through land reform (Korea and Taiwan) or investment in rural infrastructure and agricultural technologies (Indonesia and Thailand). During the infrequent downturns in the urban manufacturing sector, the countryside was able to absorb displaced workers.
- There was a strong tradition of family support, with high levels of private transfers (for example from urban workers to rural households, and between generations).
- Most notably in Korea, there was an emerging tradition in some segments of the economy that made the firm the provider of social insurance.

Notably absent from this picture was a government commitment to social insurance. This might be attributed in part to the countries' level of development, but comparisons with other middle-income countries suggest that politics also mattered. Social democratic and populist parties and movements historically had had little room to operate under authoritarian rule. Trade union movements, which historically have had a strong interest in advancing the provision of social services, were weak, repressed or both. Even with the transition to democratic rule, trade union movements outside Korea were not influential political actors. Other features of Asian societies noted above, including the tradition of private social assistance, extended family networks and flexible labour markets linking the urban and rural sectors, reduced the demand for an extensive state role in the provision of social insurance.

As a result of these factors, the countries most adversely affected by the crisis had neither social insurance mechanisms to serve as automatic stabilizers nor the capacity to identify and target those most seriously affected by the crisis. Nonetheless, the governments in the region quickly acknowledged the need to deal with the likely social costs. Encouraged by international financial institutions, they introduced a mixture of programmes under the general rubric of 'social safety net'. As the effects of the initial fiscal and monetary stance became obvious, the IMF endorsed higher fiscal deficits and the use of the additional spending for employment and other income-generating programmes. The World Bank and the Asian Development Bank negotiated social adjustment loans, which were tied to the maintenance of government spending levels on health and education, and a mix of other initiatives that largely built on pre-existing programmes: stay-in-school subsidies in Indonesia, social investment funds at the community level in Thailand, broadened eligibility for unemployment insurance in Korea and efforts in all the countries to mount some form of comprehensive public works employment programmes.

Whatever the successes and failures of these programmes in the short term, the more interesting question is what the long-term social contract will look like. One can imagine several possibilities. It is possible that political forces could arise to push for a European-style welfare state. The one country in which this could conceivably happen is Korea, where the labour movement is strongest. Indeed, Kim Dae Jung used his credentials with the movement to convene a tripartite committee in early 1998, and in the process extended unemployment insurance to a broader group of workers and increased the available benefits. But the Korean exercise was relatively modest, and was aimed in no small part at extracting concessions from workers in respect of labour-market flexibility. Workers fully understood the downside of this bargain, and the more progressive of the two main unions boycotted subsequent tripartite meetings. This casts doubt on the viability of the welfare state option in the absence of a strong and unified labour movement and social democratic parties.

A second option would be more conservative. During the crisis, the governments of Malaysia and Thailand outlined a conservative critique of the European welfare experience, citing the traditional reliance on family and community in Asia, and their past success in harnessing work, discipline and responsibility at the individual level to produce high growth. The idea of social welfare programmes that included entitlement to government transfers, they argued, contradicted the roots of past success based on productivity-enhancing investment in health, education and performance-based small credit programmes. Business groups also expressed scepticism about any further extension of the safety net on the ground that it would adversely affect recovery in the short term and competitiveness in the long term.

Large real devaluations and the corresponding fall in unit labour costs made this strategy tempting. Of course, the exchange rate adjustments were designed precisely to promote expenditure switching in favour of exports. But relying on real wage adjustments as a solution to problems in the manufacturing and service sectors seems self-defeating in the long run, particularly given the close proximity of China's massively labour-abundant economy. Moreover, such a strategy would deflect attention from the fact that in some countries, and particularly Thailand, the tight labour markets caused by economic booms masked weaknesses in the quality of the workforce that need to be addressed by upgrading the workforce and improving productivity.

A third, middle-way option would be to build on the strengths of East Asia's precrisis equitable growth while addressing the new requirements of those vulnerable to external shocks. This might emphasize continuing commitment to education, including state support to keep children in school in the event of future shocks (as with the Indonesian and Thai programmes along these lines), and increased incentives for training, both public and private, in return for workers' commitment to labour-market flexibility.

Yet, however great the emphasis on education and labour-market flexibility, it would probably not be enough to deal with the insecurities associated with slower and more erratic growth. Although recovery began in earnest in 1999 the region was exposed to a substantial global slowdown in 2001 that severely affected recovery. Moreover, a host of new uncertainties emerged in the second half of 2002 that included not only continued economic sluggishness in Europe and Japan but the threat of war with Iraq, rising oil prices and new political challenges, as exemplified by the terrorist bombing in Bali.

The option that would be most likely to fit East Asia's social circumstances would be something along the lines of Singapore's Central Provident Fund, which bundles several forms of social insurance (pension, emergency medical, unemployment), rests on employer and employee contributions mandated by the government, is non-distributive in nature and emphasizes personal control. Such a programme would have a political advantage over targeted programmes in that it would set up universal benefits, and even though it would amount to a payroll tax it would be understood as providing insurance, and not an unearned transfer. It would provide security against economy-wide shocks, provide benefits that were valued by the emergent middle class, and apart from some transitional costs, it would not necessarily have adverse fiscal consequences; in any case, the fiscal position of most countries in the region has historically been good, although the massive costs associated with the recent banking crises have changed that to some extent.

The irony is that, in the past, programmes of this sort were introduced in British colonies and were implemented by paternalistic, semi-authoritarian governments; in this sense, they can be seen as Bismarckian. For such programmes to be instituted in new democracies would require pressure from middle-class parties and interest groups, including labour, and it would be necessary to overcome resistance from cost-conscious employers. Even this modest solution could prove difficult, leaving only the incremental expansion of existing provisions.

Conclusions

Authoritarian rule, close and non-transparent business–government relations and heavy reliance on high growth and an informal safety net were among the political ingredients of East Asia's rapid growth. That formula had already undergone a change prior to the crisis, driven in part by the transition to democratic rule, which required transparency in business–government relations and greater attention to social policy. The crisis accelerated this trend, contributing to a change of regime in Indonesia, new political opposition parties elsewhere and strong pressure for changes in regulatory regimes and the social contract.

However, it is still too soon to tell what the full legacy of the crisis will be. Ironically the very resilience of the Asian economies and the speed of their recovery may serve to limit the long-term impact of the crisis, except in Indonesia, allowing a reversion to politics and institutions that bear a closer resemblance to those of the past than is generally expected. Nor do all the lessons of the crisis support Western nostrums. First, while it is true that the democratic regimes avoided the type of calamity that befell Indonesia, Malaysia's semidemocratic regime fared no worse than Thailand's fragmented democracy. Second, while there was evidence of rent seeking and corruption throughout the region, and that it affected policy, liberalization was not an adequate antidote. In the absence of countervailing institutions and coalitions, private actors captured the liberalization processes. The debate on governance needs to address a fundamental political fact faced by all market economies: that the private sector is often the most daunting opponent of the regulatory framework and social safety nets are required to make a market economy both efficient and politically sustainable.

Notes

1. See Tsebelis (2002) and Cox and McCubbins (2001) for the theoretical formulation. MacIntyre (1999a, 2001, 2002) was the first to extend this observation to the context of the Asian financial crisis, and I am indebted to him for a number of points in what follows.
2. A veto gate is an institution that has the power to veto a policy proposal, thus forcing reversion to the *status quo*. Veto gates include the president, the legislature, a second chamber of the legislature, a committee within a legislature and the courts; in authoritarian governments they may include the military. The preferences of these veto gates may be more or less closely aligned; thus the president and the legislature

may represent distinct veto gates, but may either be of the same party (unified government) or of different parties (divided government).
3. The reason for the resignation was frustration over the reversal of a small petroleum tax increase a mere three days after it had been announced as part of the government's IMF-backed programme.
4. See Khan (2000a, 2000b) for a critique of the rent-seeking literature.

References

Amsden, A. (1989) *Asia's Next Giant* (New York: Oxford University Press).
Campos, J. E. and H. Root (1996) *The Key to the Asian Miracle: Making Shared Growth Credible* (Washington, DC: The Brookings Institution).
Caprio, G. (1998) 'Banking on Crises: Expensive Lessons from Recent Financial Crises' (Washington, DC: World Bank).
Claessens, S., S. Djankov and D. Klingebiel (1999) *Financial Restructuring in East Asia: Halfway There?*, The World Bank financial Sector Discussion Paper no. 3 (Washington, DC).
Cox, G. and M. McCubbins (2001) 'The Institutional Determinants of Policy Outcomes', in S. Haggard and M. McCubbins (eds), *Presidents, Parliaments and Policy* (New York: Cambridge University Press).
Evans, P. (1995) *Embedded Autonomy: States and Industrial Transformation* (Princeton, NJ: Princeton University Press).
Gomez, E. T. and K. S. Jomo (1997) *Malaysia's Political Economy: Politics, Patronage and Profits* (Cambridge, Mass.: Cambridge University Press).
Goodman, R., G. White and H.-J. Kwon (1998) *The East Asian Welfare Model: Welfare Orientalism and the State* (New York: Routledge).
Haggard, S. (1990) *Pathways from the Periphery* (Ithaca, NY: Cornell University Press).
Haggard, S. (2000) *The Political Economy of the Asian Financial Crisis* (Washington, DC: Institute for International Economics).
Haggard, S., W. Lim and E. Kim (eds) (2003) *Economic Crisis and Corporate Restructuring in Korea: Reforming the Chaebol* (Melbourne: Cambridge University Press).
Hicken, A. (1999) 'Parties, Policy and Patronage: Governance and Growth in Thailand', unpublished manuscript, University of California, San Diego.
Johnson, C. (1982) *MITI and the Japanese Miracle: The Growth of Industrial Policy 1925–1975* (Stanford, CA: Stanford University Press).
Johnson, C. (1999) 'The Developmental State: Odyssey of a Concept', in M. Woo-Cumings (ed.), *The Developmental State* (Ithaca, NY: Cornell University Press).
Jomo, K. S. (1998) *Tigers in Trouble: Financial Governance, Liberalization and Crises in East Asia* (London: Zed Books).
Khan, Mushtaq H. (2000a) 'Rents, Efficiency and Growth', in Mushtaq H. Khan and Jomo K. S. (eds), *Rents, Rent-seeking and Economic Development: Theory and Evidence in Asia* (New York: Cambridge University Press).
Khan, Mushtaq H. (2000b) 'Rent-seeking as Process', in Mushtaq H. Khan and Jomo K. S. (eds), *Rents, Rent-seeking and Economic Development: Theory and Evidence in Asia.* (New York: Cambridge University Press).
Kim, E. (1997) *Big Business, Strong State: Collusion and Conflict in South Korean Development, 1960–1990* (Albany, NY: State University of New York Press).
Krause, L. (1998) *The Economics and Politics of the Asian Financial Crisis of 1997–98* (New York: Council on Foreign Relations).

Krugman, P. (1998) 'What Happened to Asia?', http://web.mit.edu/krugman/www/disinter.html.

Leblang, D. (1999) 'Political Uncertainty and Speculative Attacks', unpublished manuscript, University of North Texas, Denton, Texas.

MacIntyre, A. (ed.) (1994) *Business and Government in Industrializing Asia* (Ithaca, NY: Cornell University Press).

MacIntyre, A. (1999a) 'Political Institutions and the Economic Crisis in Thailand and Indonesia', in T. J. Pempel (ed.), *The Politics of the Asian Economic Crisis* (Ithaca, NY: Cornell University Press).

MacIntyre, A. (1999b) 'Political Parties, Accountability, and Economic Governance in Indonesia', in J. Blondel, T. Inoguchi, and I. Marsh (eds), *Democracy, Governance, and Economic Performance: East and Southeast Asia in the 1990s* (Tokyo: UN University Press).

MacIntyre, A. (2001) 'Institutions and Investors: The Politics of the Economic Crisis in Southeast Asia', *International Organization*, vol. 55, no. 1, pp. 81–122.

MacIntyre, A. (2002) *The Power of Institutions: Political Architecture and Governance* (Ithaca, NY: Cornell University Press).

Maxfield, S. and B. R. Schneider (eds) (1997) *Business and the State in Developing Countries* (Ithaca, NY: Cornell University Press).

Mei, J. (1999) 'Political Election, Financial Crisis and Market Volatility', unpublished manuscript, Princeton University, Princeton, NJ.

Pempel, T. J. (1999) *The Politics of the Asian Economic Crisis* (Ithaca, NY: Cornell University Press).

Phongpaichit, P. and S. Piriyarangsan (1994) *Corruption and Democracy in Thailand* (Bangkok: Silkwork Books).

Robison, R. (1986) *Indonesia: the Rise of Capital* (Sydney: Allen and Unwin).

Shinn, J. (2001) 'Globalization, Governance and the State', unpublished PhD dissertation, Princeton University, Princeton, NJ.

Stiglitz, J. E. (2002) *Globalization and Its Discontents* (New York: W.W. Norton).

Tsebelis, G. (2002) *Veto Players: How Political Institutions Work* (Princeton, NJ: Princeton University Press).

World Bank (1993) *The East Asian Miracle* (New York: Oxford University Press).

9
Re-examination of Korea's Economic Adjustment Policies since the 1997 Crisis[1]

Yoon Je Cho

Introduction

Korea's experience since the 1997 economic crisis has prompted many questions about its development policies and strategy towards the transition of the economy, whose rapid growth in the past had been based on a government-led development strategy, with heavy protection and intervention, in the move towards a fully market-based economy.

The 1997 crisis was mainly due to Korea's deep-rooted structural problems,[2] which had been accumulating for many years and had produced large corporate losses, which were concealed under irregular and dishonest accounting practices and supported by imprudent credit expansion. The progress of trade liberalization under the WTO system, however, limited the opportunity for monopolistic or oligopolistic domestic *chaebol* to pass on the costs of their inefficiency to consumers. Financial liberalization increased the country's financial fragility by expanding short-term financing (Cho, 2001) and limiting the government's ability to manage bail-out programmes for deeply troubled firms.

The immediate causes of the 1997 crisis may have been a severe maturity mismatch between the foreign debts and assets of the Korean banking sector and the contagion effect from neighbouring countries. But a more fundamental cause was related to the transition process. The economy was opened and liberalized without proper attention being paid to accumulated corporate losses and the extremely high corporate debt ratio, which were legacies of the past development model, and without changing the old style of economic management. With the old model, the government, businesses and banks had formed an implicit risk partnership that had facilitated rapid investment expansion and high economic growth. However, the institutions and market infrastructure required to make a market-based economy efficient and stable had not been developed, which made the economy extremely vulnerable to external shocks. The gap between the speed of changes in the economic environment brought by liberalization and the speed of changes in the expectations of market players (or 'the rule of game') and the development of institutions meant that sooner or later a crisis was bound to happen.

After the 1997 crisis, Korea introduced comprehensive economic reforms under the International Monetary Fund (IMF) programme. The reforms encompassed financial and corporate restructuring, the strengthening of regulatory rules, the introduction of a corporate governance system and the adoption of global standards for a broad range of economic activities. The economy recovered quickly as a result of these reforms and the favourable turnaround of the external environment. With the injection of a large amount of public funds into the troubled financial institutions, the situation of the financial and corporate sectors improved substantially. However, the government faced many difficult choices. For example, given the wide gap that existed between the reality of the situation in the corporate and financial sectors and the introduced global standards, the government had to choose between pushing the reforms by all means or adherence to the standards. The simultaneous restructuring of the financial and corporate sectors also proved difficult and the weak financial institutions could not effectively drive the necessary corporate restructuring.

The corporate and financial sectors' problems had been acute before the currency crisis, and the introduction of global standards in banking supervision (for example rules on loan classification, provisioning, accounting and disclosure, the BIS capital adequacy ratio and so on) revealed the extent of the non-performing assets that had been concealed by the lax supervisory rules and poor or fraudulent accounting practices. The speed of flooding of non-performing assets was beyond the capacity that the political economy of the country could digest. This caused the government to return to interventionism, which compromised its stated principles of restructuring and undermined the credibility of the reform process. This suggests that overly ambitious reform programmes can easily backfire, and that programmes must be based on the economic and political realities of the countries in question.

The Korean experience also suggests that in the event of a double crisis – currency plus financial – the use of traditional measures to deal with the currency crisis (especially a policy of high interest rates) can be very costly, and the negative impact of these measures may be magnified if the financial crisis deepens. Moreover, structural reform policies such as financial restructuring and the strengthening of supervisory rules can adversely affect macroeconomic development. This highlights the necessity of coordinating macroeconomic policies and structural reform policies to avoid undesirable macroeconomic consequences.

This chapter is structured as follows. The next section discusses the speed and sequencing of economic reforms in an economy that had relied strongly on a government-led economic development strategy. The third section deals with the problems caused by an asymmetric approach to the restructuring of the banking and non-banking financial sectors. The fourth section addresses the coordination of monetary and supervisory policies during the period of financial restructuring. The fifth section considers a very controversial issue – the appropriateness of the high interest rate policy adopted in the early stage of the IMF programme. The final section provides a brief concluding remarks.

The speed and sequencing of the economic reforms

The Korea's experience has raised questions about the appropriate speed and sequencing of economic reforms. The sudden introduction of global standards in Korea, whose accounting and supervisory practices had been very lax, exposed long-accumulated, non-performing assets at a pace that the political economy of the country could not accommodate. This resulted in exceptions being made to the introduced rules, benign neglect of some rules and reliance on old measures to roll over credit to troubled firms so that they would not be classified as bad assets. All these measures undermined the credibility of the reform programme and made future restructuring more difficult.

Moreover, the simultaneous restructuring of the financial and corporate sectors proved very difficult. The banks were too weak to drive the corporate restructuring effort, so there was an incentive to bail out troubled firms in order to protect their BIS ratio. In a highly concentrated economy, such as Korea's, where conglomerates dominated, many financial institutions were involved in the affairs of single conglomerates, which made coordination very complicated. Furthermore the process of restructuring the corporate capital structure was limited by the slow progress of reform of the country's financial market structure.

Political economy considerations

In an economy with severe problems, and where the gap between international standards and domestic practices is wide, the speed of reforms, including the opening of the capital market and the introduction of global standards, has to be tuned to society's capacity to endure an economic contraction. If the social safety net is inadequate to accommodate a sharp increase in unemployment, and if growing social tension cannot be properly soothed by the political leadership, overhasty implementation of reform measures can cause the reform process to backfire.

The Korean corporate sector's problems were extraordinarily severe. According to Nam (2000), about 25 per cent of corporate firms had interest rate coverage ratio of less than one in 1999.[3] These 25 per cent of firms accounted for about 40 per cent of the total borrowing of the sample firms, as shown in Tables 9.1 and 9.2. Therefore, in terms of the amount of debt, about 40 per cent of firms were unable to pay interest out of their earnings.

Table 9.1   Interest coverage ratio and potential non-performing loans, listed firms 1995–99 (billion dollars)

	Number of firms (A)	Number of troubled firms (B)	Percentage of troubled firms (B/A)	Total borrowing (C)	Borrowing by troubled firms (D)	C/D
1995	662	109	16.5	111 462	15 680	14.1
1996	654	158	24.2	137 133	29 554	21.6
1997	641	226	35.3	192 767	65 111	33.8
1998	600	225	37.5	167 941	65 612	39.1
1999	438	94	19.5	136 984	47 549	34.7

Source: BOK (a) (various years).

Table 9.2   Interest coverage ratio and potential NPLs, unlisted firms, 1995–99 (billion dollars)

	Number of firms (A)	Number of troubled firms (B)	Percentage of troubled firms (B/A)	Total borrowing (C)	Borrowing by troubled firms (D)	C/D
1995	4623	1301	28.1	77 580	26 076	33.6
1996	4722	1463	31.0	95 191	32 459	34.1
1997	5173	1956	37.8	123 289	52 284	42.4
1998	5328	1856	34.8	109 977	52 339	47.6
1999	4804	1115	23.2	103 895	49 098	47.3

Source: BOK (a) (various years).

Other studies have produced similar results. According to a Bank of Korea analysis (BOK, 1998a), of 3701 companies in the manufacturing sector, roughly one in four were unable to pay their financial costs from their cash income in 1997. A more recent study of 1807 firms (BOK, 2000a) found that in the first half of 2000 about 27 per cent of firms still had an interest coverage ratio of less than one.

In such situations, the overnight introduction of global standards in banking supervision and accounting will cause a flood of non-performing assets in the financial sector. This will in turn cause the bankruptcy and liquidation of many insolvent firms, and consequently a sharp increase in unemployment. In order to address these problems, the economy must be able to mobilize sufficient public funds to recapitalize troubled financial institutions and purchase non-performing assets from them; and it must be able to deal with high unemployment or the resulting social tension will frustrate the reform process. Thus, crisis-hit countries face a dilemma regarding the speed of reform: if reform is too slow, confidence will take a long time to recover; if it is too fast the domestic political economy will not be able to handle it.

Difficulties with the simultaneous restructuring of the corporate and financial sectors

Because the Korean financial crisis was partly caused by the corporate debt problem, the process of financial restructuring was closely linked to the process of corporate restructuring. But as mentioned earlier the simultaneous restructuring of the corporate and financial sectors proved very difficult.

The government adopted a creditor-led, out-of-court settlement framework along the lines of the London approach to corporate restructuring. Work-out units were established in eight leading banks, which were made responsible for dealing with the problem loans to the second-tier or 6–64 largest *chaebols*. In order to reduce the difficulties that would arise from intercreditor differences (for example between banks and non-banks) the government encouraged 210 financial institutions to sign a corporate restructuring agreement (CRA) by which they are empowered to advise on the viability of corporate restructuring candidates, arbitrate intercreditor differences, provide guidelines for work-out plans proposed by creditors and so on. Although this approach was an appropriate response to the systemic crisis and achieved some temporary financial stabilization, it was not an appropriate means of promoting restructuring.

Concern about losses has made banks unwilling to enforce the necessary divestitures, assets sales, management changes and other operational improvements. Instead they have tended to provide loan-term extensions, rate reductions, grace periods and some conversion of debt into convertible bonds. As long as the financial institutions are heavily burdened with non-performing assets, and unless sufficient public funds are mobilized to recapitalize banks when their capital base is eroded by debt restructurings and the government is willing to accept the temporary existence of severe instability in the financial market, rapid progress in corporate and financial restructuring cannot be expected. Furthermore, if laying off redundant workers is difficult for firms for legal or political reasons, this too will limit the progress of corporate restructuring.

Financial market structure and corporate capital structure

Korean firms' debt ratio is extremely high by international standards – the average debt ratio of the top 30 *chaebols* was about 570 per cent at the end of 1997. If global standards were applied the majority of Korean firms would probably be classified as firms whose credit rating was below investment grade. Therefore, corporate debt restructuring will have to rely heavily on the conversion of debt to equity.

The recent corporate restructuring efforts have substantially reduced the debt–equity ratio of firms. However, this has mainly been due to asset revaluation and capital issues rather than the reduction of debt, which remains high. With this high corporate leverage ratio, the financial institutions will remain vulnerable to business cycles and external shocks. Moreover, the corporate capital structure cannot be significantly changed unless changes are also made to the financial market structure, including the establishment of vulture funds, corporate restructuring vehicles and expansion of the mutual funds sector, and this will take considerable time.

The total financial debt of Korean companies had reached approximately 700–800 trillion won by 2000.[4] Assuming that the debt ratio of the corporate sector is approximately 300 per cent, its total capital will be approximately 200 trillion won. To decrease the debt–equity ratio to, say, 200 per cent, either its capital should increase by approximately 100 trillion won or its debt should decrease by 200 trillion won. However, this must be supported by a deepening of the equity market, which will require changes in the pattern of household savings. In other words, the job of financial restructuring in Korea is equivalent to the enormous job of reconstructing the balance sheet of the national economy.

Table 9.3 provides an example of the restructuring process the Korean economy will have to go through. Ultimately, the balance sheets of the corporate, financial and household sectors should be as shown in section (d) of the table. Making the transition from (a) to (d) will be an enormous task, and can be reasonably expected to take more than a decade. In the meantime, the opening of the capital market and the adoption of global standards will make the overall economy vulnerable to a financial crisis.

Financial restructuring and its impact

The way in which financial restructuring was approached in Korea after the crisis seems to have strongly affected the subsequent development of the financial market structure and macroeconomic development, as well as the progress of corporate restructuring.

The IMF's financial restructuring programme initially underestimated the depth and breadth of Korea's problems, and as a result it concentrated mainly on the restructuring of banks and merchant banking companies. The strengthening of regulatory standards also focused on these institutions. This was not surprising since the origin of the crisis was the run on banks and merchant banks by foreign creditors as the asset position of these institutions became increasingly in doubt.[5] However, the problems were equally or even more serious in the case of non-banking financial institutions, including investment and trust companies, mutual savings and insurance companies, but when the IMF programme began in 1998 these institutions were largely out of the focus and their irregularities in fund mobilization and management were benignly neglected by the supervisory authorities. As a result these institutions, and especially the investment trust companies, took advantage of the regulatory oversight and engaged in explosive expansion.

Table 9.3 Required evolution of the corporate, financial and household balance sheets (an illustrative example)

	Corporate firms — Assets	Corporate firms — Liabilities	Banks — Assets	Banks — Liabilities	Households — Assets	Households — Liabilities
(a) Precrisis	1000	Debt, 800; Capital, 200	Loans, 800	Deposits, 700; Capital, 100	Deposits, 700; Stock, 300	—; —
(b) Postcrisis	700	Debt 800; Capital, 100	Loans 700	Deposits, 700; Capital, 0	Deposits, 700; Stock, 0	—; —
(c) After recapitalization of banks and debt/equity conversion	700	Debt, 500; Capital, 200	Loans, 500; Stock, 200; Govt. bonds, 100	Deposits, 700; Capital, 100	Deposits, 700; Stock 0	—; —
(d) After completion of financial market restructuring and reprivatization of banks	700	Debt, 500; Capital, 200	Loans, 500; Govt. bonds, 50	Deposits, 450; Capital, 100	Deposits, 450; Mutual funds, 250; Stock, 100	—; —; —

Mutual funds

Assets		Liabilities	
Stock,	200	Shares,	250
Govt. bonds,	50		

This had both positive and negative effects. The positive effect was immediate: it mitigated the impact of the credit crunch in the banking and merchant banking sectors as it allowed many *chaebols* to obtain finance to tide themselves over the credit crunch and liquidity crisis. Some of them even aggressively increased their investments during this period. Overall, this aided the quick recovery of the economy in late 1998 and 1999.

The negative effects took longer to materialize. The financial restructuring that occurred during 1998–99 – by shifting funds from sectors over which regulation was strengthened to those which remained poorly regulated – did not improve the overall risks in the financial system. The rapid expansion of investment trust business sustained firms that should have been made bankrupt and increased the number of non-performing loans. When the investment trust business imploded the securities market collapsed. This also was part of the reason why the economy went into recession after its short-lived recovery.

In sum the failure to undertake a comprehensive restructuring of the financial sector and to strengthen supervision reduced (intentionally or unintentionally) the degree of economic contraction by sustaining weak *chaebols*, but it also increased both the ultimate cost of financial restructuring and the time taken for corporate and financial restructuring. Furthermore the impact of restructuring was asymmetric among firms: small and medium-sized firms who relied mainly on banks for their borrowing suffered more severely than the large *chaebols*, which were able to benefit from the expanding corporate bond market during the initial period of restructuring.

Let us look at this in more detail. The total volume of investment trust business tripled between January 1998 and June 1999, rising from 84 trillion won to 255 trillion won. Figure 9.1 compares the actual growth of this sector with its expected normal growth path between 1983 and 1999. The

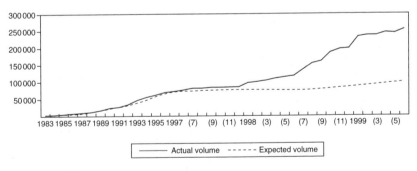

Figure 9.1 Actual versus expected normal volume of investment trust business, 1983–99 (billion won)

Note: Growth rate-increase of trust assets by annual growth rate of total savings.
Source: MOFE (various years).

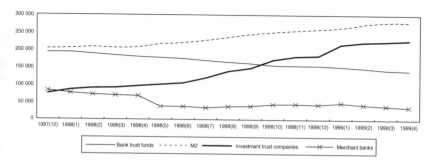

Figure 9.2 Growth of the financial sector, 1997–99 (billion won).
Source: MOFE (various years).

latter was derived by applying the growth rates of the total financial sector at the volume of investment trust business in 1983. In the past, the sector had grown at more or less the same pace as the financial sector as a whole, but from early 1998 the two paths diverged significantly. The growth of the investment trust sector was mostly at the expense of banks' trust accounts and the merchant banking sector (Figure 9.2). By April 1999 the total funds mobilized by investment trust companies had reached about 80 per cent of M2, up from about 40 per cent at the end of 1997.

The extraordinary expansion of the investment trust sector during this period was due to two main factors. First, a sharp reduction in interest rates in early 1998 resulted in large capital gains for the funds established by investment trust companies and investment trust management companies in late 1997 and early 1998.[6] Second, these companies used the capital gains to offer higher than the prevailing market interest rates (market rate plus 'alpha') by illegally transferring high-yielding bonds from the old funds to new ones, and this was not properly regulated by the supervisory authorities or monitored by investors. Many of the investment trust management companies controlled by *chaebols* aggressively mobilized funds – sometimes by means of misleading advertisements – through their affiliated security companies. As Figure 9.3 shows, the yields from the beneficiary certificates offered by investment trust and investment trust management companies rose substantially higher than those from corporate bonds from the second half of 1998, even though the former had shorter maturities. This was made possible by the illegal transfer of high-yield bonds from existing funds to the newly established ones, which attracted many individual investors as well as institutional investors seeking interest rate arbitrage (Figure 9.4).

This rapid growth took place despite the extremely poor financial status of the investment trust companies,[7] which had been in negative capital for long time especially the three largest ones.[8] Although their financial situation further deteriorated through economic crisis they were not made

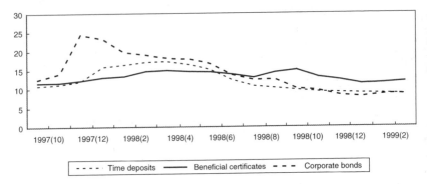

Figure 9.3   Interest rates of corporate bonds, time deposits and beneficial certificates, 1997–99 (per cent)
Notes: Time deposits: terms of one to two years; beneficial certificates: long-term bond funds; corporate bonds: three-year term.
Source: BOK (c) (various years).

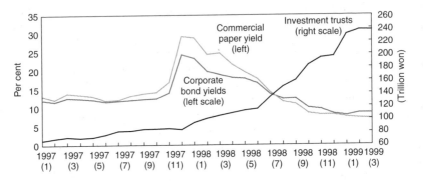

Figure 9.4   Interest rate movement and growth of investment trust companies, 1997–99
Source: BOK (c) various years.

subject to corrective action by the supervisory authorities and their irregular practices were ignored.[9] Table 9.4 shows the balance sheets of six companies for the period 1997–99.

Because the investment trust and investment trust management companies were not properly monitored by investors or the supervisory authorities, banks and merchant banks shifted funds to them, leaving the overall risks and distortions in the financial system unchanged or making them even more severe. This can be compared with the 1993–96 experience of lack of regulatory oversight of the commercial paper market and the merchant banking sector, which facilitated their rapid expansion. As a result, corporate firms

Table 9.4 Balance sheets of the three largest investment trust companies and three regional companies, 1997–99 (billion won)

	1997		1998		1999	
	Big three	Regional	Big three	Regional	Big three	Regional
Assets	6805.7	2748.0	6 570.0	3809.8	7 705.8	1132.9
Current	5686.1	2217.9	4 393.6	3285.4	2 925.0	670.8
Non-current	1119.6	530.1	2 176.1	524.1	4 780.9	462.1
Liabilities	7579.3	2589.1	10 129.5	3869.3	10 448.8	1125.2
Current	7366.5	2538.5	10 068.8	3831.6	8 291.1	1114.0
(Debt)	(7057.8)	(2362.4)	(9 827.9)	(3379.6)	(5 525.6)	(1089.9)
Non-current	212.6	50.5	60.4	37.3	2 157.7	11.2
Owner's equity	−773.6	158.9	−3 559.5	−59.6	−2 743.0	7.7
Contributed capital	520.0	600.0	610.2	280.0	610.2	370.0
Capital surplus	−1293.6	−141.1	−4 169.7	−339.6	−3 353.2	−362.3
(Net income)	(−933.2)	(−104.5)	(−2 966.2)	(−301.6)	(199.1)	(−91.6)

Source: Korea Investment-Trust Companies Association.

increasingly financed their investments by means of short-term funds, creating a severe maturity mismatch between their financing and investment. Moreover, because they were inadequately monitored by the financial market and the banking sector they were able to engage in reckless investment expansion, which further damaged their financial situation and eventually led to the bankruptcy of firms that bad borrowed heavily from the commercial paper market in 1997. This eventually became a force behind the financial crisis of 1997 (Cho, 2000).[10]

The lack of regulatory oversight of the investment trust sector in 1998–99 led to funding being provided to large *chaebol*-affiliated firms whose financial health should have precluded financial support. Many of the large investment trust management companies and securities companies were owned by *chaebols* and they mobilized the huge amount of 130 trillion won within a year, equivalent to 11 per cent of total financial savings in Korea. The top four of these (Hyundai, Samsung, Daewoo and LG) alone mobilized 77 trillion won. To aid the survival of their affiliated firms they purchased commercial paper issued by affiliated firms of placing them in affiliated investment trust management companies or other such companies (to circumvent the regulatory rules) with the implicit mutual agreement to cross-purchase the bonds or commercial paper of their affiliated non-financial firms.

Table 9.5 shows the amount of commercial papers and corporate bonds purchased by investment trust and investment trust management companies for the top five *chaebols*. As of April 1999, the top five *chaebols* obtained

Table 9.5 Trust assets purchased for the top five *chaebols*, as of 30 April 1999 (billion won)

	Total	Total	Hyundai	Samsung	Daewoo	LG	SK
Commercial paper	510 886	247 972	85 402	41 068	59 385	45 345	16 773
		(48.5%)	(16.7%)	(8.0%)	(11.6%)	(8.9%)	(3.3%)
Stock	99 258	47 125	9 077	16 234	1 646	10 185	9 982
		(47.5%)	(9.1%)	(16.36%)	(1.7%)	(10.3%)	(10.1%)
Corporate bonds	1 543 219	626 339	148 354	123 574	188 469	103 991	61 950
		(40.5%)	(9.6%)	(8.01%)	(12.2%)	(6.7%)	(4.0%)
Subtotal	2 153 363	921 437	242 834	180 876	249 500	159 521	88 705
		(42.8%)	(11.3%)	(8.40%)	(11.6%)	(7.4%)	(4.1%)
Total trust assets	2 447 233	37.7%	9.9%	7.4%	10.2%	6.5%	3.6%

92 trillion won from the investment trust sector compared with 70.2 trillion won from the banking sector. Twenty-five trillion won was used to purchase Daewoo securities and another 24 trillion won to purchase Hyundai securities, so these two *chaebols* substantially increased their domestic debt in the midst of economic crisis and bank restructuring. Daewoo's total debt increased by 17 trillion won in 1998, most of which was provided by the investment trust sector to fund the company's continuing expansion. A similar pattern can be found in the case of Hyundai.

About 22 per cent of the corporate bonds issued between December 1997 and December 1999 were subsequently defaulted as the companies that had issued them went bankrupt by the end of 2000 (Oh and Rhee, 2001). This suggests that the sector's capacity to assess the risk of firms was even poorer than that of the banking sector, and as a result the country's financial savings were further frittered away. The provision of finance to insolvent firms limited the opportunities for more profitable and promising firms to obtain finance, which served to erode the long-term growth potential of the economy.

The rapid expansion of investment trust companies and the corporate bond market in 1998, when the domestic interest rates were high, also had the effect of lengthening the period in which firms were burdened by high interest payments. As shown in Table 9.6, the firms' repayment of short-term loans and commercial papers was heavily dependent on the issuing of bonds, most of them with a maturity of three years. Corporate bond issues increased sharply between December 1997 and March 1999. This switch from short-term to long-term debts at a time when interest rates were kept relatively high extended the adverse impact of the high interest rate policy adopted immediately after the crisis.

Thus the asymmetric approach to financial restructuring and the poor regulatory oversight of investment trust companies delayed corporate

Table 9.6 Financing of non-financial firms: composition, 1981–99 (average share, percent)

	1981–85	1986–90	1991–95	1996	1997	1998	1999
Bonds	10.5	13.6	19.5	18.0	23.9	180.0	72.1
Equity	13.6	22.9	15.6	11.0	7.8	53.0	7.6
Commercial paper	3.0	5.9	8.1	17.6	3.9	−45.8	−32.3
Subtotal	27.1	42.4	43.2	46.7	35.6	187.3	47.4
Loans	48.0	35.0	38.2	28.3	37.8	−63.9	4.1
Foreign	1.6	3.2	3.5	10.5	5.7	−38.5	19.7
Others	23.3	19.4	15.1	14.5	20.9	15.1	28.8
Total	100.0	100.0	100.0	100.0	100.0	100.0	100.0

Source: BOK (b) (various years).

restructuring and deepened the financial sector's problems. Increased market uncertainty and the resulting collapse of the securities market meant that the economic recovery discussed earlier was short-lived. The substantial amount of corporate bonds issued between mid 1998 and mid 1999 fell due in 2001 and 2002. Of the 65 trillion won of bonds that fell due in 2001, about 25 trillion's worth were rated below investment grade. The full impact of the investment trust debacle has yet to be felt, but it will continue to exert a strain on and cause uncertainty in the financial market.

The above analysis suggests that, when designing a financial restructuring strategy, allowance should be made for unexpected developments in the financial market, the regulatory rules should be enforced equally across all sectors, and there should be a simultaneous restructuring of all financial institutions and market segments.

Coordinating monetary policy with supervisory policy

After the crisis, Korea's monetary stance was dominated more by the supervisory policies of the financial restructuring authority (FSC) than by the monetary policy of the central bank (Bank of Korea, BOK). The money multipliers were volatile and their change depended on the timing of financial restructuring (of banks and non-bank financial institutions) and the strengthening of regulatory rules. In fact these factors had a strong contractionary effect. Figures 9.5 and 9.6 show the monetary aggregates and the multipliers for each aggregate, respectively.

The loan to deposit ratio fell sharply as the banks and other depository institutions became subject to restructuring and regulation, and as they grew increasingly concerned about their BIS capital ratio and a possible run by depositors. As Figure 9.7 shows, the loan to deposit ratio of commercial

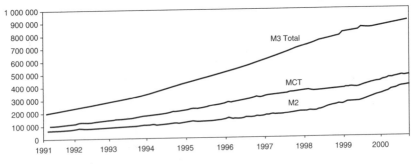

Figure 9.5   Monetary aggregates, 1991–2000 (billion won)
Source: BOK (c) (various years).

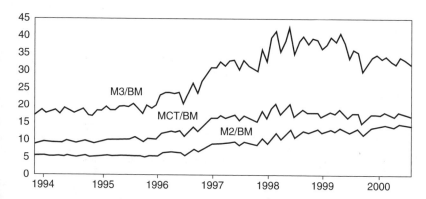

Figure 9.6 Monetary multipliers, 1994–2000
Source: BOK (c) (various years).

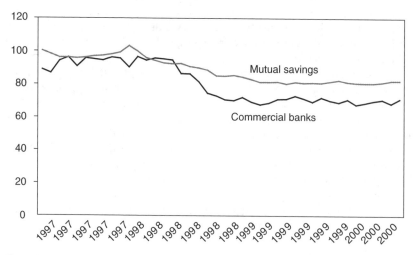

Figure 9.7 Loan to deposit ratio, 1997–2000 (per cent)
Source: BOK (c) (various years).

banks and mutual savings companies fell significantly from 1998. On the other hand, financial institutions significantly increased their holdings of public securities during this period. For example commercial banks' total holdings of government bonds increased more than three fold from 6.7 trillion won at the end of 1997 to 19.5 trillion at the end of 1999. Bonds issued by government-owned entities such as the KDB, KDIC and KAMCO increased from 47 billion won to 110 billion won during the same period, rising from 23 per cent to 44 per cent of their total loans.

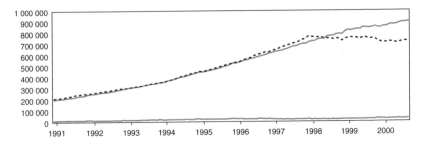

Figure 9.8   Domestic credit, M3 and reserve money, 1991–2000 (billion won)
Source: BOK (c) (various years).

Figure 9.8 shows the movement of M3 and total domestic credit.[11] Despite the rapid growth of base money and M2, total domestic credit stagnated, and total domestic credit to the private sector actually declined from the end of 1997. This reflects the unwillingness of financial institutions to lend to the private sector while the supervisory rules were being strengthened and the financial institutions were being subjected to corrective action based on their BIS ratio.

The above discussion suggests that, during the period when regulatory rules are being tightened in developing countries and/or financial restructuring is initiated, the central bank's monetary policy needs to be closely coordinated with the supervisory authorities' policy. The central bank should take into account the effect of the latter on the actual monetary stance in order to achieve the intended goal of the monetary policies. It also suggests that in the future the macroeconomic policy components and structural reform components of IMF programmes should be carefully coordinated with each other to avoid unexpected macroeconomic consequences, especially in countries where regulatory standards and practices have been very slack.

High interest rate policy

The initial crisis resolution strategy under the IMF programme consisted largely of two parts: macroeconomic policies and structural adjustment measures. The macroeconomic policies were traditional IMF stabilization policies with a tight monetary and fiscal stance. The main goal of these policies was to stabilize the exchange market and improve the current account by means of financial restructuring and the adoption of global standards in financial supervision (for example loan classification and provisioning), accounting, disclosure and corporate governance. This would improve transparency and accountability and therefore economic efficiency. The direction and goals of each of these policies were uncontroversial. However

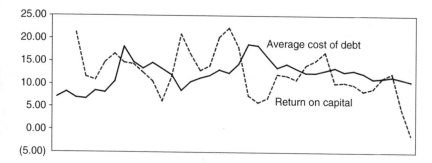

Figure 9.9 Return on and cost of capital investment, 1960–97
Source: BOK (d) (various years).

it seems that the measure adopted to deal with the currency crisis – that is, the high interest rate policy – in fact aggravated the financial crisis. Hence the 1997 crisis was a double one – currency and financial.

With regard to the corporate aspect of the crisis, the corporate sector had long suffered from severe debt repayment problems and accumulated losses that had been veiled behind irregular accounting practices. They had relied for their survival on continuous credit expansion by banks and foreign creditors. Overinvestment, a high leverage ratio with overreliance on short-term debt, and poor earnings were common to most corporate firms. This was caused by Korea's distorted incentive structure and the misalignment of relative prices, such as wages, interest rates and exchange rates. Lack of adequate competition policies, poor corporate governance and poor banking supervision gave rise to reckless expansion. This sustained the high demand for capital and labour despite the deterioration of corporate profitability, and allowed the persistence of high interest rates that exceedeed the rates of return on investments, and high wages that exceeded labour productivity (Cho, 1998). Moreover the overvalued exchange rate aggravated the profitability of exporting firms. Finally, poor accounting and disclosure practices and the lack of financial market governance over corporate firms served to worsen the situation.

The Korean economy experienced three major crises after its take-off in the 1960s (in 1971–72, the early 1980s and 1997–98), each of which followed a sustained period of overheated investment and returns on corporate investments that were lower than the average cost of debt (Figure 9.9). In each crisis the government intervened heavily in the financial system. Interest rate cuts, a massive rescheduling of existing debts, the extension of new loans, forced mergers and takeovers of firms, and tax exemptions were common strategies. The currency crisis[12] (the near default of foreign debt) was dealt with mainly by revolving of debt and finding new sources of borrowing (including bilateral loans), plus IMF-supported stabilization policies. The

(a)

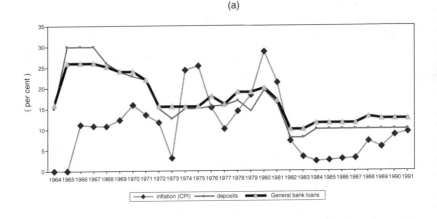

(b)

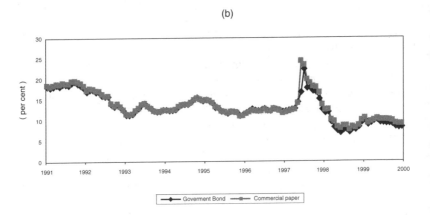

Figure 9.10   Interest rates: (a) 1964–91; (b) 1991–2000
Source: BOK (c) (various years).

stabilization policies relied mainly on the direct control of credit rather than
high interest rates, and in fact the interest rates were cut substantially in the
first two crises (Figure 9.10a). However the 1997 crisis occurred suddenly
when there was a drastic reversal of capital flows, so a high interest rate
policy was needed to curb speculation in the foreign exchange market
(Figure 9.10b). But this was very costly for the economy as Korean firms
were extremely highly leveraged (Figure 9.11).

Total corporate debt was already more than 1.5 times the annual GDP[13] – an
extremely high level even compared with the most advanced economies – and
about one third of this was accounted for by firms whose pretax
earnings were lower than their interest payment obligations (see below).
The sharp interest rate increase in this situation magnified the size of

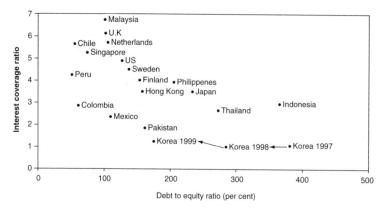

Figure 9.11   Interest coverage and debt to equity ratios

non-performing assets, thus deepening the financial crisis and increasing the ultimate burden on taxpayers.

The currency crisis was basically due to a run by foreign creditors (banks) on domestic banks after refusing to revolve short-term loans. Until that point, Korea had had control over inbound and outbound foreign portfolio investment so there had been little possibility of a massive outflow of portfolio investment.[14] Several writers (Fuman and Stiglitz, 1998; Goldfajn and Baig, 1998; Barsuto and Ghosh, 2000; Ohno *et al.*, 2000) suggest that the high interest rate policy was not effective in stabilizing exchange rates.[15] Nor did the overall macroeconomic policy stance need to be so tight if it was aimed at improving the current account position, as the latter was already turning into a surplus when the currency crisis broke out (see Figures 9.12 and 9.13). Household consumption and investment were also falling rapidly.

The high interest rate policy did not stop the run by foreign banks, and may even have aggravated it by increasing scepticism about the health of Korean banks. This suggests that, when dealing with a currency crisis in a highly leveraged economy with substantial foreign exchange control, the appropriateness of traditional policy responses, especially a high interest rate policy, may need to be reconsidered.

Concluding remarks

The Korean experience of the 1997 crisis has raised many questions about the process of structural reforms and market opening. Korea, like many other developing countries in East Asia, achieved rapid economic growth

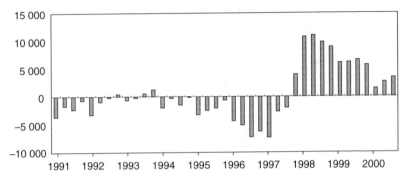

Figure 9.12   Current account, 1991–2000 (hundred million dollars)
Source: BOK (c) (various years).

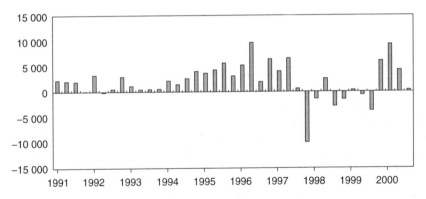

Figure 9.13   Capital flows, 1991–2000 (hundred million dollars)
Source: BOK (c) (various years).

by means of a development strategy that included strong government intervention in the market. It now faces the challenge of rapid economic liberalization and globalization. It took centuries for the Western economies to industrialize themselves, so they were able to establish the necessary institutions and market infrastructures over many generations and tailor them in accordance with the experience of many crises.

The East Asian economies achieved their industrialization in just a generation or two through heavy protectionism and government intervention in resource allocation. But the rapid integration of the global economy and the revolution in telecommunication and information technology, from which the East Asian economies cannot isolate themselves, require them to open and liberalize their economies at great speed. As discussed in this chapter, the lack of necessary institutions and social safety nets, and the economic incentive structures they have created, will make it extremely difficult to organize their rapid transition to fully liberalized and open economies. Moreover, domestic political economy factors will make it hard for them to digest a sudden shift in economic policy.

The introduction of global standards under the IMF programme flooded the non-performing assets, which had long been accumulated behind loose regulatory standards and accounting practices. It also required massive corporate and bank restructuring, and this led to unemployment and public debt on a scale never experienced in the past. This was not easy to deal with, given the political reality in most of these countries. Either the speed of reform or adherence to the new rules had to be compromised. With regard to the first of these, the international capital market became impatient and made its feelings manifest by means of adverse capital flows; and with the second the credibility of the reform programme was undermined.

In summary, the Korean economy achieved rapid economic growth in a comparatively short time, and now it is having to address the challenge of rapid economic transition, which so far has been bumpy and uncertain. Similar problems will soon be faced by other East Asian economies, including China, that are going through market opening and greater integration into the global economy.

This chapter has not provided suggestions for dealing with the enormous challenge of economic transition. What it has done is to illustrate the problems faced in the process of economic transition, based on Korea's experiences since the 1997 crisis. These issues involved deserve considerable further study.

Appendix 9.1

Table A9.1 Macroeconomic indicators, Korea, 1996–2000 (per cent)

	1996	1997	1998					1999					2000				
			1st qtr	2nd qtr	3rd qtr	4th qtr	Total	1st qtr	2nd qtr	3rd qtr	4th qtr	Total	1st qtr	2nd qtr	3rd qtr	4th qtr	Average
GDP (%)	6.8	5.0	−4.6	−8.0	−8.1	−5.9	−6.7	5.8	11.2	13.0	13.0	10.9	13.1	10.2	10.0	5.0	9.3
Export growth	3.9	5.0	8.4	−1.8	−10.8	−5.5	−2.8	−6.1	2.5	15.1	22.9	8.6	29.8	21.5	26.5	6.1	19.9
Import growth	11.3	−3.8	−36.2	−37.0	−39.9	−28.7	−35.5	8.1	22.2	38.7	44.8	28.4	51.9	38.4	35.8	16.2	34.0
Inflation																	
CPI	4.9	4.4	8.9	8.2	7.0	6.0	7.5	0.7	0.6	0.7	1.3	0.8	2.0	1.6	3.0	2.5	2.3
WPI	3.2	3.9	14.4	13.9	12.0	8.6	12.2	−3.5	−3.3	−1.9	0.5	−2.1	3.1	2.2	2.4	0.6	2.0
Current account	−4.4	−1.7	16.0	14.2	11.9	9.5	12.7	6.7	6.3	6.5	4.8	6.0	1.5	2.6	3.6	2.8	2.7
Real wage growth	6.7	2.5	−8.1	−8.6	−14.2	−5.8	−9.3	4.8	9.9	14.8	14.5	11.0	6.9	7.0	5.6	3.3	5.6
Unemployment	2.0	2.6	5.8	6.9	7.5	7.5	7.0	8.5	6.7	5.6	4.9	6.3	5.2	3.9	3.9	3.8	4.1

Notes

1. This chapter is a revised version of a paper presented at a workshop organized by the Institute of Developing Economies in Tokyo on 21–2 March 2001. I appreciate comments made by the participants of the workshop and Akira Kohsaka.
2. See Cho (1998) for a discussion of Korea's structural problems.
3. Nam (2000) used balance sheet and income statement data for firms with assets of more than 7 billion won. His sample included both listed and unlisted firms.
4. This is an approximate figure after subtracting 'stocks' and 'other equities' from 'total external financing'.
5. In fact only these two types of financial institution had been allowed to engage in foreign borrowing until the crisis.
6. During 1997–99, two types of investment and mutual companies were allowed; investment trust companies, which mobilized and managed funds; and investment trust management companies, which managed funds mobilized by their affiliated securities companies. Investment trust companies were also allowed investment by borrowing from proprietary accounts.
7. Investment trust companies have been converted to investment trust securities companies and investment trust management companies with the latter as subsidiaries.
8. The problems of three largest companies had been aggravated by government intervention in asset management for policy goals such as sustaining the stock market value, and by a lack of professional management.
9. The investment trust companies' financial insolvency problem eventually prompted the government to take supervisory action as it feared the possibility of a run.
10. Cho (2001) discusses how the asymmetric liberalization of interest rates and regulatory oversight led to the rapid expansion of the commercial paper market and the 'short-termization' of corporate finance during 1993–97.
11. These figures are taken from a BOK financial survey that includes the assets and liabilities of banks and non-bank financial institutions.
12. In my view Korea faced several currency crises before 1997: in the early 1970s when the large foreign debt incurred in the second half of the 1960s fell, in 1975 after first oil shock, and in 1980 due to heavy borrowing from the eurocurrency market in the second half of 1970s and the second oil shock.
13. According to the BOK (1998) the corporate sector's total borrowing from financial institutions and direct financing through commercial papers, bonds and trade credits exceeded 650 trillion won at the end of 1997.
14. There was a possibility of speculation on foreign currency by domestic residents, but this could be addressed by temporarily (and partially) limiting the conversion of domestic deposits to foreign deposits by residents.
15. Many analysts have empirically tested the effectiveness of interest rate policy in supporting exchange rates (Barsuto and Ghosh, 2000; Kraay, 2000; Flood and Rose, 2001). Barsuto and Ghosh (2000) argue that the fact that the coefficient of the real interest rate on the risk premium on Korean bonds issued abroad was positive (albeit not statistically significant) suggests that tightening would have been unlikely to improve the exchange rate and may have been counter-productive.

References

Bank of Korea (BOK a) (various years) *Financial Statement Analysis* (Seoul: BOK).

Bank of Korea (BOK b) (various issues) *Flow of Funds* (Seoul: BOK).

Bank of Korea (BOK c) (various years) *Monthly Bulletin* (Seoul: BOK).

Bank of Korea (BOK d) (various years) *Analysis of Financial Statements of Corporate Firms* (Seoul: BOK).

Barsuto, G. and A. R. Ghosh (2000) 'The Interest Rate–Exchange Rate Nexus in the Asian Crisis Countries', IMF Working Paper no. 00/19 (Washington, DC: IMF).

Cho, Y. J. (1998) 'The Structural Reform Issues of The Korean Economy', Sogang Institute of International and Area Studies Working Paper no. 98-01 (SIIAS).

Cho, Y. J. (2000) 'Restructuring the Financial System in Korea – Key Issues', Sogang Institute of International and Area Studies Working Paper no. 00-01 (SIIAS).

Cho, Y. J. (2001) 'The Financial Crisis of Korea: A Consequence of Poorly Phased Liberalization?', in G. Caprio, P. Honohan and J. Stiglitz (eds), *Financial Liberalization: How Far? How Fast?* (Cambridge: Cambridge University Press).

Dekle, R., C. Haiao and S. Wang (1999) 'Do High Interest Rates Appreciate Exchange Rates during Crisis?', *Oxford Bulletin of Economics and Statistics*.

Flood, R. and A. K. Rose (2001) 'Uncovered Interests Parity in Crisis: The Interest Rate Defense in the 1990s', mimeo.

Furman, J. and J. E. Stiglitz (1998) 'Economic Crises: Evidence and Insights from East Asia', *Brookings Papers on Economic Activity*, vol. 2, pp. 1–135.

Goldfajn, I., and T. Baig (1998) 'Monetary Policy in the Aftermath of Currency Crises: The Case of Asia', IMF Working Paper no. 98/170 (Washington, DC: IMF).

Goldfajn, I. and P. Gupta (1999) 'Does Monetary Policy Stabilize the Exchange Rate Following a Currency Crisis?', IMF Working Paper no. 99/42 (Washington, DC: IMF).

Kraay, A. (2000) 'Do High Interest Rates Defend Currencies during Speculative Attacks?', World Bank Policy Research Working Paper no. 2267 (Washington, DC: World Bank).

Ministry of Finance and Economy (MOFE) (various years) *Financial Statistic Bulletin* (Seoul: MOFE).

Nam, J.-H. (2000) 'Non-Performing Assets of the Korean Banks', mimeo, Sogang University (in Korean).

Oh, K.-T. and C.-R. Rhee (2001) 'Bond Market Development after the Currency Crisis', mimeo (in Korean).

Ohno, K., K. Shirono and E. Sisli (2000) 'Can High Interest Rates Stop Regional Currency Falls?', ADB Institute Working Paper no. 6: ADB.

Radelet, S. and J. D. Sachs (1999) 'What Have We Learned, So Far, from the Asian Financial Crisis?', paper presented at the NBER Conference on the Korean Currency Crisis.

10
The Regulator's Dilemma: Hedge Funds in the International Financial Architecture[1]

Barry Eichengreen

Introduction

Hedge funds have been the subject of considerable recent commentary, much of it not entirely favorable. Malaysia's Mahathir bin Mohamad famously accused them of precipitating the Asian currency and financial crisis. Joseph Yam of the Hong Kong Monetary Authority accused them of coordinating short sales on the Hong Kong Exchange with short sales of the Hong Kong dollar (the so-called 'double whammy' or 'double play'). And the Reserve Bank of Australia has accused them of manipulating the market in the Australian dollar by coordinating their position taking and signalling that they were about to attack the currency. Hedge funds had substantial positions in Russian GKDs in the summer of 1998 and suffered large losses from Russia's default; in the rush to cover their positions and restore their liquidity, they may have played a major role in last autumn's credit crunch. And then there was the all-but-failure of Long-Term Capital Management (LTCM) and the threat this may have posed to the stability of the global financial system.

Whether hedge funds deserve the influence ascribed to them is another matter. Public information on their activities is, to put it mildly, incomplete. In the absence of facts, there may be a tendency to romanticize and exaggerate their role.

This paper is an attempt to sort through the issues and available evidence on the role of hedge funds in international financial markets, with a focus on market manipulation (the issue of concern of smaller countries) and systemic stability (the issue of concern to larger ones). Data problems notwithstanding, a reasonably clear picture emerges. While the hedge fund industry is large relative to the typical emerging market, it is small in comparison to other financial-market participants that engage in many of the same activities. It is hard to see why the situation in emerging markets would be much different, in other words, were hedge funds somehow to disappear overnight.

The paper then turns to the implications of hedge funds for systemic stability and asks what lessons can be drawn from the LTCM episode. I consider the origins of LTCM's difficulties, the way they were handled, and implications for prudential supervision. I conclude that while certain aspects of this episode were sui generis, it still raises valid concerns about systemic stability.

Even those who attach heavy weight to these systemic-stability and market integrity issues have few options for action. Direct regulation of hedge funds is out of the question, since they would simply respond by moving offshore. Higher margin requirements would be vitiated by market migration and the growth of over-the-counter transactions. For emerging markets concerned about the implications for the stability and integrity of their markets, this leaves entry and exit taxes to discourage the kind of short round-trips in which hedge funds engage, and more flexible exchange rates to avoid offering the one-way bets hedge fund managers find so appealing. Neither policy will totally eliminate potential threats to market integrity, but these are the only available instruments whose costs do not exceed their benefits. For regulators concerned with systemic stability, the most effective approach will involve operating via hedge funds' counterparties, which means strengthening the incentive and capacity of the banks to manage their exposures to highly-leveraged institutions. Unfortunately, differential capital charges on lending to hedge funds that do not disclose their financial position or are located offshore, as popularly suggested, are likely to be subverted by regulatory arbitrage. This leaves market discipline, which could be strengthened by greater reliance on subordinated debt. But recent experience casts doubt on the vigour of market discipline, and subordinated debt remains unproven. Again, there are no perfect solutions.

The contours of the hedge fund industry

Hedge funds are collective investment vehicles, organized typically as limited liability partnerships. They use high-powered incentives to compensate managers, do not advertize to solicit investors, and require advance notification by shareholders wishing to withdraw their funds. Their investment activities are subject to few restrictions, and they are subject to few disclosure requirements; in the United States they are generally exempt from the investor-protection regulations of the Investment Company Act of 1940. (See Appendix to this chapter.)

Most modern-day hedge funds, unlike their ancestors, do not hedge; the name has thus become a source of confusion. In the years following the industry's inception in the 1940s, the standard hedge-fund investment strategy was to combine leverage with short selling (placing half the portfolio in short positions in order to hedge returns against aggregate market moves, while using leverage to magnify the difference between the high returns expected to obtain on long positions and the low returns on shorts). Early hedge funds took these positions mainly on US markets (Caldwell 1995).

Today, none of these generalizations is valid. Hedge funds pursue a variety of investment strategies, including some that involve neither short selling nor leverage. Moreover, the 1980s saw the growth of 'macro' hedge funds that take positions on markets around the world; and with the spread of privatization and financial liberalization in the 1990s these funds diversified into emerging markets.

In addition to hedge funds domiciled in the US and other major financial centres, there are hedge funds domiciled offshore (as explained in Box 10.1). Moreover, other collective investment vehicles, managed futures funds for

---

Box 10.1   Hedge fund regulation: the US case

Collective investment vehicles are exempt from the investor-protection regulations of the Investment Company Act of 1940 if they have fewer than 100 accredited investors (or partners) and do not make a public offering of their securities. Accredited investors each must have a net worth of $1 million and an income of at least $200,000 in each of the last two years. Alternatively, joint spousal income must have been in excess of $300,000 in the each of the last two years.[41] Such firms are then exempt under Section 3(c)(1) of the Investment Company Act. The National Securities Markets Improvement Act of 1996 amended the Investment Company Act to provide a second exclusion (Section 3(c)(7)), which allows for as many as 499 investors, each with net worth of at least $5 million. Not only are such entities exempt from disclosure and reporting requirements imposed on firms not meeting these conditions, but voluntary disclosure of positions and other investment information could be construed as soliciting business and thereby precipitate regulation under the Investment Company Act. (Offshore hedge funds are, by definition, exempt from even these limitations. Organized as private partnerships, they can offer unlimited numbers of accounts. Hence, many major hedge funds operating in the US also have offshore vehicles.)

Hedge funds are also exempt from regulation under the Securities Act of 1933 because they offer their securities privately. But even exempt funds are still required under US law to report information on their financial activities to their shareholders (as opposed to the regulators or the public). And hedge funds which trade on futures and option exchanges and accept investments from US citizens must register with the Commodity Futures Trading Commission as Commodity Pool Operators and are therefore subject to disclosure, reporting and record keeping requirements and fraud prohibitions under the provisions of the Commodity Exchange Act. Note that the Commodity Futures Trading Commission does not impose capital requirements on Commodity Pool Operators, nor does it normally receive detailed information about their off-exchange trading of over-the-counter derivatives.

example, follow many of the same practices. The facts help to explain why estimates of hedge fund capital and the number of funds vary by factors of 3 to 5.[2] Conceptually, they raise the issue of what exactly is a hedge fund. For present purposes, we can do no better than to define hedge funds as collective investment vehicles that operate largely outside the regulatory net, are largely free of disclosure requirements, and have maximum flexibility in their investment strategies.

$300 billion or even $100 billion, figures which bound the range of estimates of hedge fund capital as of the end of 1997, are large amounts relative to the size of most emerging financial markets and the resources of central banks and governments. To the extent that hedge funds lever their capital (more on this in a moment), the disproportion is more striking still. Hence the fear that large hedge funds corner and manipulate small markets.

The question is whether the world would be any different were hedge funds somehow prevented from taking positions in emerging markets or if they could be magically made to disappear overnight. There are reasons for thinking not. Hedge fund capital is small relative to that of other international investors, a significant share of which (the assets managed by the proprietary trading desks of investment banks, for example) is devoted to exactly the same activities as hedge-fund capital.[3] In the US, UK, Germany and Japan alone, the holdings of securities and money market instruments by financial institutions exceed $20 trillion, compared to which hedge funds are small potatoes. Even LTCM's $80 billion in balance-sheet arbitrage positions in US treasury markets is less impressive when one notes that commercial banks had some $3 trillion of such exposures. Thus, one can reasonably question whether hedge funds regularly move markets on the grounds that other investors follow many of the same trading and investment strategies and have many times more equity.

To be sure, hedge funds leverage their capital. But industry surveys like that in Table 10.1 suggest that a third of hedge funds do not use leverage at all, and fewer than one in six lever their assets more than twice. Such simple measures of leverage are highest for market neutral-arbitrage funds, understandably so, since the volatility of an unlevered market-portfolio would normally be low.[4] Macro funds use moderate leverage on average: nearly 70 percent claim to lever their capital less than two times.[5]

Moreover, banks are even more leveraged than hedge funds as a group. The typical gearing ratio for commercial banks is on the order of ten to one, while the ratio of total assets to equity, or gross leverage, for the top investment banks ranges from 25 to 35 (the ratio of gross assets excluding matched-book financing to equity, or net leverage, ranges from 10 to 25).[6] To be sure, investment banks and other institutional investors have more diversified portfolios; they are unlikely to concentrate their positions in particular markets.[7] But their capital is several orders of magnitude larger, so even a small portfolio share can swamp the entire hedge fund industry.

Table 10.1 Largest hedge funds according to capitalization, August 1998 (in US $ billions)

Domestic		Offshore	
Tiger	$5.1	Jaguar Fund NV	$10.0
Moore Global Investment	4.0	Quantum Fund NV	6.0
Highbridge Capital Corp	1.4	Quantum Industrial Fund	2.4
Intercap	1.3	Quota Fund NV	1.7
Rosenberg Market Neutral	1.2	Omega Overseas Partners	1.7
Ellington Composite	1.1	Maverick Fund	1.7
Hedged Taxable-Equivalent	1.0	Zweig Dimenna International	1.6
Quantitative Long/Short	0.9	Quasar International Fund NV	1.5
Sr International Fund	0.9	SBC Currency Portfolio	1.5
Perry Partners	0.8	Perry Partners International	1.3

Source: MAR/Hedge.

Thus, even if it is right to regard highly-leveraged institutions as a threat to systemic stability, it is still important to recognize that hedge funds are only a small subset of the institutions in question. That recent reports concerned with the issue have discarded the term 'hedge funds' in favour of 'highly-leveraged institutions' may seem like a bureaucratic waffle, but it actually represents intellectual progress.

One can reasonably question the accuracy of such comparisons. Data like those in Table 10.2 are provided voluntarily and not verified independently. Moreover, the omission of off-balance sheet items, which may be particularly important for certain classes of hedge funds, may lead their leverage to be understated.

In the end, what one makes of a given leverage ratio depends on with what one is concerned. If the issue is counterparty risk and systemic stability, then the standard deviation of the overall return on capital is more relevant than the leverage ratio, which should be adjusted for the riskiness of an entity's underlying investment business. And if the issue is the integrity of small markets, then the relevant metric is not just assets under management but the share devoted to positions in the relevant markets.

Hedge funds and market turbulence

The plural of anecdote may be data, but evidence of the role of hedge funds in major market moves is decidedly anecdotal. Many accounts read more like military than economic history. Yam's (1999) description of the double play in Hong Kong is representative of the genre:

> The hedge funds launched their attack on Hong Kong after careful planning. First, the hedge funds pre-funded themselves by borrowing HK$, a move designed to insulate themselves from the sharp rise in HK$

Table 10.2   Use of leverage as of December 1997

Hedge fund style	Don't use Leverage	Use leverage Low (<2.0:1)	Use leverage High (>2.0:1)	Use leverage Total
Aggressive growth	35.0%	58.4%	6.6%	65.0%
Distressed securities	61.0%	35.6%	3.4%	39.0%
Emerging markets	36.1%	56.6%	7.3%	63.9%
Fund of funds	21.6%	58.4%	20.0%	78.4%
Income	35.4%	51.2%	13.4%	64.6%
Macro	16.9%	52.3%	30.8%	83.1%
Market neutral – arbitrage	18.2%	22.7%	59.1%	81.8%
Market neutral – securities hedging	31.5%	42.5%	26.0%	68.5%
Market timing	32.1%	35.8%	32.1%	67.9%
Opportunistic	24.4%	56.0%	19.7%	75.6%
Several strategies	45.1%	52.9%	2.0%	54.9%
Short-selling	22.2%	75.0%	2.8%	77.8%
Special situations	19.9%	73.0%	7.1%	80.1%
Value	35.7%	61.0%	3.3%	64.3%
Total sample	30.1%	54.3%	15.6%	69.9%

Source: Yago *et al.* (1998).

interest rates when short-selling of HK$ began...Secondly, the hedge funds built up short positions in the cash and equity markets. The gross open interest of Hang Seng Index Futures more than doubled, to 103,101 contracts (valued at US$4.7 billion), in the five months to end-August. Finally, they launched the attack in August by selling large amount (sic) of HKI$ in the spot and forward markets, with a view to push interest rates sharply higher, thereby causing the stock and futures prices to collapse or even the HK$ peg to break.

Reserve Bank of Australia's (1999) account of the activities of hedge funds in early 1998 is in a similar spirit. Hedge funds

first emerged as large-scale players in the March and June quarters of 1998 when the exchange rate was around US$65 cents – ie after it had already fallen by 15 per cent. During this period they quietly established large short positions in the Australian dollar. Reports from dealers suggested that the positions were on the order of $A10–15 billion...The second stage involved a more aggressive stance as the exchange rate approached its post-float lows around US$60 cents, a time when the market was naturally quite sensitive. The key features of hedge funds' activities were the signalling to other market players that they were about to attack the $A (a move which heightened uncertainty and deterred potential buyers from remaining in the market); lowering offer prices in the brokers even though they were able to sell all they had on offer at the existing price; and concentrating sales into periods of thin trading... The third stage involved the hedge funds taking advantage of other participants' desire to sell by quietly buying back, unwinding their short position, and thereby taking profits.

These stories may be accurate, but their evidentiary basis is uncertain.

Some investigators attempt to draw more systematic inferences from the returns reported by hedge funds in periods of major market moves. For instance, the fact that macro funds reported disappointing returns in 1994, the end of a period when the dollar weakened against the yen and the Deutschmark, is taken to suggest that their positions contributed first to the dollar's strength and then to its weakness.[8] The large losses reported by global and macro funds in August 1998 (Table 10.3) are similarly thought to indicate their exposure to Russia and to the emerging markets adversely affected by the subsequent flight to quality.[9]

A somewhat more sophisticated way of inferring positions is to estimate a regression model of hedge fund returns on asset price changes. Brown, Goetzmann and Park (1998) regress the monthly returns of ten large hedge funds on changes in a vector of Asian exchange rates to infer hedge funds' underlying investment positions. The results do not indicate that hedge funds consistently had short positions against the Asian currencies that came under attack in 1997. These estimates may suffer from model misspecification, however, in that only a limited number of exchange rates are included as independent variables, while the prices of other assets in which hedge funds may have had positions are omitted.[10]

More rigorous analysis requires information on hedge funds' trades and positions (rather than blithely attempting to infer these from correlations). Information on hedge funds' large trades and positions in five major currencies, in three month Eurodollar contracts, and in the S&P 500 futures market, for example, is available from the Large Trade Reporting System of the Commodity Futures Trading Commission (CFTC). Using these data, Kodres and Pritsker (1997) find that the trades and positions of different hedge funds move together in the S&P 500 index contract and the three-month Eurodollar contract and to an extent in the Japanese yen contract. For those so disposed, this can be taken as evidence of herding or collusion. But whether unembellished co-movements justify this interpretation is open to question.

Eichengreen and Mathieson *et al.* (1998) use these data to test whether other large investors take the same positions as hedge funds in the current or following period, a tendency that would magnify the impact of hedge funds' positions and trades. In fact, there is a negative correlation between

Table 10.3 Monthly Returns by Investment Style, August 1998

AUG-98	Market neutral	Global macro	Short sellers	Event driven	Global mgrs*	Fund of funds	International	Regional emerging	Regional established
High	9.67	4.00	24.07	−0.55	4.84	1.56	8.95	−2.29	5.06
Median	0.40	0.07	21.81	−6.40	−8.83	−3.04	−7.27	−20.98	−6.80
Low	10.97	−19.87	19.55	−15.90	−29.68	−8.95	−40.34	−38.36	−26.10

*Sub Median for Global Managers.
Source: MAR/Hedge (http://www.marhedge.com/whatsnew/hpr0998.htm).

the large positions of hedge funds and the large positions of other traders in the same period, and little correlation between the large positions of hedge funds in the previous period and the large positions of other traders in the current period. Contrary to assertions by, *inter alia,* Yam (1999), then, there is little *systematic* evidence that hedge funds play a catalytic role in herding behaviour.[11]

National responses

Malaysia

Malaysia's was perhaps the most notable response to the perception that hedge funds are a threat to market integrity. In response to the perception that hedge funds were destabilizing Asian currencies, the country imposed capital controls in September 1998. Approval was made obligatory for outward portfolio or foreign direct investments of more than M$10,000. Lending by foreign banks to Malaysian residents or by Malaysian banks to nonresidents was prohibited, and banks and residents were barred from engaging in offshore trading of the ringget. A one-year holding period was imposed to lock hedge funds and other portfolio investors into their positions. The policy was designed to give the central bank leeway to reduce interest rates, the idea being that lower interest rates and a sharply expansionary fiscal policy would insulate the economy from the Asian recession.

Hedge fund managers value the ability to put on and take off positions quickly at low cost. Malaysia's controls thereby made it less attractive for them to attempt to speculate against the ringgit. But there was never any question that countries can cut themselves off from international markets. The question is rather whether strategy has benefits or costs.

While Malaysia's policies have raised new doubts among international investors about the attractions of the country as a place to invest, there is little evidence that they helped to jump-start its economy. At the time of writing, the evolution of interest rates and output has been essentially the same in Malaysia and in other Asian countries that shunned controls.[12] Malaysian interest rates came down, but interest rates came down as quickly in Thailand and South Korea. While manufacturing production bottomed out by October of 1998, it was still some 15 per cent below the levels of a year earlier.[13] Fiscal spending has been restrained by the weakness of the banking system and the difficulties the authorities have had in obtaining financing.

This difficulty of obtaining domestic finance and a growing appreciation of the need to borrow offshore appear to have been what led the Malaysian authorities to rethink their controls. They replaced the one-year holding period for portfolio investment with an exit tax at rates ranging from 30 per cent for investments that have been held for less than seven months to zero for investments that have been held for more than a year. Money brought into the country after February 15, 1999 is exempt from taxes on principal repatriation, while profits are taxed at 30 per cent if taken out before one year, and at 10 per cent otherwise. Restrictions on outward investment and on lending to nonresidents by Malaysian banks remain in place, although removal of the one-year holding period requirement was widely seen as the first step in a more general liberalization.

Thus, Malaysia's experiment suggests that while controls can succeed in limiting hedge fund operations in emerging markets, they come at a price for countries with weak financial systems and heavy dependence on external finance.

Hong Kong

The other notable response was Hong Kong's in the summer of 1998. The authorities there complained that hedge funds were simultaneously selling the Hong Kong dollar short, forcing up interest rates as the supply of credit contracted, and shorting the Hang Seng in anticipation that the higher interest rates would depress equity prices. It is worth making two observations about this strategy. First, it hinged on Hong Kong's maintenance of a pegged exchange rate. The province's currency board law meant that the authorities had to accede to the rise in interest rates; maintenance of the peg left them no choice. They could not inflict losses on hedge funds that had shorted the currency by widening the band and creating scope for the currency to appreciate as well as depreciate. Second, central to the official analysis of the problem was the belief that hedge funds were colluding, since it seems unlikely that sales of the currency by any one fund could have put such dramatic upward pressure on interest rates.

The Hong Kong Monetary Authority responded by purchasing nearly $20 billion's worth of shares on the Hang Seng. Its intervention was successful in the sense that equity prices recovered quickly, making profits for the Monetary Authority and averting the kind of collapse that might have jeopardized the currency board. Having been shown that speculating against the HK$ and the Hang Seng was not a one-way bet, the hedge funds withdrew from the market. Moreover, the Monetary Authority made considerable profits on its intervention.

Whether other countries have the capacity to emulate Hong Kong is another matter. The Monetary Authority had ample reserves, enabling it to intervene without igniting fears of inflation; not many other central banks would be in the same position. Its autonomy minimized the pressure for it to favour some companies over others, although it can still be argued that this kind of intervention favors large-capitalization, liquid stocks.[14] For the vast majority of countries, the safer response to this problem would be to simply eliminate the one-way currency-cum-interest rate by adopting a more flexible exchange rate.

Together, then, Hong Kong and Malaysia point to the kind of policies that should be contemplated by emerging markets concerned about the impact of hedge funds on the stability and integrity of their markets. They should consider entry and exit taxes for capital flows to discourage the kind of short round-trips in which hedge funds engage without also making themselves less attractive to investors prepared to stay for the duration. They should shun pegged exchange rates to avoid offering hedge fund managers the one-way bets they find so irresistible. Alternatively, economies like Hong Kong and Argentina, which have good reasons to resist the pressure to adopt more flexible exchange rates, may ultimately be forced to take one more step in the other direction, by going all the way to dollarization or its euro equivalent as a way of rigidly linking their interest rates to those prevailing in the U.S. or Euroland and thereby removing all scope for a double play. Neither measure will provide complete insulation, nor should it to the extent that market discipline is usefully applied to the public as well as the private sector. But such policies are likely to reduce the pressures to levels where they can be viewed as constructive and not as a threat to a country's very existence.

Hedge funds and systematic stability

Russia's default, the rescue of LTCM, and the flight to quality in 1998 raised two additional concerns about hedge fund operations. One is that hedge funds may be important transmissions belts for contagion. This could be the case insofar as hedge funds use leverage and concentrate their portfolios in risky securities. Losses in one market, say Russia, may therefore force them to liquidate positions in other markets in order to raise liquidity.[15]

Recall that this concern also arose toward the beginning of the Asian crisis when volatility spread from Korea to Brazil. Then, however, it seems to have been commercial and investment banks, including Korean banks, that were liquidating their Brazilian Brady bonds to raise funds following losses on their Korean holdings. While this channel for contagion may be at work, the Korean episode reminds us not to attribute its operation to hedge funds alone. Indeed, the fact that the risk management practices of most major investment banks leads them to cut positions across the board after they have suffered losses causes them to behave very similarly to hedge funds in this respect.

The second concern is whether hedge fund operations can threaten systemic stability. Some who subscribe to this view cite the exposure of leading international banks and securities firms to LTCM, which understandably raised a red flag about the riskiness of banks' and securities firms' investments in and loans to the hedge fund industry as a whole. Regulators also worried that forcing LTCM to unwind its positions would precipitate large movements in the prices of US government securities and associated derivatives, causing distress for others with positions in those same markets.[16]

Before drawing sweeping conclusions regarding systemic risk, it is worth asking how likely these events are to recur. Inevitably, outsiders are at a disadvantage in attempting to put the events at LTCM in context. (One might say that they suffer from the same informational disadvantage as the regulators!) Still, it is useful to see how far the available information permits us to go.

LTCM started trading in 1994 as a relative-value fund with a glittering cast of Wall Street veterans, Nobel Laureates, and MIT Ph.D's. From its inception it pursued both fixed-income and equity relative-value investment opportunities, utilizing both model-based techniques and market intelligence. Its portfolio was dominated by US treasury securities and related derivatives. The market in US treasuries being relatively efficient, price discrepancies were small. To attain an attractive return on capital, the firm consequently needed large amounts of credit, which it obtained via collateralized credits provided by counterparties in markets for stocks, bonds and derivative instruments and uncollateralized credit lines extended by a syndicate of international banks.[17] Its access to unsecured credit lines appears to have been exceptional, a fact which is now explained by referring to the sterling reputation of its partners and the low risk that was therefore presumed to be attached to its portfolio.

Although LTCM produced admirable returns in its early years (43 per cent in 1995 and 41 per cent in 1996, after fees), its return on capital declined in 1997 (to 17 per cent). A simple explanation is that the firm's very success lured competitors into the field.[18] This increased the difficulty of keeping the fund's capital profitably invested and of maintaining the rates of return to which shareholders had grown accustomed. Management responded by returning roughly half of the fund's capital to investors on December 31st, 1997 (taking a larger share for itself, and therefore keeping management's incentives properly aligned) and diversifying into new investments.

Many of these investments were predicated on the assumption of falling liquidity premiums. LTCM bought assets with below-average liquidity and sold assets with above-average liquidity, ideally with both sides of the strategy having the same credit quality. Since the two sides of the trade would differ only in their liquidity characteristics (i.e., they would pay equal and offsetting cash flows), pricing discrepancies could be captured if the positions could be held until maturity. In 1998 this was not the case. The fallout from Russia's default caused the price of liquidity to skyrocket, and LTCM ran out of equity capital and was unable to hold onto the positions. There may have been good reasons for believing that the underlying strategy was sound (LTCM's subsequent return to profitability provides some vindication of this view), but this was cold comfort to a highly-levered hedge fund that suddenly found itself lacking the money to pay the mark to market.

LTCM's rescue is controversial. The Federal Reserve Bank of New York brought together 14 of the firm's principal institutional creditors, who agreed to inject $3.6 billion in return for 90 per cent ownership. Federal Reserve officials were concerned for the stability of the financial system, as noted above, not for the survival of LTCM *per se*. But they worried that placing the firm into receivership and forcing it to liquidate its positions might add to the volatility of already volatile financial markets. Had LTCM been forced to file for bankruptcy protection, repurchase and reverse repurchase agreements containing acceleration clauses would have permitted its creditors immediately to sell the collateral securing those repos and swaps.[19]

The Fed's actions are said to have created moral hazard.[20] The knowledge that it was prepared to arrange a meeting of the firm's creditors, it is alleged, allowed LTCM's partners to reject a competing proposal (by Warren Buffet and Maurice Greenberg) that would have wiped out 100 per cent of their stake.[21] The Fed thus missed the chance to teach a painful lesson.

While the moral-hazard argument cannot be dismissed, it is hard to lend it too much credence, given that the partners in LTCM still lost 90 per cent of their investment.[22] Beyond that, there is the fact that the Fed put up no money of its own. Its effort to facilitate a lifeboat operation in which other financial institutions took over the portfolio and operations of a fundamentally-sound financial institution has precedents stretching back to the (first) Baring Crisis. It is not clear that this operation could have been arranged without Fed help; not only were there free-rider problems, but commercial and investment banks that otherwise might have been prepared to collaborate in LTCM's rescue required assurances that they would not be subject to legal action for having shared information.

Counterparties now appear to have tightened up their extension of credit to hedge funds and to have begun demanding more information on their positions, leverage and investment strategies. Whether this new vigour is permanent or lenders will again find it irresistible to hand over very large amounts of cash on terms that are less than prudential to the next set of high-powered theorists who come along with a novel investment strategy is, of course, impossible to say.

The ultimate unanswerable question is whether this episode was *sui generis*, in which case the moral-hazard concern is essentially a red herring – along, perhaps, with concerns for systemic stability themselves – or whether there is a real danger of similar problems recurring. The argument that the episode was unique rests on the unusual attributes of both LTCM and global market conditions. The firm had a larger portfolio than any other hedge fund. It enjoyed access to unsecured bank credit lines, exceptionally for a hedge fund, as a result of its partners' sterling reputation. At the same time, it is implausible to think that the extraordinary conjuncture of events that caused risk premiums to explode in August of 1998 will occur again. That said, with the growth of the hedge fund industry, there will be other large limited partnerships making heavy use of leverage; and it is not hard to imagine that they might be hit by some other, different, but equally devastating shock. The safest conclusion is probably that while history repeats itself, it never repeats itself in precisely the same way. Systemic stability should be a concern, although regulators should be careful not to extrapolate mechanically future threats from past experience.

Implications for regulatory policy

Before arguing for tighter control of hedge fund operations, it is important to recall the justification for regulating financial markets. The three conventional rationales are consumer protection, market integrity and systemic stability. The dilemma in the context of hedge funds is that strengthening measures in one area may be counterproductive for the others.

Consumer protection

The long-standing view of legislators and regulators (implicit in the US Investment Company Act of 1940, for example) is that there is no need to regulate hedge funds on consumer protection grounds, since their high-income shareholders can fend for themselves. LTCM, for example, required a minimum investment of $10 million. To be sure, when the extent of its difficulties was revealed, some investors complained that they had not been provided adequate information, warning of impending difficulties, or opportunity to comment on takeover plans. To some extent, such problems are unavoidable: a hedge fund will hesitate to reveal its difficulties to its shareholders for fear that news of its distress will leak to the markets, with adverse consequences as other investors react.[23] Similarly, it is difficult to give 499 shareholders the opportunity to comment on a takeover plan when the goal is quick action that avoids the need to appeal to the bankruptcy court or to liquidate the portfolio. But these are risks with which high-income investors, who allocate only a fraction of their investment portfolios to hedge funds, can presumably cope.

The LTCM episode does point up the question of whether institutional investors, some of whom took large losses, require additional protection through, *inter alia*, requirements for hedge funds to disclose further information about their financial condition. The argument is that counterparties did not have adequate information on LTCM's investments, leverage, or exposure to market risk. The firm provided them with monthly information on net asset value; quarterly balance-sheet information on debt, equity, total liabilities, total assets and leverage; and annual financial statements including audited balance sheets and off-balance-sheet information on both contractual and derivative obligations. But in today's fast moving markets, annual or even quarter information on these magnitudes may not be enough.[24] And in any case, individual positions were not disclosed.

A problem with this argument is that banks are already required to do due diligence (which means, in the present context, analyzing offering circulars, private placement memoranda, partnership agreements, performance history, liquidity, on- and off-balance sheet leverage, risk management, and front and back office operations). They can demand to inspect the books of an entity to which they lend at any time, and at any frequency, as a condition for extending credit. Management is responsible for protecting itself, and shareholders can apply the relevant sanctions where its diligence falls short. And if market discipline is inadequate, supervisors already have the authority to scrutinize the adequacy of the banks' due diligence and to initiate discussions with and seek corrective commitments from management when substandard practices are detected.

Moreover, stronger incentives for shareholders and creditors in particular to demand more information on hedge funds' positions, trades and investment strategies may be counterproductive from the viewpoint of market integrity, since it could encourage front-running. I turn to this problem next.

Market integrity

Outside the United States, the key question is whether hedge funds collude, corner or manipulate markets. The same market-integrity arguments governments use to demand information about possible collusive practices in other markets (the case of Archer-Daniels-Midland springs to mind) can be invoked to justify regulations requiring financial-market participants to provide information about their trades and positions. In the United States, the Large Trade and Position Reporting System (LTPRS) operated by the CFTC is justified on these grounds. The LTPRS requires entities with foreign exchange futures positions in excess of $50 million to report these to the CFTC. At present, the US system mandates reporting of positions in five currencies.

To address the concerns of emerging markets, such reporting would have to be extended to other currencies, and the threshold above which positions had to be reported would have to be lowered. Reporting would have to apply not only to exchange-traded products like futures but also to products traded over the counter like forwards.[25] Above all, it would be necessary to establish reporting requirements like those operated by the CFTC in other national markets. Given the high mobility of the foreign exchange market, an effective reporting system would have to embrace all the leading financial centres. And national authorities would have to share the information they obtained, given the ease with which market participants can split their transactions between markets.[26]

Even then, large trade and position reporting will not suffice to determine the existence of collusion. Similar positions are not necessarily signs of collusion; they may just be independent responses to the same information.

Interpretation requires the authorities to supplement LTPRS data with other information. The argument for LTPRS is then weaker. It becomes that while such information is only one input into the process of protecting market integrity, this knowledge plus fear of detection will still discourage those who might otherwise be tempted to collude.

Another threat to market integrity is front running by creditors and counterparties. Recall the allegation that LTCM's counterparties sold into the markets in which it was known to have positions in anticipation of its need to raise liquidity, which is said to have unjustifiably aggravated that firm's financial difficulties. It is alleged that information about LTCM's trades and positions flowed from the credit departments and agency sales traders of the commercial banks to those same banks' position traders, who had an incentive to front run.

It is not clear what can be done about this problem so long as hedge funds continue to rely on investment banks for information about market conditions and to place their trades. Hedge funds, like other clients, obtain information on market prices from sales traders in investment banks, who get the price quotes from their dealers, who in turn become the counterparties to the trades. Dealers, however, are also position traders – as counterparties they necessarily take positions and run their proprietary books. Because dealers are both counterparties and position traders, they have an incentive to infer the positions being built up by their clients and to position themselves to exploit them. Since position traders and sales traders must talk to one another, the latter providing the price quotes to the former, there is no easy way around the problem. Higher Chinese Walls can help insofar as front running results from information spillovers from credit departments to dealers, but not insofar as the dealers are themselves necessarily the counterparties to hedge fund trades. Greater reliance on anonymous electronic trading – and less reliance on sales traders for information and position traders for their deals – is likely to be the only way for hedge funds and other large counterparties to protect themselves from front running. But it is available only in assets where exchange-based trading is well advanced.

Systemic stability

Because private risk management is not always optimal – especially when financial institutions are sheltered from the adverse consequences of their decisions by the financial safety net – and because individual banks do not have incentives to internalize fully the systemic implications of their actions, there is a role for supervisors concerned with systemic stability to monitor exposures and demand corrective action. The steps that need to be taken are well known and the problem is by no means peculiar to the business that banks do with hedge funds.[27] But the LTCM episode raises questions about whether supervision of banks doing business with hedge funds, and possibly of hedge funds themselves, requires special attention.

It has been suggested that a more extensive system of large trade and position reporting would be desirable from the viewpoint of systemic stability. Frankly, it is hard to see why. Hedge funds like LTCM spread their positions over many different assets and markets; for the regulators to gauge effectively the implications for systemic stability, they would have to be able to stress test the entire portfolio. Large trades and positions would not be enough; the regulators would have to know the hedge fund's entire balance sheet. And any attempt to apply this kind of comprehensive disclosure requirement would only drive the more hedge funds offshore.

In addition, no one regulator will know the exposure of financial intermediaries as a whole to hedge funds that obtain credit from banks in different countries. This was a problem with LTCM, where even if US regulators knew the exposure of US banks and Swiss regulators knew the exposure of Swiss banks, they did not know the exposure of one another's banks and therefore of the financial system as a whole.[28] This too is a generic problem – it applies to other large borrowers as well as hedge funds – and there is a generic solution: bank supervisors should systematically share information as recommended by, *inter alia*, the Core Principles for Banking Supervision of the Basle Committee. Hedge funds are different from other borrowers in this respect only insofar as they tend to be highly leveraged, so that when things go wrong, they go very wrong.

One idea, tabled by US and German regulators (and resisted by their other European counterparts), is to establish a clearing house or credit registry to assemble information from different countries on the borrowings of highly leveraged institutions.[29] To be sure, assembling such figures might create a spurious sense that regulators really know the exposure of the regulated to hedge-fund counterparties (in derivatives, for example) where in fact they do not. It might create moral hazard if lenders thought that the authorities, as a result of operating the clearing house, felt obliged to run to the rescue of investment banks and others providing information.[30] But moral hazard for counterparties and the danger of overestimating the accuracy of information on the industry already exist, and it is not clear that an international registry would aggravate either problem significantly.

It has been suggested that the danger that excessive risk taking by the borrower could create problems for its lenders could be addressed by raising capital risk weights on bank lending to hedge funds and by applying capital surcharges on bank lending to entities not providing their counterparties with information on their trades and positions. But banks have proven themselves adept at regulatory arbitrage, shifting assets subject to high capital charges off balance sheet through securitization without modifying their underlying positions. Surely an attempt to make lending to hedge funds more expensive by imposing differential capital charges would elicit just such a response (particularly in light of some hedge funds' heavy utilization of derivative instruments and off-balance-sheet transactions).

The risk that distress sales by a major hedge fund might destabilize securities markets might be addressed by raising margin requirements on exchange-traded products, including exchange-traded derivatives, which would further limit the ability of hedge funds and other investors to lever their capital. To be effective, however, this would have to be coordinated internationally. Many of the same securities are traded in multiple markets. While the Federal Reserve's Regulation T requires purchasers to put up 50 per cent of the cost when they buy stocks on margin, it can be easily circumvented by channelling business to offshore prime brokerage affiliates like Goldman Sachs's and Morgan Stanley's London prime brokerage offices.[31] And the willingness to cooperate of the relevant exchanges, many of which are private, for-profit organizations, should not be assumed. The business of exchange-traded derivatives is fiercely competitive: witness the life-and-death battles between Chicago, London and Frankfurt.

In any case, the vast majority of derivatives are traded over the counter rather than on organized exchanges and are therefore not subject to margin requirements. Indeed, the OTC market would swamp exchange-traded products to an even greater extent if margin requirements were raised on the latter. In the absence of formal requirements, one must hope for voluntary action. The recent agreement by 12 leading international banks, together with senior U.S. government officials including the chairman of the Securities and Exchange Commission, to set voluntary guidelines for the extension of credit to participants in derivatives markets, is a step in this direction.[32] But what is in the collective interest of the group is not necessarily in the self interest of each individual institution, which has an incentive to chisel on the agreement. And the very fact that 12 leading banks have agreed to increase the cost of credit for certain derivatives-related transactions will create an incentive for other banks to enter the market.

At a more fundamental level, raising the cost of all derivative transactions is a rather indirect way of addressing the problem of lenders having insufficient knowledge or concern about their counterparties' use of leverage. Much of that leverage has nothing to do with derivatives *per se*. And clamping down on the derivatives market would interfere with the constructive risk-management uses of those instruments.

These doubts about the effectiveness of regulatory oversight and about the effects (and side effects) of capital and margin requirements lead many observers to conclude that there is no workable alternative to market discipline. Instead of fine-tuning capital requirements, regulators would be better advised to require their banks to issue unguaranteed subordinated debt, which would work to strengthen their own creditors' oversight of bank risk-management practices. Banks will then have stronger incentives to assemble and use information on the financial condition of their hedge-fund counterparties and to deal with them in a way that maximizes the economic value of the relationship.

This is not the place to rehearse the arguments for and against subordinated debt. Questions can be raised about the vigour and effectiveness of market discipline, even when market participants, like holders of subordinated debt, stand to lose from excessive risk taking but not gain from excess returns. It is also possible to question the assumption – for ultimately it is only an assumption – that subordinated debt would be unguaranteed. Note, however, the following implication. Relying for a solution to the hedge fund problem on risk management by bank counterparties presumably requires making full use of the information flows into and within the counterparty institution. It requires pooling the information resources of the trading and credit departments of the banks. How otherwise could the bank prudently manage the risk confronting the institution as a whole? An LTCM-like situation where it is in the interest of the proprietary trading desk but not the counterparty institution as a whole to front run a hedge fund in distress is to be avoided by breaking down the Chinese Walls between the two departments within the bank. But what is desirable from a systemic-stability point of view is undesirable for market integrity. In a world where banks can act as lenders to hedge funds but also engage in hedge-fund-like activities of their own, there may be a conflict between these goals. Narrow banking is a solution, but not one that is likely to receive much political support in an era when regulatory reform is moving in precisely the opposite direction.

Are the official assesments adequate?

Several official bodies, led by the Basle Committee and a U.S. government task force, have considered the implications of hedge fund operations for regulatory policy. But are their assessments adequate?

The Brockmeijer Group

First off the mark was the Basle Committee on Banking Supervision Working Group (or the Brockmeijer Group – see BIS 1999), which focused on systemic stability. It criticized the banks for failing to adequately assess LTCM's creditworthiness and for relying on collateral in the form of government securities.[33] As its report points out, the value of many of these securities fell sharply with the flight to quality, leaving collateral in practice worth less than collateral on paper.[34] In addition, there were delays in identifying the need for additional margin and in rebalancing positions in rapidly moving markets.[35]

Many of the committee's recommendations are uncontroversial: banks should improve their procedures for assessing the risks of lending to hedge funds, stress test their balance sheets, and impose firm-wide credit limits on lending to individual hedge funds. They should stay in touch with highly-leveraged institutions on a 'timely and ongoing basis.'[36] The report echoes the risk management guidelines issued by the Committee of Banking

Supervisors in 1995 for assessing risk to counterparties in over-the-counter derivatives markets.[37] Banks are again urged to develop more useful measures of potential future exposure that provide a meaningful estimate of the extent of a bank's involvement with such counterparties, allow them to convert derivatives contracts into loan equivalent amounts, and permit them to aggregate counterparty credit exposures across products and instruments.

More controversially, the report recommends that different departments within an institution should take into account one another's exposures *vis-à-vis* their hedge fund customers. As already noted, this idea has merit from the viewpoint of systemic stability, the Basle Committee's bread and butter, but has worrisome implications for market integrity. It is not likely to appeal to the emerging markets to which the BIS is currently reaching out.

The president's working group on financial markets

A second report was issued in April 1999 by an interagency task force consisting of senior staff of the US Treasury, Federal Reserve, Securities and Exchange Commission, and Commodity Futures Trading Commission. While it, like the Brockmeijer Report, emphasizes that responsibility for preventing excessive risk rests first and foremost with hedge fund shareholders and counterparties, it warns that market discipline tends to weaken in good times. In addition to a variety of BIS-like recommendations, the report concludes that hedge funds should be required to disclose more frequent and detailed information on their operations. Specifically, it recommends that hedge funds registered as Commodity Pool Operators and therefore required to report to the CFTC should be made to file more comprehensive reports on a quarterly rather than an annual basis and that this information should be made public. Funds that are not registered as CPOs should be required to disclose similar financial information, presumably also on a quarterly basis.[38] Financial institutions, for their part, should be required to disclose a summary of their exposure to hedge fund counterparties.

Serious questions can be raised about these recommendations. First, will quarterly reports be a significant improvement over annual reports, given the speed with which hedge funds put on and take off positions and conditions in world markets change? Would a report for the second quarter of 1998, made available to the public in the third quarter, have provided significant advance warning of the difficulties of LTCM and have invigorated the operation of market discipline? This seems unlikely.

Second, mandating additional disclosure may lead hedge funds that regard the requirement as onerous to relocate to offshore jurisdictions. The task force therefore recommends that offshore financial centres should adopt and comply with internationally-agreed upon standards for disclosure and prudential supervision. Recommend it can, but in the absence of specific actions the problem of offshore financial centres and tax havens will not go away.

This realization presumably was what prompted the task force to recommend that regulators attach higher capital requirements to banks doing business with financial entities offshore. But whether this capital-based approach would be circumvented by regulatory arbitrage is not addressed. In any case, the real issue is not differential charges for on- and offshore entities but differential charges for entities that do and do not disclose information to their counterparties.

Above all, there is the question of whether there is justification for *public* disclosure, as recommended in the report. The task force appears to believe that public disclosure will strengthen market discipline on hedge-fund counterparties (as opposed to hedge funds themselves, on which few members of the public hold claims). Not only is the route circuitous, but the recommendation runs the risk of driving hedge funds, asked to reveal proprietary information, further offshore.[39] One is reminded of Chairman Greenspan's remark that 'most hedge funds are only a short step from cyberspace.'[40]

Conclusion

Hedge funds are here to stay, reflecting the growth of a clientele of high-income investors seeking to diversify their portfolios to include high-risk, high-return elements. So long as the demand exists, attempts to suppress hedge-fund-like investment vehicles in one place will only cause them to pop up in another.

Some modest steps can be taken to address the challenges they pose for public policy. Expanding the coverage of the US Large Trade and Position Reporting System and establishing analogous reporting mechanisms in other countries where they do not exist would provide information to officials concerned about the implications for market integrity of the existence of small numbers of large investors. Obliging them to report their trades would cause hedge funds and other market participants tempted to collude to think twice. But more heavy-handed regulation is unlikely to succeed. It would have to be universal, since hedge funds are mobile. It would have to be applied by tax havens and offshore financial centres.

This means that emerging markets at risk from hedge-fund operations have to protect themselves. Self protection means adopting more flexible exchange rates as a way of removing the one-way bets that hedge funds find so irresistible (or, alternatively, going all the way to dollarization as a way of eliminating the scope for a speculative 'double play'), and placing holding period taxes on foreign investment (the kind of system that Chile has long had in place and to which Malaysia has now begun to turn) to increase the cost of getting in and out of domestic markets. But while such measures will help, they provide no guarantee of insulation from pressures from hedge funds and other market participants. Nor, of course, should they.

Regulators are responsible for seeing that banks and other credit providers stay on top of the operations of their hedge-fund customers. They should continue to scrutinize these functions in the course of the normal surveillance process. In addition, regulators should more systematically share information on the exposure of the intermediaries for which they are responsible. To this end, the idea of a clearing house or credit registry to assemble information from national sources should be revived.

Attempts at more heavy-handed regulation are likely to be frustrated, and not only by the mobility of hedge funds themselves. Raising capital requirements for banks lending to highly-leveraged customers, requiring more margin on exchange-traded products, and adopting standards for the extension of credit to participants in derivatives markets are likely to be frustrated by regulatory arbitrage, the growth of over-the-counter transactions, and the difficulty of enforcing any informal agreement governing the extension of credit for derivatives transactions. This creates is a danger that, having made such changes, policy makers will sit back in the erroneous belief that they have made the world a significantly safer financial place.

Notes

1. This chapter previously appeared in *International Finance*, vol. 2, no. 3, November 1999, and is reprinted here with the permission of Blackwell Publishers. An earlier version was prepared for the Institute for Developing Economies and presented at a symposium in Tokyo on 22–23 March 1999. The analysis builds on my previous work on the subject, including an Occasional Paper published by the International Monetary Fund (Eichengreen *et al.*, 1998). I thank Benn Steil, Adam Posen, Lee Hennessee, Charles Calomiris, Alberto Giovannini, Daniel Gros, David Modest, Joseph Yam and two anonymous referees for *International Finance* for helpful comments, and seminar participants at IDE for their reactions. The usual disclaimer – that any views expressed here are not necessarily shared by these commentators – applies with special force. The Ford Foundation provided partial financial support through the Berkeley Project on New International Financial Architecture.
2. Thus, while MAR/Hedge estimates there to have been 1,115 hedge funds with $109 billion capital under management at the end of 1997, Van Hedge Fund Advisors estimates there to have been 5,500 funds with a capital of $295 billion.
3. Reinforcing this point, there is the fact that only a fraction of hedge fund capital is devoted to activities in emerging markets. The best estimates suggest that roughly a third, circa the end of 1997, was in the hands of the 'macro' funds that take positions in emerging as well as advanced-industrial-country markets, and that only a fraction of that third was devoted to emerging-market investments.
4. This is, of course, the category in which LTCM is traditionally placed. This suggests that some hedge funds with exceptionally high investment to capital ratios may be lurking in the survey returns reported in high-leverage column of Table 10.2. LTCM normally leveraged its capital 20 to 30 times; the much higher ratios circa September 1998 that were reported in the press reflected the extraordinary losses of capital following Russia's default. US Government (1999) reports that

as of September 1998, it was aware, on the basis of CPO filings, of ten hedge funds (out of the population with capital exceeding $100 million) with on-balance-sheet leverage of more than ten to one, and one hedge fund with leverage of more than 30 to one. Unpublished data from Hennessee Associates suggests that 12 per cent of all hedge funds had leverage ratios greater than eight to one at the end of 1998, including 8 per cent of macro funds, 33 per cent of emerging market funds, 25 per cent of technology funds, and 71 per cent of distressed securities funds. I thank Lee Hennessee for this information.

5. Roach and Montgomery (1998), using a simulation methodology, estimate in contrast that industry-wide leverage is on the order of eight.

6. As reported in International Monetary Fund (1998). The five largest commercial bank holding companies had average leverage ratios of 14 to 1 at the end of 1998 according to US Government (1999).

7. As argued by Reserve Bank of Australia (1999), p. 5.

8. Hedge funds had presumably taken long positions on the dollar while shorting the yen and the DM and were forced to close out those positions when the market began to move against them, accounting for both the disappointing returns and the currency-market volatility.

9. 'Global' funds invest globally but attempt to pick individual stocks, while macro funds take positions in different markets on the basis of expectations of economy-wide conditions.

10. The fact that the authors find extremely large short positions in periods when their results do point in this direction lends substance to the critique. Thus, when estimated for the Malaysian ringgit, the model implies short positions in various recent periods of more than $200 billion, 2 2 times Malaysian GDP and a year's turnover in the foreign exchange market (Reserve Bank of Australia 1999, Attachment 2).

11. To be fair, the issue cannot be regarded as settled. For one thing, the CFTC data do not provide information on positions in emerging-market currencies. For another, they pertain to currency futures and not forward markets.

12. This paragraph draws on Armstrong *et al.* (1999).

13. Data for GDP growth point in the same direction, with a fall of some 6 per cent in the most recent year in Malaysia compared to 8 per cent in Thailand.

14. Thus, its intervention in the Hang Seng made the Hong Kong Monetary Authority the largest shareholder in the Hong Kong and Shanghai Bank, whose shares appreciated while those of other leading Hong Kong banks were falling sharply. The Monetary Authority's concentrated stake also raised difficult issues of how it should carry out its responsibility for corporate governance. Hale (1998) has suggested that governments could deal with this problem by setting up separate, independent agencies ('government hedge funds') to undertake this kind of contrary speculation.

15. A model of this mechanism is provided by Calvo (1999). Historically, returns on, say, Russian and Latin American government securities are imperfectly correlated; hence, holding a diversified portfolio including both is a way to limit the volatility of the return on the overall portfolio, a fact which may have encouraged hedge funds like LTCM to increase their positions in the sum of these markets. In the aftermath of Russia's default and the subsequent flight to quality, however, the historically low correlation between the returns on these different classes of assets no longer held. Losses on different components of the portfolio occurred simultaneously, heightening the need for institutional investors to liquidate

related holdings in order to raise capital. Again, however, the question is whether this tendency is particularly prevalent among hedge funds as opposed to other investors.

16. This fear was cited by the Chairman of the Federal Reserve Board and the President of the Federal Reserve Bank of New York as the rationale for Federal Reserve efforts to facilitate the private rescue and takeover of LTCM. See Greenspan (1998) and McDonough (1998).

17. Credit to hedge funds is typically collateralized by the securities that the hedge funds purchase with the funds thereby obtained. Banks apply haircuts to the securities taken as collateral, discounting them relative to current market value to account for the possibility that their price may have fallen by the time they are liquidated in response to the default of the counterparty. In addition, LTCM obtained unsecured credit lines for which no such collateral was required, although it is not clear that these were heavily drawn upon prior to the summer of 1998, when the firm was in serious financial stress. Estimates of LTCM's leverage range as high as that reported in Wolffe (1999), that it used less than $1 billion of capital to purchase the above-mentioned $120 billion of securities and derivatives with a notional value of $1.3 trillion. IMF (1998) reports that as of Tuesday, September 23rd, 1998, LTCM's capital had fallen to just $600 million, which still supported balance sheet positions in excess of $100 billion. That these figures are much higher than the leverage ratios of 20 to 30 noted in footnote 5 above indicates the extent to which LTCM's leverage was boosted by the loss-induced erosion of its capital. In any case, to the extent that some of these open positions were offsetting, such figures are spurious, although there are some who would argue that the gross positions are a better measure of counterparty risk. In fact, of course, neither gross nor net positions are an ideal measure of counterparty risk; ideally, one would want detailed information on the exposure of individual counterparties to the event of an LTCM default.

18. As additional resources were devoted to arbitraging price discrepancies between closely related US treasury securities, fewer such discrepancies remained. As Alan Greenspan put the point, 'it is the nature of the competitive process driving financial innovation that such techniques would be emulated, making it ever more difficult to find market anomalies that provided shareholders with a high return. Indeed, the very efficiencies that LTCM and its competitors brought to the overall financial system gradually reduced the opportunities for above-normal profits' (Greenspan 1998, p. 2).

19. Since derivatives are exempt from the automatic stay provision of the bankruptcy code. A valid question is whether the counterparties to these repurchase agreements would have dumped the securities on the market when they foreclosed and took possession. Mayer (1998) suggests not, since they didn't need the cash. But this neglects the distinction between collective action and individual action: the fear that other counterparties were prepared to dump their holdings may have strengthened the incentive for each individual counterparty to do so to beat the subsequent price fall, as Edwards (1999) also implies. In addition, it is important to recall that Russia's default and the subsequent flight to quality had already reduced the liquidity of other institutional investors and raised fears of a credit crunch.

20. While suggestions continue to circulate that the Fed did more than provide a conference room and a coffee machine (Edwards 1999), Chairman Greenspan has reiterated that 'no Federal Reserve funds were put at risk, no promises were made

by the Federal Reserve, and no individual firms were pressured to participate.' (Greenspan 1998, 1).

21. The 'allegation' part of this sentence is important, since there is a question of whether the Buffet-Greenberg offer was in fact valid (in the sense that it may have required LTCM to liquidate all outside investors on terms that may not have been legal).

22. Here it is important to distinguish between the losses of Long-Term Capital's partners, which were diluted by 90 per cent, and the assets of the management company itself, which were essentially wiped out.

23. Thus, when on 2 September 1998, LTCM sent its investors a letter announcing 52 per cent losses in the first eight months of the year, the contents became widely known, allegedly leading other investors to sell into the markets into which LTCM was long, an anticipation of the latter's fire sale, compounding the difficulties of the fund.

24. In addition, LTCM made its principals available to creditors with other questions, and made occasional presentations to all creditors to update them on developments affecting the fund. There is still a question, of course, of whether this substitutes adequately for high-frequency balance-sheet information.

25. This appears to be the preferred approach of Japanese officials (Feldman 1998).

26. This may not be as easy as it sounds. For example, the Counterparty Risk Management Policy Group has expressed concern about the obligation of counterparties and regulators to respect client confidentiality and potential legal obstacles to sharing regulatory information. Sharing would require a very high degree of policy commitment at the international level as well as effective cooperation by the private sector.

27. See Basle Committee on Banking Regulation and Supervision (1998) and Folkerts-Landau and Lindgren (1998). The challenges posed by hedge funds are not unique, that is, aside from the fact that their especially heavy use of derivative financial instruments compounds problems of information and evaluation for bank management and supervisors alike.

28. Graham (1999) argues that this was true of banks as well as regulators.

29. National supervisors could collect information on the exposure to such institutions of their banks and report these to an international registry. The procedure would not be unlike that which underlies the quarterly figures on international banks' cross-board exposures already collected and published by the BIS or the triennial survey of derivatives, transactions recently inaugurated by that same institution.

30. In addition there are the legal, administrative and political obstacles to effective information sharing.

31. In addition, there is the possibility of the prime broker and the hedge fund setting up an unregistered joint back office, in which the hedge fund takes part ownership in the separately established broker dealer, which is itself exempt from Regulation T.

32. See Corrigan and Thieke (1999).

33. 'In some cases, competitive forces and the desire to conduct business with certain counterparties may have led banks to make exceptions to their firm-wide credit standards' (BIS 1999, p. 1 of preface). A more revealing sentence later in the report (p. 5) states, 'However, a bank should not grant credit solely because the counterparty, or key members of its management, are familiar to the bank or are perceived to be highly reputable.'

34. 'Full collateralization of mark-to-market positions does not eliminate exposure to secondary risks such as declines in the value of securities pledged as collateral

from a volatile market environment that could follow the default or disorderly liquidation of a major HLI [highly-leveraged institution]' (p. 5).
35. Margin on collateral tends to be called the day after the position has been marked to market (Celarier 1998).
36. Since the unusual flexibility enjoyed by their management permit radical changes ins trading activities and investment strategies (a lesson from the late days of LTCM).
37. Bank for International Settlements (1994).
38. This would require Congress to enact legislation requiring this and setting up a mechanism for disclosure.
39. Presumably in response to this problem, the task force suggests that disclosure statements could concentrate on measures of value at risk (VAR) and stress-test results. Requiring the publication of VAR results but not the proprietary information on trades and positions on which they are based is presumably intended to avoid driving hedge funds offshore. Given the exceptional mobility of hedge funds, however, the result remains to be seen. The publication of stress tests, for its part, is presumably intended to enable market participants and regulators to predict future problems from past behaviour. Given the limitations of existing stress tests and VAR models, it similarly remains to be seen how effective this approach would be.
40. Greenspan (1998), p. 6.
41. Hedge funds also have as shareholders pension funds, university endowments, and corporate clients (for whom they invest corporate cash), which must meet additional criteria in order to be accredited. These alternative sources of capital are important; for example, among the macro funds that have been so controversial of late, these other sources of capital combined are more important than that contributed by individual investors (Hennessee Group 1998).

References

Armstrong, A., M. Spencer, S. Lin, S. Sanyal and A. Wong (1999) 'Malaysia's Return to Normality', *Deutsche Bank Asia Economics Weekly*, vol. 29, pp. 2–4.
Bank for International Settlements (BIS) (1994) *Public Disclosure of Market and Credit Risks by Financial Intermediaries* (Basle: Bank for International Settlements).
Basle Committee on Banking Regulation and Supervision (1998) *Core Principles for Effective Banking Supervision* (Basle: Bank for International Settlements).
Basle Committee on Banking Regulation and Supervision (1999) *Sound Practices for Banks' Interactions with Highly Leveraged Institutions* (Basle: Bank for International Settlements).
Brown, S. J., W. N. Goetzmann and R. G. Ibbotson (1997) 'Offshore Hedge Funds: Survival and Performance 1989–1995', *NBER Working Paper*, no. 5909 (Cambridge, Mass.: NBER).
Brown, S. J., W. N. Goetzmann and J. Park (1998) 'Hedge Funds and the Asian Currency Crisis of 1997', *NBER Working Paper*, no. 6227 (Cambridge, Mass.: NBER).
Caldwell, T. (1995) 'Introduction: The Model for Superior Performance', in J. Lederman and R. Klein (eds), *Hedge Funds: Investment and Portfolio Strategies for the Institutional Investor* (New York: Irwin), pp. 1–17.
Calvo, G. (1999) 'The Asian Flu and the Russian Crisis', unpublished manuscript, University of Maryland.
Celarier, M. (1998) 'Collateral Damage', *Euromoney Online* (November). *http://www.emwl.com*.

Corrigan, E. G. and S. G. Thieke (1999) 'Testimony on Behalf of Counterparty Risk management Policy Group', Subcommittee on Capital Markets, Securities, and Government Sponsored Enterprises, Committee on Banking and Financial Services, US House of Representatives, 3 March, http:www.house.gov/banking/3399 coth.htm.

Edwards, F. R. (1999) 'Hedge Funds and the Collapse of Long-Term Capital Management', *Journal of Economic Perspectives*, vol. 13, pp. 189–210.

Eichengreen, B. and D. Mathieson, with B. Chadha, A. Jansen, L. Kodres and S. Sharma (1998) *Hedge Funds and Financial Market Dynamics*, Occasional Paper no.155 (Washington, DC: IMF.

Feldman, R. A. (1998) 'Agenda of the Japanese Policy Elite', *Global Economic Forum* (Morgan Stanley Dean Witter), 19 October, pp. 8–12.

Folkerts-Landau, D. and C.-J. Lindgren (1998) *Toward a Framework for Financial Stability* (Washington, DC: International Monetary Fund).

Graham, G. (1999) 'Call for Better Monitoring of Lending to Hedge Funds', *Financial Times*, 25 January, p. 2.

Greenspan, A. (1998)'Private-Sector Refinancing of the Large Hedge Fund, Long-Term Capital Management', Testimony of Chairman Alan Greenspan Before the Committee on Banking and Financial Services, U.S. House of Representatives (Washington, DC: Board of Governors of the Federal Reserve System, 1 October).

Hale, D. D. (1998) 'Will Malaysia and Hong Kong Change the Rules of the International Financial Game?', unpublished manuscript, Zurich Group.

Hennessee Group LLC (1998) *Annual Hennessee Hedge Fund Manager Survey* (New York: Hennessee Group).

International Monetary Fund (IMF) (1998) *Interim World Economic Outlook and International Capital Markets Report* (Washington, DC: IMF).

Kodres, L. E. and M. Pritsker (1997) 'Directionally-Similar Position Taking and Herding by Large Futures Market Participants', unpublished manuscript, International Monetary Fund and Board of Governors of the Federal Reserve System, Washington, DC.

Lewis, M. (1999) 'How the Eggheads Cracked', *New York Times Magazine*, 24 January.

Mayer, M. (1998) 'The Big Bailout', unpublished manuscript, The Brookings Institution, Washington, DC.

McDonough, W. J. (1998) 'Statement by William J. McDonough, President Federal Reserve Bank of New York Before the Committee on Banking and Financial Services U.S. House of Representatives', (New York: Federal Reserve Bank of New York, 1 October).

Reserve Bank of Australia (1999) 'The Impact of Hedge Funds on Financial Markets', paper submitted to House of Representatives Standing Committee on Economics, Finance and Public Administration's Inquiry into the International Financial Markets' Effects on Government Policy.

Roach, S. and J. Montgomery (1998) 'Hedge Funds – Scale, Scope and Impact', Morgan Stanley Dean Witter Equity Research Briefing Note (Morgan Stanley Dean Witter, 13 October).

United States Government (1999) *Hedge Funds, Leverage, and the Lessons of Long-Term Capital Management*, report of the President's Working Group on Financial Markets (Washington, DC: GPO).

Wolffe, R. (1998) 'Washington Plans Powers to Cut Hedge Fund Risks', *Financial Times*, 17 December, p. A15.

Yago, G., L. Ramesh and N. E. Hochman (1998) 'Hedge Funds and Systemic Risk Demystified', *Milken Institute Policy Brief* (Santa Monica, CA: Milken Institute).

Yam, J. (1999) 'Capital Flows, Hedge Funds and Market Failure: A Hong Kong Perspective', paper presented at the Reserve Bank of Australia Conference on Capital Flows and the International Monetary System, 9–10 August.

Part IV

Transition to a Market Economy

11
Market Creation in Transition Economies: Reconstruction of Production Linkages in Kazakhstan[1]

Koji Nishikimi

Introduction

Since the fall of the Berlin Wall in 1989 and the collapse of the Soviet Union in 1991, countries in Central and Southeastern Europe and the Baltics (CSB), as well as the Commonwealth of Independent States (CIS), have been struggling to create market economies, in contrast with the booming transitions in China and Vietnam, which will be discussed in the next chapter.[2] While the transition experiences of the CSB countries and the CIS have been similar in several aspects, the most striking similarity is the substantial magnitude of the drop in GDP (de Melo *et al.*, 1996; de Melo *et al.*, 1997; de Broeck and Koen, 2000; Campos and Coricelli, 2002; World Bank, 2002a). This fall took place immediately after the beginning of the transition and lasted three to six years in the CSB countries and four to ten years in the CIS. As a consequence these countries generally suffered from serious contractions of production and income in the 1990s, in sharp contrast with the perpetual double-digit growth in China and Vietnam. Indeed 21 of the 25 countries in question had lower GDPs in 1999 than in 1989; in the most serious cases, real GDP plummeted by more than 50 per cent during the decade (CIS Stat, 1996, 2000; EBRD, 2000; World Bank, 2002a).

Several causes of the fall in output have been studied to date. Of these, the disorganizational effect of economic liberalization has recently attracted considerable attention among researchers (Blanchard and Kremer, 1997; Blanchard, 1997; Konings and Walsh, 1999; Roland and Verdier, 1999; Marin and Schnitzer, 1999; Roland, 2000; Campos and Coricelli, 2002). In this view, input supply networks can be easily disrupted in circumstances where doubts beget doubts, which is likely in an economy that is full of uncertainty due to economic transition. Moreover this process is irreversible – that is, once distrust arises and prevails among the members of an economy, it persists. To return to smooth and normal transactions, people must make an enormous joint effort to accumulate the social capital needed to reestablish customs and institutions that are in harmony with the developing market system (World Bank, 2002b). In a traditional society, all these things are usually achieved over time in a recursive trial-and-error process.

When confronted with economy-wide disorganization, transition economies need to set up second-stage strategies to reconnect their disrupted production linkages. However there is no easy policy short-cut to this, only step-by-step efforts by individual producers and traders. Using the case of wheat farming in Kazakhstan as an example, this chapter examines how people in a transition economy try to reconstruct the broken nexus of input procurement for production. As will be discussed in detail later, Kazakhstan is a typical CIS economy in that total production and income decreased continuously during the 1990s. Wheat, which is one of its major export products, suffered a long-term fall in production and productivity, mainly due to the breakdown of production linkages. In the struggle to resolve the problem, not only farmers but also the government, traders and sometimes food manufacturers, have tried to establish a well-functioning input supply system to provide farmers with sufficient seed, fuel, fertilizer and spare parts for agricultural machinery, as well as the financial resources to purchase them. Reflecting the challenge to produce a better system, contract institutions and organizational structures for wheat production evolved during the 1990s. Some partially succeeded, others failed and quickly disappeared.

The remainder of this chapter is organized as follows. The next section looks at output falls in the transitional CSB and CIS economies and discusses the major causes of these falls. The third section provides an overview of the agricultural reforms in Kazakhstan and evaluates the productive performance of private wheat farms. The fourth section discusses how farms, including family farms and collectives, have tried to establish a reliable input supply system.

General aspects of the CSB and CIS transition economies

Output fall

Campos and Coricelli (2002) present seven stylized facts on the transition process in the CSB countries and the CIS: output fall, capital contraction, labour shift, trade reorientation, industrial structure change, institutional collapse and poverty increase.[3] Of these, output fall is the most striking and painful. Consequently it has sparked growing concern among policy makers and researchers.[4] Figure 11.1 shows the real GDP indexes of the CSB and CIS countries in the 1990s.[5] In the first years of transition all countries experienced a fall in production of 15–65 per cent. In the CSB group, the Czech Republic, Hungary, Poland, the Slovak Republic and Slovenia experienced relatively moderate falls (about 20 per cent) within three to four years. Croatia, Estonia, Lithuania, Macedonia and Latvia experienced contractions of 30–40 per cent, and in 1999 their GDP was lower than in 1989. Meanwhile

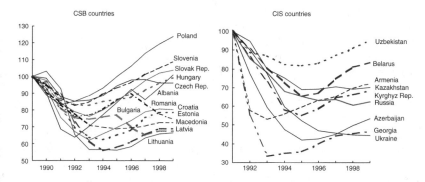

Figure 11.1 GDP index in the CSB and CIS countries, 1989–99
Sources: CIS Stat (1996, 2000); EBRD (2000)

the CIS countries, which began their transition two years after the CSB countries, experienced an even more tragic situation: most of them suffered 30–65 per cent falls, and in the severest cases production in 1999 was less than half that in 1989.[6]

Causes of the fall in output

The sudden collapse of output prompted a heated debate on its causes.[7] In the early days it was generally claimed that the fall in GDP was due to a decrease in consumer demand following the implementation of stabilization policies (see for example Lipton and Sachs, 1990; Blanchard *et al*. 1991; Berg and Sachs, 1992; Rosati, 1994). However the contraction was greater in both magnitude and duration than could be expected from a simple Keynesian recession. In addition several surveys have revealed that a large proportion of firms in the transition economies cited a shortage of materials as a major problem for their business (Windell *et al*., 1995; Blanchard and Kremer, 1997). As a result, in the latter half of the 1990s more attention was paid to supply-side problems, particularly the breakdown of production linkages (Blanchard and Kremer, 1997; Blanchard, 1997; Konings and Walsh, 1999; Roland and Verdier, 1999; Marin and Schnitzer, 1999; Roland, 2000; Campos and Coricelli, 2002).[8]

Blanchard and Kremer (1997) have developed a formal model of the production linkage breakdown. In their model the basic force of the disruption is distrust among producers (employers), workers and input suppliers.[9] Imagine, for example, that under a socialist regime ten engineering specialists in ten different technical fields are assigned to work at a steel mill. Their skills are assumed to be essential for steel production, so that production will decrease by a substantial magnitude, say 50 per cent, if any of them becomes unavailable. With the launching of a liberal market economy the engineers gain the freedom to work at any firm they want. Some of them may actually change their jobs if they receive better offers from other companies. However their decisions are made in very uncertain circumstances. On the one hand, since jobs are offered personally (as in most Western economies), individuals cannot know what offers have been made to the others. On the other hand, because of the complementarity in production, each engineer's productivity and income will depend on whether all the other engineers decide to stay on at the steel mill. In such a situation an individual may well accept a less than favourable offer if it seems probable that everybody else will leave the mill. Blanchard and Kremer show that, at equilibrium, the critical wage offer that makes each engineer indifferent to the choice of quitting or remaining can be much lower than that currently earned at the mill. This encourages essential production factors to move to less productive (lower income-yielding) sectors, resulting in a substantial fall in GDP.[10] The same mechanism applies, of course, to complementary inputs such as raw materials, energy, and other intermediate products. In either case, economic liberalization causes serious disruption of the input supply network.[11]

Wheat production in Kazakhstan during the transition

In this section we shall look at details of wheat production in Kazakhstan as a specific example of production linkage disruption during transition.[12] As briefly discussed in the introduction, Kazakhstan has suffered bitter experiences, including a substantial fall in GDP. Before delving further into the problem, we shall first look at the general features of agriculture in Kazakhstan. In 1997 the sector accounted for 11.3 per cent of GDP and 18.1 per cent of total employment. The main products are wheat (59.1 per cent of total cultivated land), barley (11.7 per cent), cotton, potatoes, vegetables and melons. Kazakh wheat is well known for its high protein content and 30–40 per cent of the yield is exported, the rest being consumed domestically as the staple food.[13] The northern provinces (Akmola, Kostanai, Pavlodar and North Kazakhstan) specialize in grain production, while the southern provinces (Almaty, Zhambul, Kzyl-orda and South Kazakhstan) produce cotton, vegetables, melons and sugar beet. Due to the lack of irrigation in the north, wheat production is highly dependent on there being sufficient rainfall.[14] In 1991, 1995 and 1998 Kazakhstan experienced three severe droughts each of which reduced the wheat yield to half that in an average year.[15]

Agricultural reforms in Kazakhstan

The reform of Kazakhstani agriculture has been carried out in the three strategic areas: farm restructuring, property right reforms and market liberalization.

Farm restructuring

Since the beginning of the transition the majority of *kolkhozes* (collective farms) and *sovkhozes* (state farms) have been broken up and converted into private farms. The total number of those Soviet-type farms fell from 2520 in 1990 to 1189 in 1994 and just 88 in 2000, while the number of private farms rose from 324 in 1990 to 25,219 in 1994 and 91,653 in 2000.[16] Thus about 97 per cent of agricultural land in Kazakhstan was privately farmed in 2000 (Agenstvo Respubliki Kazakhstan po statistike, 2000).

There are three categories of private farm in Kazakhstan: family farms, private agricultural enterprises (PAEs) and personal auxiliary plots (PAPs). Family farms are defined as those operated by a single family. Since the government of the Soviet Union experimentally permitted the establishment of such farms in 1989 the number has grown continuously. By 2000 there were 76,373 family farms occupying 4848 thousand hectares (29.9 per cent of total cultivated land). PAEs are farms that are collectively managed by multiple families in various organizational forms such as joint stock companies, partnerships and cooperatives. The size of PAEs varies widely, ranging from a handful of families farming a few hundred hectares of land to more than 100 families farming 30,000 hectares. In total PAEs account for 10,855 thousand hectares of land, or 67.0 per cent of total cultivated land in Kazakhstan. The third category of private farms, PAPs, are defined as farm production that is individually conducted by member families of PAEs. Production is usually carried out in kitchen gardens, the gardens of *dachas* (summer cottages) and collectively managed plots. In all cases the individuals concerned make all the decisions about and enjoy all the revenues from the PAP operations, so the latter are fully separated from the management of PAEs. In this sense they can be thought of as a form of family farm. Recently PAPs and family farms have come to dominate the markets for various agricultural products. Their share of vegetable, potato, melon, milk and meat production was above 90 per cent in 2000, though their share of wheat production was just 37 per cent.

Property rights

Private land ownership in Kazakhstan has not yet been established, so all agricultural land is still in the hands of the state.[17] Farmers are granted the right to use the land allotted to them for a maximum of 49 years free of charge. In addition they are able to buy the right to extra land. These rights can be handed down to their children and sold to others, as well as served as collateral. In this sense the usage right appears to be almost equivalent to a property right, but there is a special rule that creates a clear distinction between the two, that is, land use rights can be withdrawn by the local governor if the latter deems that the land is being used inappropriately. Farmers are in constant fear that their land will suddenly be confiscated, which discourages them from looking after it with a long-term view. Furthermore, since money lenders are aware of the threat of confiscation, farmers find it difficult to secure a loan against their right to the land even if their husbandry is appraised as excellent. To date the land use right has not significantly boosted the circumstances of individual farmers.

Market liberalization

By the mid 1990s the government had more or less completed the liberalization of markets for agricultural products and inputs, as well as foreign exchange, which has substantially affected the trading conditions open to farmers. Wheat is the only agricultural commodity for which the government procurement system has remained in force in the twenty-first century. However the share of government procurement in total production decreased to 29.0 per cent in 1991–95 and 6.8 per cent in 1996–97, and it is continuing to fall (Shevchik, 1998).

Production and productivity of private farms

Production and productivity trends

Figure 11.2(a) shows the production indexes of major crops in Kazakhstan in the 1990s. Each index is valued so that production equals 100 in 1991, and a five-year average is used to smooth out annual fluctuations due to weather conditions. During the period 1991–97 there was a general downward trend in the production of the six crops shown. In particular, sugar beet decreased by 70 per cent, wheat by 40 per cent and the other four crops by 20–30 per cent. This trend can be explained by the simultaneous fall in land productivity (Figure 11.2b) and cultivated land area. Productivity fell by 40–50 per cent for sugar beet and sunflower seed, 20–30 per cent for wheat and 10–20 per cent for potatoes, melons and vegetables. In the case of wheat, productivity fell to 520 kilogrammes per hectare, equivalent to the level in 1913

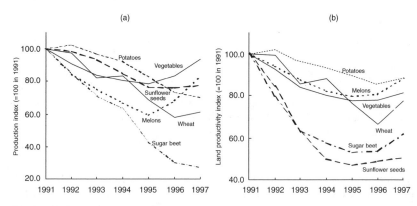

Figure 11.2 Agriculture in Kazakhstan: (a) production (five-year average); (b) land productivity (five-year average), 1991–97
Source: CIS Stat (1996); Agenstvo Respubliki Kazakhstan po statistike (1999, 2000).

(Shevchik, 1998). In general, therefore, agriculture in Kazakhstan has suffered since independence.

Farm productivity

We shall now examine the production efficiency of individual wheat farms. Table 11.1 shows the land productivity of wheat in PAEs and family farms. Although the average productivity shown in the last column fluctuated from year to year, largely due to weather, it shows a clear downward trend in the 1990s, as we also observed in Figure 11.2(b). The land productivity of PAEs and family farms does not appear to differ systematically, but this does not necessarily imply that the two groups of farms produce wheat in an identical way. In fact PAEs generally carry out much more extensive cultivation than family farms, which is likely to raise PAEs' productivity of inputs other than land and lower their land productivity. To evaluate the overall productivity of the two types of farm, therefore, we need also to look at factor inputs other than land, such as labour and machinery, but little information on such inputs is available in the official statistics of Kazakhstan. However we can look at data obtained from a small-scale survey conducted in Akmola province in 1996. Table 11.2 summarizes the main results of the survey. As can be seen, there was a large difference between the scale of operations of PAEs and family farms, that is, 4500 versus 134 hectares on average. With regard to land productivity, the values for Akmola were slightly higher than the national averages shown in Table 11.1. PAE yields were 815 kilogrammes of wheat per hectare of land, while family farms produced 756 kilogrammes per hectare. A much more striking contrast appears in labour productivity, which was almost twice as high in PAEs as it was in family farms.[18]

Does the fact that family farms were less productive than PAEs with respect to land and labour imply that they were absolutely inefficient? The answer

Table 11.1 Land productivity, wheat, Kazakhstan, 1985–2000 (tonnes per hectare)

	Private agricultural enterprises (PAEs)	Family farms	All farms
1985–89	0.91 (100.0)	–	0.91 (100.0)
1990	1.15 (100.0)	1.49 (0.0)	1.15 (100.0)
1995	0.52 (95.3)	0.43 (4.6)	0.52 (100.0)
1996	0.62 (90.4)	0.63 (9.6)	0.63 (100.0)
1997	0.85 (82.5)	0.83 (16.8)	0.84 (100.0)
1998	0.49 (72.1)	0.63 (27.0)	0.52 (100.0)
1999	1.29 (72.9)	1.27 (26.5)	1.29 (100.0)
2000	0.82 (63.0)	1.08 (36.2)	0.90 (100.0)

Note: Output shares (in per cent) are shown in parentheses.
source: CIS Stat (1996); Agenstvo Respubliki Kazakhstan po statistike (1998, 1999).

Table 11.2   Wheat production in Akmola province, 1996

	Private agricultural enterprises (PAEs)	Family farms
Number of sample farms	29	30
Area of wheat-growing land (hectares)	4,526.3	133.5
Land productivity (tonnes per hectare)	0.815	0.756
Labour productivity (tonnes per person)	67.6	34.3
Land–labour ratio (hectares per person)	81.4	45.0
Fuel consumption (litres per hectare)	70.1	48.7
TFP (average = 100)	104.0	96.1

Source: Nishikimi (1998).

is no, because they intensively used those inputs in order to save on the use of machinery. Tractors and combines are, of course, essential inputs in large-scale wheat farming. But in Kazakhstan farmers generally use very old Soviet machines such as the Enisei 120, which are prone to breaking down and hence are in constant need of maintenance and expensive spare parts. In the 1990s especially it was quite difficult, regardless of the type of farm, to raise sufficient funds to buy spare parts. However the PAEs were able to use their many in operable machines as sources of spare parts for a limited number of working machines. Family farms could not do this as they had only a few tractors and combines, and therefore had to restrict their use of machinery. This is reflected in fuel consumption (Table 11.2), which on average was 44 per cent less in family farms than in PAEs. In other words, if we measure machinery service using the proxy of fuel consumption, productivity was 1.4 times higher in family farms than in PAEs.

The above fact suggests that the productivity differences were partly the result of factor substitutions in wheat production rather than the technical superiority (or inferiority) of either group of farms. To examine the productivity difference between family farms and PAEs more closely it is necessary to measure the total factor productivity (TFP) of each farm. TFP is a measure of technical efficiency and is defined as the fraction of output change that cannot be explained by changes in inputs.[19] It is regularly applied to the analysis called growth accounting, in which TFP accounts for the productivity change along the time axis, that is, in comparison with base year production. In such applications TFP is usually interpreted as reflecting the effects of changes in technologies, labour skills, institutions and so on, but in our analysis we shall calculate the TFP of each farm at the same point in time (1996) by comparing it with a benchmark farm instead of a benchmark year. Accordingly our TFP measures the technical efficiency of each farm relative to a standard farm in Akmola province.

In our calculation of the TFP of the individual farms in the 1996 survey, land, labour and fuel consumption (the proxy for machinery use) were treated as production factors. The results show that the average TFP of PAEs was about 8 per cent higher than that of family farms, that is, 104.0 for PAEs and 96.1 for family farms.[20] However if we look more carefully at TFP in relation to farm size we find some interesting features in terms of distribution. Figure 11.3 plots the TFP of wheat production against the wheat-growing area of each farm. When farms of similar size (about 100–500 hectares) are compared, most family farms appear to have been more productive than PAEs. Furthermore family farms cultivating about 300 hectares fall into in the highest TFP group. The second point to be noted is that family farms exhibit a clear tendency towards economies of scale, in that the TFPs of farms with 300 hectares of land are about three times higher than those with 10 hectares. In contrast there is no significant correlation between size and TFP in the case of PAEs.[21]

That there were economies of scale in family farms sounds reasonable considering the nature of wheat production, with cultivation taking place in

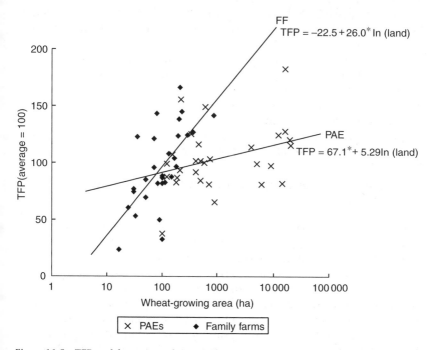

Figure 11.3 TFP and farm size, wheat production, 1996
* Significant at the 1 per cent level.
Source: Nishikimi (1998).

large swathes of land and reliance on large Soviet-type machinery. However, if the economies of scale were the result of the technical nature of wheat production, why were they seemingly absent from PAEs? The probable reason is diseconomies of scale in farm management. As discussed earlier, PAEs comprise multiple families, and in extreme cases more than 100 families work together. Given their limited monitoring capacity, it would have been difficult for those involved in large farms to prevent member families from free riding, which would have had a serious effect on the organizational efficiency of the farms. Consequently in PAEs the technical economies of scale were probably cancelled out by organizational diseconomies of scale.

While the production data show that family farms with approximately 300 hectares were the most efficient wheat producers in 1996, those farms have never dominated wheat market. In fact, in 2000 about 70 per cent of the total wheat-growing land was still farmed by collectives (Agenstvo Respubliki Kazakhstan po statistike, 2000).[22] Why do not individual member families of giant PAEs become independent in order fully to exploit technical economies of scale? Why do small family farms never turn to large-scale cultivation in order to become more productive and profitable? In both cases the main obstacle is input procurement. While most farms in the north are, to varying degrees, hindered by a shortage of working capital, the problem tends to be more serious among family farms, which have insufficient machinery or livestock to serve as collateral.[23] Those farms have often faced the start of the growing season without essential inputs such as seed, fuel and fertilizer, especially in the early 1990s. In addition, as discussed above, the antiquity of the agricultural machinery discourages individual farming families from breaking away from their PAEs, where spare parts can be obtained from a large stock of broken equipment. In general the immaturity of the input and credit markets tends to have a more severe effect on family farms than on PAEs, inhibiting the decollectivization of wheat farms in Kazakhstan.[24]

The institutional and organizational evolution of input procurement

When the Soviet input supply systems collapsed at the beginning of the transition, private suppliers were not immediately able to substitute for them due to the prevailing atmosphere of distrust and coordination failures. Consequently, farms suffered a serious shortage of most inputs, especially seed, fuel and fertilizer, as well as financial resources. Indeed, wheat farmers in Kazakhstan, as discussed above, have tended to remain in the PAE in order to obtain essential inputs, in spite of the significant hindrance this causes to production efficiency. If the input supply linkages improve in the future it is likely that a number of PAEs will be decollectivized into family farms, resulting in significant progress in wheat production as a whole. However the establishment of well-functioning production linkages will require the transformation of transaction practices in related sectors. The process of market creation is closely linked to institutional evolution and organizational change. In the following subsections, we shall look at the trial-and-error process of market creation in Kazakhstan.

Government support

The Kazakhstani government has experimented with two policy measures to support farmers: The *veksel* scheme and the public provision of inputs.

The veksel scheme

With the *veksel* scheme, which was introduced in the mid 1990s, the government acted as an endorser of farmers' bills for inputs. More specifically, when they purchased inputs farmers could issue *veksels* (promissory notes) up to an amount predetermined by the government, calculated in proportion to the amount of wheat they had supplied in the previous year to the state Food Contract Cooperation (FCC). If a farmer failed to honour a bill the amount in question would be paid by the government. This scheme was supposed to help both farmers and input suppliers by eliminating uncertainty about payment, but in practice it never worked, mainly because people did not trust *veksels* due to the lack of decision-making transparency at the FCC and the Ministry of Agriculture. Suppliers refused to sell inputs in exchange for *veksels* and the policy failed.

Public provision of inputs

In 1999 the government set up the Grain Committee to supply inputs to farms. The Committee sells fuel, fertilizers and chemicals, with the payment becoming due after harvest at 1 per cent interest. While this interest rate is lower than the market rate of 15–24 per cent, the price the Committee changes for fuel is rather high.[25] Moreover, the Committee is restricted from supplying more than 45 per cent of the total demand of any one farm. For these reasons most farms are not attracted to the programme and prefer to engage privately with large traders and manufacturers, as will be discussed below. Consequently, the programme mainly serves small family farms that are unable to enter private contracts under favourable terms. In this sense the Committee is a complement to the markets, but it can never play a principal role in market construction.

Interlinked transactions with wheat traders

In the mid 1990s, when the *veksel* scheme was obviously failing, there spontaneously emerged a private system of input supply in which wheat traders played a key part. In particular the traders provided farms with seed, fuel and agricultural chemicals in the spring before the start of cultivation, with the payment (usually in form of wheat) falling due after harvest in the autumn. Wheat traders had a stronger motivation to supply inputs to farms than did other organizations, since greater inputs would lead to greater yields, which were what the traders were interested in. For their part, farmers tended to make a considerable effort to repay the costs since they did not want to lose the major purchaser of their crops. This encouraged the formation of mutual trust between farmers and traders, and as a result the practice spread rapidly throughout north Kazakhstan from the mid 1990s onwards.

Such transactions are frequently observed in agricultural finance, particularly in developing economies, although in many cases the transactions take place between farmers and landlords rather than crop traders. These practices are usually called interlinked transactions and have been studied by many scholars (for example Braverman and Stiglitz, 1982; Basu, 1983, 1997; Platteau and Abraham, 1987; Bell and Srinivasan, 1989; Otsuka *et al.*, 1992; Hayami and Otsuka, 1993; Ray, 1998; Bardhan and Udry, 1999; Kurosaki, 2001). A distinctive feature of interlinked transactions is that the equilibrium prices are determined flexibly. In the case of input lending by a trader who will purchase wheat from the debtor, for instance, the trader's expected profit can come either from a high lending charge (interest) on inputs and a high purchase price for wheat, or from low interest on inputs and a low purchase price for wheat. Hence traders receive profits in the form of high interest charges or discounted purchase prices.[26] In between these two extremes lie a large number of other charging structures.

In input lending by wheat traders in Kazakhstan in the 1990s, the charges varied from one input to another. For instance farms usually paid two tonnes of wheat in the autumn for one tonne of seed in the spring, and three tonnes of wheat for one tonne of diesel fuel. Using spot market prices we can calculate the associated interest rates as 0 per cent for seed and 60 per cent for fuel. This large difference is probably related to the resalability of the inputs. Since fuel was required by many non-farming people for various purposes, farmers could make a profit by reselling it if the traders provided it at a comparatively low rate.[27] In the case of seed, however, there was little outside demand, hence the lower charge.

In transactions involving non-resalable inputs such as seed, both farmers and traders generally tend to prefer contracts with low interest rates and low purchase prices. As mentioned above, there are numerous combinations of interest rates and purchase prices that can result in the same expected total payment from farmer to trader. However the allocation of risks is strongly influenced by how they combine the two terms of payment. To illustrate this, let us examine a simple model of an interlinked seed transaction. Suppose that a trader lends seed to a farmer at interest rate i and purchases all the farmer's wheat at price p. The trader can borrow money from a bank at interest rate r and sell the wheat at market price q, while farmers cannot obtain loans directly from banks due to lack of trust. The market price, q, is assumed to be independent of fluctuations in domestic production since the market is open to the world. If the farmer sells all the yield to the trader who have supplied the seed in the spring, the respective profits for the farmer (π^F) and the trader (π^T) can be given as follows.

$$\pi^F = pWHEAT - (1+i) \, p_S \, SEED \tag{11.1}$$

$$\pi^T = (q-p) \, WHEAT + (i-r) \, p_S \, SEED \tag{11.2}$$

where p_S is the spot price of seed, and $WHEAT$ and $SEED$ are the farmer's wheat production and seed input respectively. We assume for simplicity that all inputs other than seed, such as land, labour and machinery, are constant during the period of analysis, and that production can be simply described by

$$WHEAT = F(SEED) + \varepsilon, \tag{11.3}$$

where $F(\bullet)$ represents the production process of wheat with diminishing returns, and ε is a stochastic variable with a mean of zero, which exhibits production risks from unpredictable factors such as drought, crop diseases and pests. Due to the lack of irrigation, wheat production in Kazakhstan is highly dependent on rainfall, and in a drought year annual production can fall to half the average yield, creating a major problem for farmers as they cannot borrow money to get by. Accordingly most farmers tend to behave as risk averters.

Let us investigate which equilibrium is likely to emerge in the above transaction, assuming that the farmer and trader are respectively risk averse and risk neutral. We also assume that farmer decides how much seed to sow, and that the conditions of the contract (interest rate and wheat price) are determined through negotiations between farmer and trader. The possible contracts are depicted in Figure 11.4. First, point E_0 shows the interest

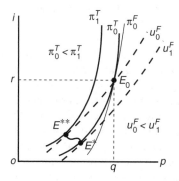

Figure 11.4   Equilibria in interlinked transactions

rate and wheat price on the spot market. If a trader lends seed to a farmer on these terms, on average no extra profit can be expected (see Equations 11.2 and 11.3). There is a whole set of terms that yield zero expected extra profit to the trader, as shown by curve π_0^T.[28] Likewise curve π_1^T shows the set of terms that yield an identical positive profit. We designate these curves 'isoprofit curves for traders'. In the figure an 'isoprofit curve for farmers' is given by curve π_0^F. It can be shown that the isoprofit curve for farmers has less curvature than that for traders and that the curves π_0^F and π_0^T are tangential to each other at point E_0.

Since the trader is risk neutral she prefers contract terms that yield greater expected profits, regardless of the magnitude of uncertainty. The farmer, in contrast, loathes uncertainty so his choice is not determined solely by expected profits. We need to take into account his risk preference. The broken curves in Figure 11.4 are drawn as indifference (iso-utility) curves for a risk-averse farmer, where all sets (p, i) on each curve realize the same utility $(u_0^F < u_1^F)$. They have flatter slopes than the isoprofit curve for farmers, π_0^F, since a risk-averse farmer is willing to accept a higher interest rate and lower expected profit if a fraction of the risks can be transfered to the trader by lowering the wheat price, p.

A possible equilibrium is indicated by E^*, at which the trader earns the same profit as in the spot market and the farmer enjoys greater welfare. Tangent point E^{**} also represents an equilibrium. Likewise all the sets (p, i) on the locus E^*–E^{**} are candidates for the equilibrium contract.[29] It should be noted that, in either case, the wheat price and interest rate tend to be lower than those on the spot market, E_0. Both farmer and trader are likely to preferred the lower wheat price. This is mainly because of the special function of the interlinked transaction, that is, risk sharing. When the farmer pays the seed cost in the form of a wheat price discount, the total payment changes according to the annual yield of the farm. He pays more in a good harvest year and less in a bad one. The farmer can transfer a portion of the production risks to the trader by making a contract at a low wheat price. The trader, on the other hand, obtains greater expected profits in the form of a risk premium. In sum, the interlinked transactions benefit both farmer and trader.

As noted earlier, such transactions emerged spontaneously in Kazakhstan in the mid 1990s and made a great contribution towards the achievement of a smooth input supply and risk sharing. Indeed in the latter half of the 1990s most wheat farmers obtained seed and fuel, their two most essential inputs, through this transaction system. However the system had a significant side effect – price distortion. We observed above that the equilibrium price in an interlinked transaction generally reflected not only the productive value of inputs but also the risk premium. This would cause farmers to misallocate inputs by showing them wrong price signals. The most obvious consequence was that most farmers did not apply fertilizers to their land, mainly because the wheat price paid by traders was too low. According to official statistics, during the 1990s the total area of land that received mineral or chemical fertilizers fell to one hundredth of what it had been at the end of the Soviet regime. In fact, of 100 the farms that the author's team had interviewed by 1998, approximately 90 had ceased using fertilizer since 1991. Not surprisingly this had resulted in a long-term decrease in land productivity, as shown in Figure 11.2 above.

Integration into food production companies

As noted above, during the 1990s the interlinked transactions between farmers and wheat traders were not able to eliminate all the problems involved in production linkages. Particularly they could not provide farmers with fertilizer, partly due to their unexpected side effects on wheat price. To counter this a new arrangement emerged and quickly replaced interlinked transactions at the end of the century. The new organizational arrangement involved the integration of wheat farms into trade/manufacturing companies. A critical trigger for this movement was a severe drought in 1998, which brought most farmers near to ruin. By that time agrotrading companies such as Golden Grain, Agrocenter Astana and Golden Ear had met success in the food processing industry,[30] and these successful firms began to absorb the nearly bankrupt farms into their organizations. For instance Golden Grain incorporated 10 PAEs in 1999 and started to grow wheat on 92,000 hectares of land.

On the integrated farms, nowadays all production operations, including cultivation, sowing and harvesting, are governed by a plan of operation drawn up by the farm manager and submitted to the company for approval. The wage payment to individual farmers is also governed by a plan that determines how many workers are assigned to each operation. On average, companies pay each farmer 5000–8000 tenge (US $40–60) per month plus about 10 per cent of the harvest as rent for the land use rights. In total this is slightly more than the average revenue received by family farms. It should also be noted that farmers' incomes have been stabilized by integration, since wages are now paid on the basis of operations rather than harvest. Therefore the new system works as a risk-sharing device, but without the distortional changes in prices and input allocations that occurred with interlinked transactions.

Another striking change is that many of the farms operating in this system have begun to use fertilizers again. Of the ten or more large companies interviewed by the author during the past few years, only one uses no fertilizer on its farms. Thus it seems that the new system has encouraged farmers to tend to the fertility of their land, although admittedly this assumption is based on a limited number of observations. Company directors, who are the principal decision makers under the new system, have a considerable incentive to use fertilizers since the price of wheat is determined by the spot market price, which is higher than the equilibrium price under interlinked transactions. In 1999 the average land productivity of wheat in Kazakhstan recovered to 1.29 tonnes per hectare, which was approximately 2.5 times higher than the level in 1998. Substantial part of this productivity rise should be attributed to the fertilization by the integrated farms.[31]

Despite the above benefits of integration, there may be adverse effects in terms of efficiency. As individual farmers receive fixed wages, moral hazard and/or free rider problems could appear unless companies can monitor farmers and force them to work hard, which would be reminiscent of the old *kolkhoz* style of production. Nonetheless future results will depend heavily on how efficiently the integrated companies can monitor the affiliated farms.

Concluding remarks

As we have seen, in Kazakhstan the process of economic transition started with the collapse of production but then moved towards the reconstruction of linkages. Transitional markets are often disordered, so production linkages have been disconnected everywhere, resulting in the sudden collapse of production and a drastic fall in GDP. Reconstruction of production linkages is not easy once they have been broken, and a government can play a limited part in it. Indeed when the shortage of inputs became a serious problem in Kazakhstani agriculture the government introduced several policies to inspire the markets, but these fell short almost every time. In the private sector, by contrast, workable new ideas spontaneously emerged and were developed through a process of trial and error by farmers, wheat traders and food manufacturers. The resulting practices, however, cannot be seen as a panacea and they can have serious side effects, as in the case of the interlinked transactions discussed above. Similarly the organizational integration of wheat farming, which has spread widely in recent years, may involve serious problems with moral hazard and free riding. The solution to this would be efficient monitoring, but if the problems turn out to be serious, the search will have to begin again for a more efficient transaction system. Eventually superior institutions that are really suitable for the village economies of Kazakhstan will surely emerge. Today, all the transition economies are on similar quests.

Notes

1. An earlier version of this chapter was presented at an IDE workshop held at Keio University, Tokyo, on 30 January 2002. The author wishes to thank Kaushik Basu, Takashi Kurosaki, Jeffrey Nugent, Hitoshi Yonekura and other workshop participants for their constructive comments and encouragement.
2. The CSB consists of 13 countries: Albania, Bulgaria, Croatia, the Czech Republic, Estonia, Hungary, Latvia, Lithuania, Macedonia, Poland, Romania, the Slovak Republic and Slovenia. The CIS comprises 12 countries: Armenia, Azerbaijan, Belarus, Georgia, Kazakhstan, the Kyrgyz Republic, Moldova, the Russian Federation, Tajikistan, Turkmenistan, Ukraine and Uzbekistan.

3. For details see Campos and Coricelli (2002). De Melo *et al.* (1996), de Broeck and Koen (2000) and World Bank (2002b) present alternative but quite similar sets of stylized facts.

4. There is another focus of study, namely whether liberalization policy as a whole affects transition economies positively or negatively. To the best of my knowledge, all studies have found that liberalization has a significantly positive effect on economic growth, which suggests that transition economies should continue their liberalization policies to achieve long-term growth. (see de Melo *et al.*, 1996; de Melo *et al.*, 1997; de Broeck and Koen, 2000; Macours and Swinnen, 2000.)

5. The falls shown in the figure may be partially due to systematic biases in official statistics (Broeck and Koen, 2000; Schneider and Enste, 2000; Campos and Coricelli, 2002). In addition, as discussed by Cochrane and Ickes (1995) and de Broeck and Koen (2000), real income may fall less than production in transitional CSB and CIS economies.

6. Four countries in the CIS (Armenia, Azerbaijan, Georgia and Tajikistan) and two in the CSB (Croatia and Macedonia) experienced civil wars during the transition period, which would have considerably affected their economic performance.

7. For detailed discussions of the debate see Roland (2000) and Campos and Coricelli (2002).

8. In addition to the above factor there are several other possible causes, such as partial reforms (Murphy *et al.*, 1992), credit crunch problems (Calvo and Coricelli, 1992) and the monopolistic structure of input markets (Blanchard, 1997; Li, 1999), which are considered to be important in the earlier phases of transition.

9. Roland and Verdier (1999) propose that disorganization is the result of search frictions and investment specificity.

10. The disorganization effect mainly affects sectors with complex production processes for which a large variety of essential inputs are required. Those inputs tend to move out to relatively simple production sectors where the rewards are relatively low but assured. In more established market economies the input vacuum can be immediately filled by substitutes available on thick input markets. Hence the disorganization effect is not significant in such economies.

11. Blanchard and Kremer (1997) and Konings and Walsh (1999) cite results of empirical analyses that support the above hypothesis.

12. For general overviews of the Kazakhstan and Central Asian economies, see Pomfret (1995), Hunter (1996), Kenzheguzin (1997), Rumer and Zhukov (1998), Kalyuzhnova (1998) and Agency on Statistics of the Republic of Kazakhstan (2000).

13. Shevchik (1998) reports that in 1992 Kazakh wheat contained 28.3 per cent gluten on average; better farmers produced wheat containing more than 35 per cent gluten.

14. In 1997 only 10 per cent of cultivated land was irrigated in Kazakhstan.

15. The average wheat harvest in 1990 was 1.15 tonnes per hectare, compared with 0.51, 0.52 and 0.44 in 1991, 1994 and 1998 respectively. Land productivity is much lower than in developed countries, even in an average year. This is mainly due to the lack of irrigation and fertilizers.

16. Three hundred and twenty four farms were privately operated with special licences issued by the Gorbachov government at the end of socialist regime.

17. The government has started to examine the feasibility of legislating land property rights, in response to a presidential decree in 2002.

18. The difference in labour productivity would be larger still if we accounted for the fact that labourers on family farms worked longer hours and usually harder than labourers in PAEs.

19. For more details see Ray (1998).
20. The TFP difference between the two groups is not statistically significant because the standard deviation of TFP is as large as shown in Figure 11.4.
21. A direct estimation of the Cobb–Douglas production function gives the same results, that is, scale economies in family farms but not in PAEs.
22. Collectives include PAEs and state farms.
23. Land use rights are not easily used as collateral, as discussed earlier.
24. In more general circumstances, several other factors influence farm decollectivization, including economies of scale, farmers' management skills, terms of trade and the presence of risk. For details see Carter (1987), Deininger (1995), Mathijs and Swinnen (1998) and Sedik *et al.*, (1999).
25. Several PAE managers told the author that they never bought fuel from the Grain Committee because of its high cost, but the Committee insisted that its price was less than the market one by about 10 dollars per tonne.
26. To obtain this result traders require farmers to guarantee that they will sell them a predetermined quantity of their product. This condition was likely to hold in Kazakhstan in the 1990s as there were a limited number of large trading companies in each region. Usually each farmer sold the farm's entire yield to a single trader.
27. Of course resale is not necessarily profitable for farmers even with a low interest charge because they must pay the remaining cost in the form of price discount in autumn. However, since the amount of this payment is given in proportion to the yield, the low interest would encourage farmers to shift fuel from productive use to resale.
28. It can be shown that curves π^T and π^F are upward sloping and convex to downward.
29. The equilibrium locus may be extended in the northwest of E^{**} since farmer cannot obtain loan from a bank at interest rate r.
30. There are many other successful companies, such as Agroexport, Alebi, Cenegole, Export Astik, Astana Astik and Seimar.
31. The remarkable recovery in productivity is partly due to favourable weather in 1999. In 2000 the land productivity fell to 0.90 tonnes per hectare.

References

Agency on Statistics of the Republic of Kazakhstan (various years) *Statistical Year-book of Kazakhstan* (Almaty: Agency on Statistics of the Republic of Kazakhstan).
Agenstvo Respubliki Kazakhstan po statistike (various years) *Sel'skoe, lesnoe i rybnoe khoziaistvo Kazakhstana: Statisticheskii sbornik (Agriculture, Forestry and Fishery of Kazakhstan: Statistical book* [in Russian]) (Almaty: Agenstvo Respubliki Kazakhstan po statistike).
Bardhan, P. and C. Udry (1999) *Development Microeconomics* (Oxford: Oxford University Press).
Basu, K. (1983) 'The Emergence of Isolation and Interlinkage in Rural Markets', *Oxford Economic Papers*, vol. 35, pp. 262–80.
Basu, K. (1997) *Analytical Development Economics: The Less Developed Economy Revisited* (Cambridge, Mass.: MIT Press).
Bell, C. and T. N. Srinivasan (1989) 'Some Aspects of Linked Product and Credit Market', in P. Bardhan (ed.), *The Economic Theory of Agrarian Institutions* (Oxford: Clarendon Press), ch. 11.

Berg, A. and J. Sachs (1992) 'Structural Adjustment and International Trade in Eastern Europe: The Case of Poland', *Economic Policy: A European Forum*, vol. 14, pp. 117–74.

Blanchard, O. (1997) *The Economics of Post-Communist Transition* (Oxford: Clarendon Press).

Blanchard, O., R. Dornbusch, P. Krugman, R. Layard and L. Summers (1991) *Economic Transition in Eastern Europe* (Cambridge, Mass.: MIT Press).

Blanchard, O. and M. Kremer (1997) 'Disorganization', *Quarterly Journal of Economics*, vol. 112, pp. 1091–126.

Braverman, A. and J. E. Stiglitz (1982) 'Sharecropping and the Interlinking of Agrarian Markets', *American Economic Review*, vol. 72, pp. 695–715.

Calvo, G. and F. Coricelli (1992) 'Stabilizing a Previously Centrally Planned Economy: Poland 1990', *Economic Policy*, vol. 14, pp. 175–208.

Campos, N. F. and F. Coricelli (2002) 'Growth in Transition: What We Know, What We Don't, and What We Should', *Journal of Economic Literature*, vol. 40, pp. 793–836.

Carter, M. (1987) 'Risk Sharing and Incentives in the Decollectivization of Agriculture', *Oxford Economic Papers*, vol. 39, pp. 577–95.

CIS Stat (Interstate Statistical Committee of the Commonwealth of Independent States) (various years), *Official Statistics of the Countries of the Commonwealth of Independent States*, CD-ROM version (Moscow: CIS Stat).

CIS Stat (2002) 'Main Macroeconomic Indicators on CIS Countries (annual data)', http://www.cisstat.com/eng/macro_an.htm.

Cochrane, J. H. and B. W. Ickes (1995) 'Macroeconomics in Russia', in E. P. Lazear, (ed.), *Economic Transition in Eastern Europe and Russia: Realities of Reform* (Stanford, CA: Hoover Institution Press), ch. 2.

De Broeck, M. and V. Koen (2000) 'The Great Contractions in Russia, the Baltics and the Other Countries of the Former Soviet Union: A View from the Supply Side', *IMF Working Paper* WP/00/32 (Washington, DC: IMF).

Deininger, K. (1995) 'Collective Agricultural Production: A Solution for Transition Economies?', *World Development*, vol. 23, pp. 1317–34.

De Melo, M., C. Denizer and A. Gelb (1996) 'From Plan to Market: Patterns of Transition', *World Bank Working Paper Series*, no. 1564 (Washington DC: World Bank).

De Melo, M., C. Denizer, A. Gelb and S. Tenev (1997) 'Circumstance and Choice: The Role of Initial Conditions and Policies in Transition Economies', *World Bank Working Paper Series*, no. 1866 (Washington, DC: World Bank).

EBRD (various years) *Transition Report* (London: EBRD).

Hayami, Y. and K. Otsuka (1993) *The Economics of Contract Choice: An Agrarian Perspective* (Oxford: Clarendon Press).

Hunter, S. T. (1996) *Central Asia since Independence* (Washington, DC: Center for Strategic and International Studies).

Kalyuzhnova, Y. (1998) *The Kazakstani Economy: Independence and Transition* (London: Macmillan).

Kenzheguzin, M. (ed.) (1997) *Economy of Kazakstan on the Path of Reforms* (Almaty: Institute of Economics of the Ministry of Science and Academy of Sciences of the Republic of Kazakstan).

Konings, J. and P. P. Walsh (1999) 'Disorganization in the Process of Transition: Firm-level Evidence from Ukraine', *Economics of Transition*, vol. 7 pp. 29–46.

Kurosaki, T. (2001) *Kaihatsuno Mikurokeizaigaku: Riron to Ouyou* (*Microeconomics of Development: Theory and Applications* [in Japanese]) (Tokyo: Iwanami Shoten).

Li, W. (1999) 'A Tale of Two Reforms', *Rand Journal of Economics*, vol. 30, pp. 120–36.

Lipton, D. and J. Sachs (1990) 'Creating a Market Economy in Eastern Europe: The Case of Poland', *Brookings Papers on Economic Activity*, vol. 1, pp. 75–133.

Macours, K. and J. F. M. Swinnen (2000) 'Causes of Output Decline in Economic Transition: The Case of Central and Eastern European Agriculture', *Journal of Comparative Economics*, vol. 28, pp. 172–206.

Marin, D. and M. Schnitzer (1999) 'Disorganization and Financial Collapse', *William Davidson Institute Working Paper* no. 285, (Ann Arbor: University of Michigan).

Mathijs, E. and J. F. M. Swinnen (1998) 'The Economics of Agricultural Decollectivization in East Europe and the Former Soviet Union', *Economic Development and Cultural Change*, vol. 47, pp. 1–26.

Murphy, K. M., A. Shleifer and R. Vishny (1992) 'The Transition to a Market Economy: Pitfalls of Partial Reforms', *Quarterly Journal of Economics*, vol. 107, pp. 889–906.

Nishikimi, K. (1998) 'Kazafusutan niokeru Nougyouminneika no Genjou to Kadai' (Farm Privatization in Kazakhstan: Production Efficiency of Private Farms [in Japanese]), in M. Shimizu (ed.), *Chuuouajia: sijouka no Genndannkai to Kadai* (*Central Asia: Current Stage and Work to Be Done* [in Japanese]) (Tokyo: Institute of Developing Economies), ch. 4.

Otsuka, K., H. Chuma and Y. Hayami (1992) 'Land and Labor Contracts in Agrarian Economies: Theories and Facts', *Journal of Economic Literature*, vol. 30, pp. 1965–2018.

Platteau, J.-P. and A. Abraham (1987) 'An Inquiry into Quasi-credit Contracts: The Role of Reciprocal Credit and Interlinked Deals in Small-scale Fishing Communities', *Journal of Development Studies*, vol. 23, pp. 462–90.

Pomfret, R. (1995) *The Economies of Central Asia* (Princeton, NJ: Princeton University Press).

Ray, D. (1998) *Development Economics* (Princeton, NJ: Princeton University Press).

Roland, G. (2000) *Transition and Economics: Politics, Markets, and Firms* (Cambridge, Mass.: MIT Press).

Roland, G. and T. Verdier (1999) 'Transition and the Output Fall', *Economics of Transition*, vol. 7, pp. 1–28.

Rosati, D. (1994) 'Output Decline during Transition from Plan to Market', *Economics of Transition*, vol. 2, pp. 419–42.

Rumer, B. and S. Zhukov (eds) (1998) *Central Asia: The Challenges of Independence* (Armonk, NY: M. E. Sharpe).

Schneider, F. and D. Enste (2000) 'Shadow Economies: Size, Causes, and Consequences', *Journal of Economic Literature*, vol. 38, pp. 77–114.

Sedik, D., M. Trueblood and C. Amade (1999) 'Corporate Farm Performance in Russia, 1991–1995: An Efficiency Analysis', *Journal of Comparative Economics*, vol. 27, pp. 514–33.

Shevchik, P. P. (1998) *Zernovoi rynok Kazakhstana: Sostoianie, problemy i tendentsii razvitiia* (*The grain market in Kazakhstan: current state, problems and growth tendency* [in Russian]) (Almaty: Almatinckii tekhnologicheskii institut).

Windell, J., R. Anker and G. Sziraczki (1995) 'Kyrgyzstan: Enterprise Restructuring and Labour Shedding in a Free Fall Economy, 1991–1994', *ILO Labour Market Papers*, no. 5 (Geneva: ILO).

World Bank (2002a) *Transition, First Ten Years: Analysis and Lessons for Eastern Europe and the Former Soviet Union* (Washington, DC: World Bank).

World Bank (2002b) *World Development Report 2002: Building Institutions for Markets* (Washington, DC: World Bank).

Yurist (2001) *Zakon Respubliki Kazakhstan o zemle: Ofitsial'nyi tekst po sostaianiiu na 1 iiulia 2001 goda* (*Land law in Kazakhstan: An official document about the situation on July 1, 2001* [in Russian]) (Almaty: Yurist).

12
Strategic Choices for China and Vietnam in the Twenty-First Century

Dwight H. Perkins

Introduction

China since 1978 and Vietnam since 1989 have taken major steps towards becoming market economies. In the first decades of market-oriented reform the choices facing policy makers have been comparatively simple, but no reasonable person could think that active government direction is a sensible way of managing household farms, retail shops or even small industrial enterprises. If the objective is political control rather than economic growth or efficiency, of course, government intervention may make sense in almost any sphere, but the political leaders of China and Vietnam clearly want economic growth, not just political control.

Over the next decade or two, both China and Vietnam will have to make a series of hard choices about just where their economic systems are heading. Two basic conditions will make these choices difficult. First, they will involve fundamental changes that will shape the nature of ownership of and control over many key sectors of the economy, what economists some-times refer to as the 'commanding heights'. These changes will raise the question of whether the system is socialist or capitalist, and will directly affect the levers of political and economic control over society. Second, it is difficult to make choices when there is no consensus on which of two or more alternatives is likely to work best. In China and Vietnam there is no consensus on the proper role of government intervention in the economy. Equally seriously, there is no real consensus in the world outside China and Vietnam.

The principal choice facing the leaders of China and Vietnam is whether to play an active role in the economy along the lines of the Japanese and Korean models of the 1960s and 1970s, or whether they should take steps to become fully integrated into the international economic system along the lines of a typical OECD economy. This decision will not be made in a vacuum. The current rules of the international economic system are not the same as those that prevailed in the 1960s and 1970s. Of direct relevance to this discussion is that in the earlier period a country could pursue an activist industrial policy without being sanctioned by international agencies such as the General Agreement on Tariffs and Trade (GATT). By the 1990s, however, it was no longer possible to have an activist industrial policy and be accepted as a new member in good standing of the World Trade Organization (WTO). Existing members were treated with considerably greater leniency, but that fact was and is of little value either to China or to Vietnam.

The main theme of this chapter is that it would be in China's and Vietnam's best interests to move as quickly as they can towards full membership of the international economic system, and to resist pressure to maintain government direction over micro-level economic decisions in industry and the modern service sector. Integration into the world economic system would also serve the interests of that system and of the advanced industrial nations, but that is not why the leaders of these two countries should take this path. They should take it because, as will be argued at length, the alternative path would be one of growing inefficiency, corruption, slow growth and quite possibly political instability.

Slow growth and inefficiency would in part be the result of hostility by the major postindustrial economies towards the activist approach. More importantly, China and Vietnam lack the economic and political institutions that would make it possible to pursue an efficient activist industrial policy, which would require a decision-making apparatus that was largely insulated from political and rent-seeking pressures. Chinese and Vietnamese economic decisions are immersed in politics and have become increasingly subject to the personal rent-seeking goals of officials both high and low.

To argue in favour of full Chinese and Vietnamese integration into the world economy, however, is not to agree with those who think that this can or should be achieved in a few years. Some of the key steps required, for example the creation of an economic system governed by the rule of law, will take a generation or more even if the countries' commitment to the task is strong and consistent. There are also major interim hurdles that, if handled inappropriately or ineptly, could lead to political upheaval and disrupt economic progress.

This chapter begins with an overview and simplified version of the two kinds of economic system that China and Vietnam must choose between. A review of the current state of economic reform in the two countries is followed by an analysis of the recent nature of the international economic system. The latter discussion will include a brief analysis of the Asian financial crisis of 1997–99 and its implications for the system choices that Vietnam and China must make. The chapter concludes with an attempt to answer the main question posed here: what kind of economic system will best suit Vietnam and China in the first decades of the millennium.

Alternative economic systems: the interventionist model

The interventionist approach to the development of industry and the modern service sector is modelled on perceptions of the economic systems of Japan, South Korea and Taiwan. To a considerable degree, those of South Korea and Taiwan were modelled on Japan, but with significant differences, especially in the case of Taiwan.[1] There are also important elements of this system in Malaysia and Indonesia. Just what are the dominant characteristics of this system?

Central planning is a thing of the past, apart from in a few countries that still attempt to follow the old Soviet style path, such as North Korea. In contrast strategic planning, where governments promote particular industries, is still very much alive in Asia and elsewhere. The East Asian version of strategic planning is usually carried out by a powerful ministry, the Ministry of International Trade and Industry in Japan, the former Economic Planning Board in South Korea, a group of economics ministers in Taiwan, and the prime minister's office in Malaysia. In Korea in the 1970s and Malaysia to this day, the president or prime minister directly participated in the planning effort. These ministries or offices typically selected a few key industries that they believed would lead the development of industry in the coming decade.

Once the strategic industries were selected, the government became actively involved in ensuring that these industries would be established and grow. At the core of this implementation effort were a number of powerful tools. Imports of goods and services that directly competed with the new industries faced high tariffs, quotas or outright bans. When overt trade restrictions of this kind ran into determined international opposition, they were often replaced by less open methods that served much the same purpose. The government also used its influence to order or encourage the banking system to provide adequate financial support to the industrial efforts, often at subsidized rates of interest. Sometimes the banks were directly owned by the state, as was the case in South Korea, Taiwan and Indonesia.[2] In other cases the banks were private, but were generally willing to carry out the wishes of the government, as in Japan. These banks and much of the rest of the financial system were also largely sheltered from direct foreign competition in their home markets.

Government officials had a high degree of discretionary authority to carry out the decisions of the planners. The rules and regulations that governed their actions were flexible and were often known only to those inside the system; that is, the rules were not transparent to outsiders or even to some insiders. When the process functioned well, decision making was usually conducted by technically competent government bureaucrats who were relatively isolated from political pressures.

Politics, however, was never very far away. This system required a close relationship between the government and the business community.

Government planners and regulators typically retired early and moved on to well-paid positions in the industries they had hitherto regulated or influenced. Business in turn required ready access to government decision makers so that they could maintain a clear understanding of what was expected of them. Access was sometimes based on relatively objective measures of competence and performance, as was the case in Park Chung Hee's Korea and with much of the industrial policy carried out by Japan in the 1960s and 1970s. In numerous other cases, however, access could be bought. In general governments whose survival depended on an effective development policy made decisions mainly on the basis of competence, as in Taiwan and South Korea in the early years. Japan also based industrial policies, as opposed to public construction contracts, mainly on performance.

Few governments anywhere in the world have found open and honest ways to fund political parties and elections. The United States has not found such a way, nor have many countries in East and Southeast Asia. The US government, however, does not intervene in industry to anywhere near the extent that is typically found in Asia. In the past the power of governments in East Asia to determine the course of the economy, in contrast with the situation in the United States and other market-dominated economies, made it easy for ruling parties to raise money, and few resisted the temptation. The distortions created by this varied greatly between countries. In the Korea of Park Chung Hee, providing support to the governing party bought general access but not approval of specific projects, much like the ante required to stay in a poker game. At the other extreme, in the Philippines of Ferdinand Marcos support for the governing party did buy support for specific projects, often without any concern for their economic merits. Indonesia was looking more and more like Marcos's Philippines by the 1990s, and even Korea was moving in that direction, as the Hanbo steel case illustrated.

The lack of transparency in such systems is greatly facilitated when the governing party is not effectively challenged in open and relatively honest elections. Transparency is also not promoted if the governing party does participate in honest elections but opposition parties are not effective enough occasionally to receive the mandate to govern. A less than free press can also aid a government that operates behind a veil of secrecy. While full democracy and a free press do not automatically mean that industrial policies will be free from politics, demagoguery or corruption, as Korea in the 1990s demonstrated, they clearly make it much more difficult to carry out the work of government in secrecy, with results that sometimes enhance but often distort the government's industrial policies.

Finally, the interventionist industrial policy model run by government bureaucrats with considerable discretionary authority is not really consistent with a system based on the rule of law. Interventionist systems have numerous laws and regulations, but that is a very different matter from having the rule of law. A system with the rule of law is generally one in which laws are transparent and everyone must live by them. Government bureaucrats do not have the discretionary authority to decide how the laws will be applied in particular cases. That role is reserved for a court system that is independent of both government bureaucrats and politicians, and bases its decisions on the word of the law and judicial precedents. It was no accident that the interventionist industrial policies of East and Southeast Asia operated, and in many cases still operate, in countries where the legal tradition was weak and the courts were anything but independent. The two Asian economies with the strongest legal systems, Hong Kong and to a lesser degree Singapore, also became the most market oriented and this too was no accident, although the direction of causation went both ways.[3]

The decentralized market model

The decentralized market model is familiar to most educated observers in postindustrial economies because it is the system that prevails in most of these economies and the model that dominates economics textbooks. In this economic system, companies make decisions about what to produce and where to invest in response to impersonal market forces. Relative prices determine whether an industry should expand or contract and, in the global economy, the global forces of supply and demand determine those relative prices. Governments do occasionally intervene to set prices, most commonly in the agricultural sector and with respect to sunset industries, but rarely does the government involve itself in directly promoting new and cutting-edge industries.[4]

Governments do not get involved in picking industrial 'winners' because few have personnel who are sufficiently qualified to do so. An enormous quantity of quality information is required to decide where on the industrial frontier to invest. In the high-income countries, tens of thousands of highly skilled specialists spend their lives trying to understand present trends and predict future ones, and most of these people are in private business. The information requirements for developing countries that are just starting on the path to industrialization are much smaller. This group of countries can learn a great deal about their next steps by observing economies that are just ahead of them on that path. Thus information requirements virtually rule out an activist industrial policy in countries on the economic frontier, but do not do so in those in the early stages of economic development.

The roles played by government in a market economy are largely confined to macroeconomic policy and to matters of defence, education, public health and basic research when real or perceived market failures lead to underinvestment in these areas.[5] There are those who believe that private ownership governed by market forces would be desirable in many of these sectors as well, but education and basic research are predominantly public sector activities in most countries. No one thinks that defence or macro-economic policy should be privatized.

A market economy still requires rules and regulations and methods of dispute settlement. Government officials play a part in implementing such rules, but this usually involves little discretion. The rules and regulations are published and are supposed to be clear to all, although they often fail in the latter objective, thus creating space for discretionary decisions by government bureaucrats. The ultimate arbiters of disputes and interpreters of rules, however, are the courts, which are largely or completely independent of the executive authority.

There are opportunities for corruption in a market system, but they are much more circumscribed than in a system where discretionary intervention in the economy is widespread. Because the opportunities for corruption are more limited in a market system it is easier for the government to ferret out and prosecute the perpetrators of any corruption that does occur. In a true competitive market situation, neither party to a transaction gains anything from under-the-table payments as these raise the cost of the transaction and purchasers will turn to other suppliers that do not have such costs.

The corruption that does exist is usually in areas where the government still plays an active or dominant role. Road building and other government-sponsored infrastructure projects frequently attract individuals and firms that are eager and able to circumvent the competitive bidding process, if that process exists. Corruption also enters at the point when laws are being written. Many of the larger contributors to political campaigns in the United States are companies or industries with a vested interest in how new laws are worded. Once the laws are written it is still possible to bribe the officials and judges responsible for implementing them, but it is much easier to devise methods to uncover this type of corruption than is the case when discretionary intervention is legal.

A market system can operate in the absence of a democratic system and a free press, but it operates much better when the opposite is the case. A free press is often more effective in exposing and bringing about the correction of corrupt governmental acts than is a strong internal police force, although the two should be seen as complementary. Politicians are also likely to be less corrupt, even or especially at the highest levels, if they know that exposure of corrupt activities is likely to result in their being voted out of office. They can also be exposed and voted out of office for decisions that are simply mistaken. In a pure market system there is no need for this since mistaken decisions can result in reduced profits and ultimately lead to the firm going out of business.

A review of reform in China and Vietnam

Market forces alone run no economy, not even that of Hong Kong. The issue of central relevance to this chapter is where China and Vietnam stand on the spectrum from a pure market economy to a centrally planned command economy: A clearer picture of where these economies stand today will provide a foundation from which to speculate about the choices they will face in the future.

China's economic reforms began in late 1978 and those in Vietnam began in earnest in 1989, although the key political changes that made the reforms possible date back to 1986. The early stages of reform in the two countries (1978–1984 in China and 1989–1993 in Vietnam) were very similar. The key elements included abandonment of the collective system and a return to household agriculture, and the freeing of farm prices and rural markets for most but not all agricultural commodities. Closely related to this was the rapid liberalization of most retail trade and a considerable proportion of wholesale trade, a process that began in rural areas in China but quickly spread to the cities. In Vietnam the markets for most goods were liberalized within two years. The impact of these market openings was rapid and dramatic, with the formerly empty shelves of shops now teeming with goods.[6]

Another first-phase change was in the sphere of foreign trade and foreign direct investment. The key decisions were to promote foreign trade rather than trying to limit it, and to allow foreign direct investment rather than prohibiting it. In China the large state monopolies run by the Ministry of Foreign Trade were broken up into a much larger number of local state trading corporations and the currency was devalued. These steps, together with a variety of other export promotion measures, led to the rapid and steady growth of manufactured exports, which rose from around half of total exports of $9.75 billion in 1978 to 90 per cent of exports of $249.2 billion in 2000. Vietnamese exports also increased, but most were commodities rather than manufactures, including petroleum and agricultural crops such as coffee and rubber. Manufactured exports accounted for only a third of Vietnam's total exports in 2000, partly because prior to the 1990s Vietnam had had little experience of exporting manufactures to hard-currency markets, and partly because it had allowed its exchange rate to become overvalued in the 1990s.[7]

Foreign direct investment played a minor role in China in the first phase of reform and a somewhat larger though still small role in Vietnam in the same phase.[8] The main contribution of FDI was to come later, and more in China than in Vietnam. The first years of reform were mostly a learning period for both countries and for foreign investors. New laws were passed, revised and amended, and export-processing zones for foreign investors were created. In essence, institutional infrastructure was being put in place in the expectation of future pay-offs.

By the mid 1980s market forces were governing nearly half of China's economy (the one third of the economy that was in agriculture plus most commerce and a variety of other services). In Vietnam the percentage was higher, mainly because of the larger share of agriculture in GDP. Chinese manufacturing firms producing for the export market and a substantial and rising number of other manufacturers faced international market forces, although they were only beginning to be affected by domestic market pressures. In 2000, Vietnamese manufactured exports amounted to little more than $5 billion and were produced mainly by FDI firms.

In 1984 the Chinese government and in the early 1990s the Vietnamese government took the first major steps to introduce market forces into their industrial sectors. There were five main elements of the move from a centrally planned command system to a market system.

Vietnam took immediate and vigorous steps to bring inflation under control, and thereby to create the macroeconomic conditions required for markets to function well. In the early 1980s China did not have any serious macro-economic disequilibria, either in the form of inflation or a major deficit in its balance of payments. It began making a larger and larger share of industrial inputs available on the market, beginning with minority shares in the mid 1980s and rising to over 90 per cent and sometimes 100 per cent by the mid 1990s. Vietnam simply allocated most industrial inputs, including imports, through market channels in the early 1990s. Foreign exchange, and hence imports, remained administratively controlled in China throughout the 1980s, but this was less the case in Vietnam.

If goods were to be allocated through markets, prices had to reflect relative scarcities in the economy so that the goods would go where they were most needed. Vietnam solved this problem by freeing up most prices, although tariffs and other import controls kept the price of certain key products such as cement and steel from converging with world prices. China met too much resistance from the politically powerful state-owned enterprises to free up all prices, so it created a dual system where goods distributed through the market were sold at market prices while goods still allocated by the planners were distributed at lower state-set prices. While this dual price system created a bonanza for some corrupt officials, it did solve the political problem of persuading powerful interests to go along with the expansion of the market.

China introduced competition into what in the industrial sphere had been a system of local monopolies. In the 1970s county-level enterprises had a monopoly over their local markets and large Shanghai enterprises were often restricted to selling in the East China market. It was easier to plan if the planners know in advance where the products of any given firm were heading. These monopolies were abolished in most parts of China in the 1980s and firms were now able to sell anywhere they could find customers.[9] Local governments sometimes tried to protect local industries, but usually with little success. Monopoly powers were retained in areas where a competitive system would be technically and politically difficult to achieve, such as electric power generation and petroleum exploration and drilling, but even in these areas China began to introduce competition in 1999. Vietnam too introduced competition into all but a handful of heavy industrial sectors, but here the government had little choice in the matter as most of the competition was coming from imports and the government had only limited control over the goods that were flooding across its very long land border or arriving by sea.

A market system cannot function efficiently unless the producers of goods and services behave according to the rules of the market – that is, maximize profits by cutting their costs or increasing their sales. Increasing profits by obtaining larger subsidies from the state does not count. Whether the firm is privately or publicly owned, this rule must be followed, but it is the hardest market-creating element to achieve. Private firms in a market economy either maximize profits or lose business to firms that do. No such compulsion affects the typical state-owned enterprise, which habitually turns to the government for support when it cannot make profits on its own. Private firms can also become dependent on state subsidies, but the problem is much greater among state firms. Both China and Vietnam struggled with this problem and by 1999 neither had fully solved it (we shall return to this topic below.)

The two countries therefore began to introduce many of the elements of a market economy into the industrial sector, in the late 1980s in the case of China, and simultaneously with the other market reforms in the case of Vietnam. In China, but not in Vietnam, these changes led to unintended consequences that moved China's industrial sector a long way towards a full market system. The Chinese reforms, incomplete as they were, opened up opportunities for tens of thousands of enterprises that are now known as TVEs (township and village enterprises).

As is now well known, TVEs were responsible for a large share of the high GDP and industrial growth rates enjoyed by China between 1984 and 1997. Industrial value added over this period rose at an average annual rate of 13.5 per cent. The collectively owned industrial sector that included the TVEs grew by 21.1 per cent per year. State-owned industrial enterprises accounted for 77.6 per cent of gross industrial output in 1978, but their share fell to 64.9 per cent in 1985 and 25.5 per cent in 1997. From the late 1990s completely private industries and, much more importantly, FDI enterprises began to grow even faster than TVEs.

There is a large body of literature on the nature of ownership and the role of government in the development and operation of China's TVEs.[10] From the point of view of this chapter, these enterprises behaved much like privately owned firms, whatever their formal ownership category. To compete and survive they had to behave in that way because the state was not there to bail them out. The same was true of FDI enterprises and firms with other forms of ownership, apart from state-owned enterprises and particularly the larger ones.

By the late 1990s, therefore, the market-dominated sectors in China's economy accounted for at least three quarters of economic value added, and possibly more. Only the large state-owned enterprises in industry and their counterparts in the service sector, notably the banks, could be said to have been influenced as much by direct government intervention as by the market.

Surprisingly the share of the state-owned sector in Vietnam was significantly larger than it was in China in the 1990s. Despite being more of an agricultural economy than China, Vietnam's state-owned sector accounted for over 40 per cent of GDP. A major reason for this is that Vietnam experienced nothing comparable to China's TVE boom. Most of the local industries in Vietnam were state owned, although there were a few joint ventures. Analyzing the reason for this large difference between China and Vietnam is beyond the scope of this chapter, but it was partly due to China's special experience with the People's communes, its small-scale rural industry programme and its greater tolerance of quasi-private forms of ownership. China's local governments were often promoters of local industry, while Vietnam's local governments were usually tax collectors and regulators with a hostile attitude towards anything that looked like private enterprise.

Whatever the reasons for the difference, the fact that most Vietnamese industries are still state owned and most Chinese industries are not has profound implications for how the government can or should influence or control industrial development. Before we explore these implications, however, it is important to gain a clearer picture of the nature of the state-owned enterprise problem in China and Vietnam. It is also necessary to have a view of how ownership and control over industry is related to the nature of the political and legal institutions in the two countries.

The state-owned enterprise problem

State-owned enterprises in both China and Vietnam now operate mainly in a market environment, but they do not behave in the way that market-oriented enterprises should. In the 1990s and even earlier, state-owned enterprises cared about profits and no longer concentrated on meeting gross value output targets. Their primary emphasis, however, was on maintaining good relations with those government ministries and party officials who determined whether they would be promoted and whether their firms would receive the subsidies they required in order to survive. The basic problem can be broken down into two major components.

First, state enterprises faced a 'soft budget constraint'.[11] As used here, this term refers to the fact that when state enterprises lost money they could always turn to the state to cover their losses. The state could intervene by providing subsidies from the government budget, by directing a state-owned bank to make a loan even if the enterprise was in arrears on past loans, by telling the tax authorities to forgive part or all of a firm's tax obligations, and various other measures. Because of the soft budget constraint, enterprises had little incentive to use inputs efficiently. The key to continued operation and growth was to maintain close relations with the government and those party authorities who kept enterprise budgets soft.

Second, state enterprise managers were selected, promoted and fired by these same government and party officials, not by boards of directors or others whose main concern would have been the profitability of the enterprise. Government and party officials might have preferred the enterprise to be profitable, but they typically had a number of other objectives, such as encouraging the enterprise to fund a favoured project that was critical to the achievement of a political objective, or to hire more workers than it needed because the workers in question could cause political trouble. Around the world, one of the biggest problems with state-owned enterprises is that they have multiple objectives because the politicians who control them have multiple objectives. Boards of directors elected by shareholders, in contrast, are usually concerned mainly with profits.

While China, and to a lesser degree Vietnam, have made major efforts to reform their state-owned enterprises,[12] the one thing that neither country has been willing to consider has been systematic privatization of these enterprises. Rather, their objective has been to make the enterprises internationally competitive. The steps they have taken are impressive on paper, but for nearly every step towards reform there has been a countermeasure that has partially undermined what the reform is trying to accomplish. The list of reform measures is a long one.

China introduced a bankruptcy law as early as 1986, but for years there were virtually no bankruptcies. Bankruptcy is essential for hardening a soft budget constraint in that it is the standard international way of removing failed managers and either restructuring the firm to make it profitable or liquidating it. Eventually, in the late 1990s China began to force an increasing number of loss-making state enterprises either into bankruptcy or to merge with more successful firms. Over 30 million state workers lost their jobs as a result of these measures.

In the 1990s, China also took steps to counter the willingness of state-owned banks to continue to lend to state enterprises with a poor repayment record. Because raising the interest rates was not a very effective means of reducing the demand for credit, the commercial banks were given credit quotas. Consequently, state-owned enterprises found it difficult to obtain loans from banks even when there we sound commercial reasons for borrowing. Rather then cutting back their operations in order to live within these tight credit constraints, however, enterprises simply ceased paying their bills to other enterprises. In effect these other enterprises were forced to become creditors, and this interenterprise or 'triangular' debt rapidly rose to enormous proportions. It was no longer easy to tell whether or not firms were economically profitable because they typically had huge accounts receivable that might or might not be received. More recently the state has begun to swap enterprise debt to the banks for equity in the enterprise, a measure that will only solve the debt problem if it is seen as a one-off bailout that will never be repeated. It is doubtful, however, that either enterprises or the banks see it this way.

China has thoroughly reformed its tax system, at least on paper. Enterprises are supposed to pay their taxes in accordance with the new tax laws, and to pay no more or no less than is due. However firms with large surpluses of cash are regularly raided for funds by local governments and even by the Ministry of Finance,[13] and firms that are financially strapped can still negotiate tax reductions.

China and Vietnam have both introduced shareholding systems for state-owned enterprises. In Vietnam the number of 'corporatized' firms is still very small, although the number began to increase rapidly after the year 2000. In China the number of such enterprises has reached many thousands and is still rising. The shares are sold to workers, managers, the general public and even foreigners. In principle the shareholders are entitled to elect boards of directors and the boards of directors can pick the management team, but in practice this has not happened. The government and the party still pick most of the managers and there is little indication that they will surrender this power in the near future.

There are several reasons why the Chinese and Vietnamese governments have been reluctant to do what is necessary to harden the budget constraint and cut the ties that connect management to the government bureaucracy. The biggest problem is that these governments have been afraid of the political consequences of large numbers of state-owned enterprises being either cut back sharply or allowed to go out of business. China's willingness in the late 1990s to cut state enterprise employment by more than 30 million, however, is evidence that the government was at last ready to take on this political risk.

A second reason is that government officials and the Chinese and Vietnamese Communist Parties are reluctant to surrender the political control that goes with direct authority over enterprise management. The governments of the two countries did surrender much of the control they had in the countryside when they reverted to household-based agriculture, but surrendering control over urban enterprises is perceived as a threat to continued party dominance. Finally, many in government are reluctant to relinquish control over the direction of industry. For officials with a planning background, and many in the economic bureaucracy fit that description, direct control over industrial enterprises makes it easier to implement inter-ventionist industrial policies. We shall return to this issue below.

It will be impossible to reform state-owned industrial enterprises without also reforming the state-owned banking system. After all, the banking system is the main vehicle for the perpetuation of soft budgets. The reverse is also true – it will be impossible to reform the banks without ending the ability of state enterprises to pressure the banks to make unsound loans. China, and to a lesser degree Vietnam, have adopted a variety of measures to reform their banking systems. The monobank system has been abolished, and commercial bank functions have been separated from central banking functions by creating new commercial banks. In addition, jurisdiction over many of the loans in China that are dictated by government priorities, the so-called 'policy loans', has been removed from the commercial banks and given to a new group of policy banks.

In principle the commercial banks are therefore free to make or withhold loans based on their assessment of the borrowers' ability to repay the loans with interest. But in reality, political power still has a good deal of influence over who receives loans and who does not. The Chinese leadership recognizes the problem and has tried to weaken this political pressure by changing the regional jurisdiction of the various banks so that these jurisdictions do not coincide with political ones. It will take more than procedural changes of this kind, however, to remove politics from the system. Until that is accomplished, Chinese and Vietnamese banks will continue to make loans that will turn into non-performing assets, and those non-performing assets will accumulate to the point where they threaten the viability of the banks as independent commercial entities.

As long as most of the liabilities of the Chinese and Vietnamese banking systems are owed to domestic depositors, the two governments can continue to refinance the banks so that on paper they appear healthy. The amount of refinancing required is large. Even official estimates of non-performing bank assets put the total at over 25 per cent of commercial bank assets, and the true figure is probably much higher.[14] But however large the true figure, if necessary the government can simply print the money required for the refinancing. More realistically, it can issue domestic bonds to cover the costs of this effort and persuade domestic institutions to buy the bonds, either voluntarily or with the help of government pressure. A variation of the latter theme has been tried in China with the creation of asset management companies, one for each of the four large state commercial banks. To date, however, only one quarter to one third of non-performing bank loans have been transferred to these asset management companies.

Refinancing the banking system without changing the way in which the system relates to state industrial enterprises, however, will not change the underlying problem. The banks will soon be pressured into making bad loans again, and their non-performing assets will return to the high levels of the recent past. So nothing will have changed. The budgets of enterprises and banks will continue to be soft, and both sets of institutions will depend on government support for their survival.

Industrial policy

Given the nature of the partially reformed industrial enterprises and banking systems in China and Vietnam, what can one conclude about the future of industrial policy in these two economies? Chinese and Vietnamese planners, looking at the experience of Japan and South Korea, would like to pursue an interventionist policy. The Chinese car industry provides an illustration of this approach. Prior to the reform period, small numbers of vehicles were produced in dozens of enterprises scattered around the country. In more recent years the government closed down many of these factories and concentrated production in several large enterprises, most of which had some kind of joint venture or cooperative relationship with a major international car manufacturer.[15]

These new ventures initially relied heavily on imported components, but then the government imposed tough domestic content requirements that forced the firms to turn increasingly to domestic suppliers. This involved some reduction in quality, but mostly it involved a substantial increase in costs. This meant that China could not produce vehicles at costs that were internationally competitive, and therefore tariffs and other restrictions were imposed on the importation of cars. It was hoped that the sector would eventually lower its costs to internationally competitive levels, where upon the trade restrictions could be removed. With China's entry into the World Trade Organization, however, most of the restrictions will have to be eliminated much sooner than most observers anticipated.

The Chinese government's involvement in industrial development, as the above example illustrates, is pervasive in many sectors, but the degree of involvement varies considerably from sector to sector. At one end of the spectrum are the petroleum corporations, where monopoly control of major markets was not formally ended until 1998 and profits did not replace output targets until 1999. The Chinese National Petroleum Corporation was basically a government bureau. Government control is also strong in industries that produce for the armed forces, and in other sectors that the government considers strategic in some way or other.

At the other end of the spectrum are a large number of sectors where the central government relies mainly on general incentives rather than specific intervention to stimulate growth. Most consumer manufactures fall into this category, as do many producer goods that are not considered strategic. Most TVEs receive little help from the central or even the provincial governments. Joint ventures and private firms, except in such strategic sectors as car manufacturing, are generally free from direct government control.

The Chinese government is as concerned with the way in which industry is organized as it is with the kinds of products produced. Inspired in part by the Korean *chaebol*, the government has been encouraging Chinese firms to consolidate into groups (*jituan*), but these have little in common with the Korean *chaebol* or the Japanese *keiretsu*. For one thing they are much smaller and far less diversified. Almost any collection of enterprises that work together is now labelled a group, and there appear to be many thousands of such groups.

The situation in Vietnam is somewhat different. Most enterprises in the heavy industry sector continue to operate under close guidance from the central government, and enterprises in sectors such as cement, steel and refining could not operate without government support in the form of tariffs and other trade restrictions. The Vietnamese are also enamoured of the Korean *chaebol*, and an effort has been made to form a group of enterprises into a Vietnamese equivalent. But the result is more like a government industrial bureau with a new name than a genuinely independent conglomerate on the Korean model.[16]

Are either China or Vietnam capable of efficiently running an industrial policy of this sort? Nothing that has happened so far suggests that they are. The performance of state-owned enterprises that are at the centre of the new policies has been poor. Even with protection from imports, many of them have lost money. Profits in the sector did rise after 2000, but much of this rise was due to the government's decision to reduce the bad debts of many of these enterprises by converting them into equity shares. Efforts to reform the state enterprises have been going on for 15 years but their situation does not appear to have improved significantly.[17]

It is worth remembering that in the 1970s Korea's President Park met monthly with the main leaders of industry. He followed their progress carefully, and if they performed well in meeting his goals they were rewarded; the opposite pertained if they performed poorly. President Jiang Zemin could not possibly do the same thing in China as he would have to meet with thousands of managers. Equally importantly, neither President Jiang nor Premier Zhu Rongji has the personal power to dictate what is best for their countries. Rule in China is mainly by consensus and involves numerous individuals and groups. The process of reaching a consensus is a political not a technical process, and therefore the decisions reached are inevitably influenced in a major way by political considerations.

If the top leaders are not in a position to make industrial policy decisions without injecting politics, could the task be turned over to industrial ministries along the lines of what was done with Japan's Ministry of Trade and Industry (MITI)? Given the nature of the Chinese government bureaucracy, there are at least two problems with this solution. High officials are picked in part because of their technical skills, but it is often their political skills and allegiances that matter most.[18] Furthermore it is widely claimed that governmental decision making is increasingly driven by personal rent seeking by these same officials. Thus decisions often have some political or rent-seeking purpose.

The situation is similar in Vietnam, but as Vietnam is smaller than China it is conceivable that one person or a small group of leaders would be able to follow what was going on in the principal industrial enterprises. But Vietnamese decisions too are arrived at by consensus via a political process. And rent seeking is at least as pervasive in Vietnam as it is in China.[19]

266 Strategic Choices for China and Vietnam

The weaknesses of the legal systems in the two countries and the closed nature of their political processes also make it difficult to operate an industrial policy governed by technical rather than political or personal criteria. There is no free press or political opposition to restrain policies that damage the economy. The only control is exercised by public security officials who are themselves an integral part of the political leadership. Trials of higher officials accused of wrongdoing in support of particular industrial policies are also partly political since the judiciary is no more independent of the politicians than are the public security forces.

Chinese and Vietnamese industrial policies, therefore, are inevitably a product of political and personal interests conflicting with the purely technical requirements of an effective industrial development programme. With so many opportunities for rent seeking, given the discretionary powers enjoyed by so many government officials, periodic anticorruption campaigns will only dent the surface of the personal rent-seeking problem. Removing politics from the process would be an even more formidable task. Conceivably the introduction of full democracy with vigorous opposition parties, plus the creation of a free press, could reduce the political content of industrial policy decisions. But it is also possible that democratic politics would increase the political content of these decisions, just as it did in Korea in the 1990s.

If China and Vietnam cannot isolate their industrial interventions from politics and personal rent seeking, what other options do they have? The only real answer is that they should rely more on forces that are not controlled by politicians and rent-seeking government officials – that is, they need to rely more on market forces. This does not mean that China and Vietnam should become like Hong Kong or the United States overnight, but they must begin to move more vigorously in that direction if they want to achieve efficient industrial development.

The international economic environment

Up to this point the discussion of Chinese and Vietnamese industrial policies has been conducted mainly in terms of how policies would work domestically. But the Chinese and Vietnamese economies must also function well in the international environment. If autarchy had proved to be an efficient means of development, China and Vietnam might have been able to ignore international forces, but it was completely rejected by both countries when their reform processes began because it had failed to deliver economic growth at rates that were vaguely comparable to those of their Asian neighbours. Given that China and Vietnam now have to operate as a part of the international economic system, what implications does this have for our discussion of the role of government in industrial development?

As pointed out earlier in this chapter, the first problem that an interventionist policy faces is that it is not consistent with the rules that currently govern the international economic system, notably the rules of the World Trade Organization. How serious a problem is that? Some used to argue that China did not have to worry about WTO membership because it enjoyed most favoured nation (MFN) treatment by all its principal trading partners, and therefore had as much access to those country's markets as it would have as a member of the WTO.

Having MFN access to the markets of the industrial world, however, does not mean that a country can pursue an activist industrial policy without endangering that access. Most of the US Trade Representative's negotiations are with countries that have both MFN status and membership of the WTO. Most of those negotiations deal with real or perceived restrictions on US goods entering the markets of those countries. Activist industrial policies are a major reason why such restrictions on access exist. A country that wants continued access to the US market is therefore vulnerable to pressure from sources of this kind. If it is a member of the WTO, it can at least reduce any retaliation that is driven more by domestic politics than by real trade restrictions. The same argument holds for trade relations with the European Union.

The continued growth of manufactured exports is far more crucial to the economic development of China and Vietnam than is the future of a handful of industries that are perceived as strategic, such as car manufacturing. Relatively free trade might slow the development of a few import-substituting sectors by a few years, but if it allows exports to continue to grow rapidly the net impact on overall economic growth is likely to be highly positive.

It was partly considerations of this sort that led China to agree to the very stringent WTO membership conditions and why Vietnam finally concluded a trade agreement with the United States. By the time China actually joined the WTO, China's leaders had come to view the WTO rules as useful and powerful instruments for pressuring state-owned enterprises to reform.

Lessons from the Asian financial crisis

Are there lessons to be learnt from the Asian financial crisis for the issues discussed in this chapter? One lesson that some countries have learnt is that it does not pay to be too fully integrated into the international economic system, or at least in the financial sphere. China, it is argued by some, avoided the crisis because its currency was not fully convertible for capital account transactions. Vietnam was in a similar situation.

The real lessons of the financial crisis for China and Vietnam, however, lie elsewhere. Two distinct but interrelated factors provoked the Asian financial crisis.[20] One was a financial panic much like a bank run and other such panics that have occurred at various times around the world. The other was that the crisis hit countries with marked structural weaknesses in their economies, and that made the impact of the financial panic far more severe than would otherwise have been the case.

One reason why China and Vietnam managed to avoid the financial panic aspect of the Asian crisis was the existence of controls on their capital accounts. More important in the case of China was the fact that it had $140 billion in foreign exchange reserves, a very large current account surplus and most of its foreign debt was long term and hence could not be pulled out of the country at short notice. Vietnam did not have a strong reserve or balance of payments position, but it too had little short-term debt, mainly because few lenders were willing to loan money to Vietnam. Those who did were institutions such as the World Bank, which only lent long term.

While China and Vietnam were not subject to the panic aspect of the crisis they did share the structural problems that contributed to the crisis elsewhere. The core structural problem in the countries concerned, which has been described at length above, was the weakness of their financial systems, which were burdened by large amounts of risky and non-performing assets. These were the result of borrowing by state enterprises that were confident the government would bail them out if their risky investments failed. Their confidence was justified in that the governments in question had a long track record of doing precisely that. If the banks had financed these risky investments with domestic funds, none of the crisis-hit countries would have faced a panic. But instead the financial systems had borrowed heavily abroad and the governments did not have sufficient foreign exchange to bail out the system, although each crisis-hit government tried to do so.

One danger for China and Vietnam in the future is that a weakening of their balance of payments position or an increase in short-term foreign borrowing will render them vulnerable to the kind of crisis that hit elsewhere in Asia in 1997–98. In such a case they might be able to avoid the panic, but they will not be able to escape the crisis because the banking systems of the two countries are, if anything, weaker than those in the crisis-hit countries.

Is there an example of an economy that avoided the financial panic but still experienced a crisis that had a strong negative impact on long-term economic growth? The obvious example is Japan, which was one of the principal instigators of interventionist industrial policy and the institutions that go with it. In Japan's case the bubble burst in 1991 and there has been stagnation ever since, caused in large part by the weakness and paralysis of the domestic financial system.

China and Vietnam are in a very different stage of development from Japan, but this may not be the crucial variable in determining how a similarly weak financial system might affect the two economies. Both have relatively weak governments that require consensus for politically difficult decisions. Whether or not to implement radical reforms of the complex of weak banks and weak state enterprises is just such a politically difficult decision. Rather than really trying to solve the problem, the leaders of China and Vietnam could well equivocate and merely tinker with the existing systems. The end result could well be a financial system that is partially paralyzed and a state industrial sector that imposes more and more of a drain on the rest of the economy. It is unlikely that these weaknesses would lead to outright stagnation in the two countries, but their annual growth rate could be slowed by several percentage points. Given the large number of underemployed and unemployed workers in both China and Vietnam, a slowdown in growth of this magnitude could be more politically serious than the ten years of stagnation has been for Japan.

The lessons of the Asian financial crisis therefore point in the same direction as the analysis of the internal reform issues still facing China and Vietnam. Neither country has the political, legal and economic institutions needed to make an interventionist industrial policy work well enough to meet their economic needs. Korea and Japan were able to make such a system work well for a time, but today's China and Vietnam are not like the Korea and Japan of the 1970s. Furthermore there is no reason to think that realistic reform measures could make China and Vietnam enough like Korea and Japan for government-led industrial development to be made to work.

What, then, is the alternative? The only real alternative is for the two countries to move steadily towards reduced government intervention in favour of market forces. Perhaps some infant industry protection could be retained within the bounds of the WTO rules. There will also be a major role for government in the provision of badly needed infrastructure. But the governments of both countries should loosen their reins on the banking system, other than maintaining a vigorous regulatory regime, and cease trying to run large numbers of industrial enterprises.

Notes

1. There is a large body of literature on the nature of this interventionist model and how it has worked in the Asian context. For Korea, see for example Jones and Sakong (1980), Amsden (1989) and Song (1990). An influential study of the system in Taiwan is that by Wade (1990). There are also many works on this subject *vis-à-vis* Japan.
2. The Indonesian system is discussed at length in Cole and Slade (1996).
3. The Hong Kong and Singapore legal systems did not become strong and relatively independent quickly, or simply because the British colonial authorities brought in a strong system from Britain. The authorities did bring in such a system, but it was only they and a handful of local inhabitants who used it. For a very long time the majority Chinese populations of these two cities had as little to do with the courts as they could.
4. Governments do occasionally try to get involved in decisions about leading edge technologies, but this has rarely resulted in success. Most relatively successful interventions, including that in Airbus in Europe, had an existing model of success to follow.
5. Much is often made of how defence research, particularly in the United States, has produced technologies that have had later found commercial applications, and defence research is clearly led to some degree by the government. If a country does not

have a compelling security reason for conducting defence research, however, it does not make sense to undertake such research simply because it may have a non-military application. If defence research were judged solely in terms of its commercial applications, most of that research would be seen as extremely expensive and inefficient.

6. There is an enormous body of literature on the reform process and how it evolved in China, but much less has been written about Vietnam's reform experience. One example of the latter is World Bank (1997). Much of what is contained in this chapter is based on knowledge gained when working as a researcher, consultant and teacher in Vietnam from 1989.
7. In the early 1990s the overvaluation of the Vietnamese dong may have been a deliberate policy by the central bank. In the mid and late 1990s, however, the overvaluation is more likely to have resulted from the large inflow of capital in the form of World Bank loans, foreign direct investment and so on, which created a kind of 'Dutch disease' effect.
8. Foreign direct investment that was actually utilized in China in the first half of the 1980s averaged less than US$1 billion a year, whereas in the period 1995–98 the average was over US$40 billion a year (State Statistical Bureau, 1998, p. 637).
9. A good case study of how this worked can be found in Byrd and Tidrick (1992).
10. To mention just two of many articles, see Che and Qian (1998) and Chang and Wang (1994).
11. This concept was first introduced by Janos Kornai. See for example Kornai (1992).
12. For an in-depth discussion of enterprise reform in China see Jefferson and Singh (1999).
13. For a good description of how this worked in the steel industry in China see Steinfeld (1998).
14. Lardy (1998), pp. 115–24.
15. Eric Thun (1999) discusses the evolution of China's car manufacturing sector at length in his Harvard University doctoral dissertation.
16. This statement is based on interviews with Vietnamese government officials involved in the state enterprise reform process.
17. The results of efforts to measure the productivity growth and profitability of China's state-owned enterprises are controversial. See for example the debate in Jefferson and Xu (1994) versus Woo *et al.* (1994).
18. There are numerous works on Chinese politics. One that deals with personnel selection issues, among many other things, is Lieberthal (1995).
19. China and Vietnam are regularly scored as very corrupt in surveys that ask businessmen to rate countries according to the degree of corruption they have witnessed when working in them.
20. There is a growing body of literature on the causes and nature of the Asian financial crisis of 1997–98. The World Bank's view of the crisis can be found in World Bank (1998), ch. 2.

References

Amsden, A. (1989) *Asia's Next Giant* (New York: Oxford University Press).
Byrd, W. A. and G. Tidrick (1992) 'The Chongqing Clock and Watch Company', in W. A. Byrd (ed.), *Chinese Industrial Firms under Reform* (Oxford: Oxford University Press), pp. 58–119.

Chang, C. and Y. Wang (1994) 'The Nature of Township Enterprises', *Journal of Comparative Economics*, vol. 19, pp. 434–52.

Che, J. and Y. Qian (1994) 'Institutional Environment, Community Government, and Corporate Governance: Understanding China's Township and Village Enterprises', *Journal of Law, Economics, and Organization*, vol. 14, pp. 1–23.

Cole, D. C. and B. F. Slade (1996) *Building a Modern Financial System: The Indonesian Experience* (Cambridge: Cambridge University Press).

Jefferson, G. H. and I. Singh (1999) *Enterprise Reform in China: Ownership, Transition and Performance* (Oxford: Oxford University Press).

Jefferson, G. H. and W. Xu (1994) 'Assessing Gains in Efficient Production in China's Industrial Enterprises', *Economic Development and Cultural Change*, vol. 42, pp. 595–615.

Jones, L. and I. Sakong (1980) *Government, Business, and Entrepreneurship in Economic Development: The Korean Case* (Cambridge, Mass.: Council on East Asian Studies, Harvard University).

Kornai, J. (1992) *The Socialist System: The Political Economy of Communism* (Princeton, NJ: Princeton University Press).

Lardy, N. R. (1998) *China's Unfinished Economic Revolution* (Washington, DC: Brookings Institution Press).

Lieberthal, K. (1995) *Governing China: From Revolution through Reform* (New York: W. W. Norton).

Qian, Y. and J. Chan (1998) 'Constitutional Environment, Community Government and Corporate Governance: Understanding China's Township–village Enterprises', *Journal of Law, Economics and Organisation*, April, vol. 14(1), pp. 1–23.

Song, B.-N. (1990) *The Rise of the Korean Economy* (Hong Kong: Oxford University Press).

State Statistical Bureau (1998) *China Statistical Yearbook 1998* (Beijing: China Statistical Publishing House).

Steinfeld, E. S. (1998) *Forging Reform in China: The Fate of State-Owned Industry* (Cambridge: Cambridge University Press).

Thun, Eric (1999) 'Changing lanes in China: industrial development in a transition economy', Harvard University Ph.D. dissertation.

Wade, R. (1990) *Governing the Market: Economic Theory and the Role of Government in East Asian Industrialization* (Princeton, NJ: Princeton University Press).

Woo, W. T., W. Hai, Y. Jin and F. Gang (1994) 'How Successful has Chinese Enterprise Reform Been: Pitfalls in Opposite Biases and Focus', *Journal of Comparative Economics*, vol. 18, pp. 410–37.

World Bank (1997) *Vietnam: Deepening Reform for Growth: An Economic Report* (Washington, DC: World Bank).

World Bank (1998) *Global Economic Prospects, 1998–99: Beyond Financial Crisis* (Washington, DC: World Bank).

Author/Name Index

Abraham, A. 242
Acemoglu, D., *et al.* (2001) 45, 59
  Johnson, S. 59
  Robinson, J. A. 59
Agency on Statistics of Republic of
  Kazakhstan 247(n12)
Alesina, A. 46, 50
Amade, C. 250
Amsden, A. 269(n1)
Anwar bin Ibrahim, *Dato' Seri* 160
Aoki, M., *et al.* (1995) 134, 136, 150
  Kim, H. 150
  Okuno-Fujiwara, M. 150
Armstrong, A., *et al.* (1999) 223(n12), 226
  Lin, S. 226
  Sanyai, S. 226
  Spencer, M. 226
  Wong, A. 226

Baldwin, R. E. 58(n10)
Banharn, S.-A. 157
Bank for International Settlements
  (BIS) 219, 225(n33)
Bank of Korea 169, 180, 199(n11, n13)
Bardhan, P. 242
Barsuto, G. 199(n15)
Basle Committee on Banking
  Supervision 225(n27)
Basu, K. x, **4–5**, 97, 98, 112(n6, n10),
  113(n14), 242, 246(n1)
Bates, R. H. 50, 54
Bell, C. 242
Ben-David, D. 36(n11)
Berg, A. 233
Berkowitz, D., *et al.* (1999) 35, 36
  Pistor, K. 36
  Richard, J.-F. 36
Besley, T. 102
Bhagwati, J. 99
Bismarck, O. von 173
Blanchard, O. 233–4, 247(n11)
Blanchard, O., *et al.* (1991) 233, 249
  Dornbusch, R. 249
  Krugman, P. 249

Layard, R. 249
Summers, L. 249
Bordo, M. D., *et al.* (1998) 23, 36
  Goldin, C. 36
  White, E. N. 36
Bosworth, B. 16
Braverman, A. 242
Brown, S. J. 207
Buchi. H. 58(n6)
Buffet, W. 213, 225(n21)
Burgess, R. 102
Byrd, W. A. 270(n9)

Calomiris, C. 222(n1)
Calvo, G. 223(n15)
Campos, N. F. 46–7, 49, 50, 232,
  247(n3, n7)
Campos, N. F., *et al.* (2000) 49, 59
  Nugent, J. B. 59
  Robinson, J. A. 59
Carter, M. 248(n24)
Castro, S. de 58(n6)
Cavallo, D. 58(n6)
Chadha, B. 227
Chang, C. 270(n10)
Chatichai, C. 157
Chavalit, Y. 157, 158, 159, 166
Che, J. 270(n10)
Cheng, L. K. 132(n2)
Cho, Y. J. x, **7**, 199(n2, n10)
Choksi, A. M. 61
Chuan, L. 157, 159, 166
Chuma, H. 250
Claessens, S., *et al.* (1999) 166, 175
  Djankov, S. 175
  Klingebiel, D. 175
Clinton, W. J. 51
Cochrane, J. H. 247(n5)
Cole, D. C. 269(n2)
Collins, S. 16
Cooper, R. 60
Corden, W. M. 60
Coricelli, F. 232, 247(n3, n7)
Corrigan, E. G. 225(n32)

Cox, G.   174(n1)
Cukierman, A.   51

de Broeck, M.   247(n3–5)
de la Madrid Hurtado, M.   50
de Soto, H.   46
de Melo, M., *et al.* (1996)   247(n3–4), 249
 Denizer, C.   249
 Gelb, A.   249
de Melo, M., *et al.* (1997)   247(n4), 249
 Denizer, C.   249
 Gelb, A.   249
 Tenev, S.   249
Deardorff, A. V.   124, 132(n2)
Deininger, K.   248(n24)
Denizer, C.   249
Djankov, S.   175
Dollar, D.   36(n11)
Dornbusch, R.   249
Drazen, A.   50
Dreze, J.   111(n2)
Dunning, J. H.   71, 132(n4)

Easterly, W.   46
Edwards, F. R.   224(n19)
Edwards, S.   36(n11)
Eichengreen, B.   x, **7–8**
Eichengreen, B. and Mathieson, D.,
    et al. (1998)   207, 227
 Chadha, B.   227
 Jansen, A.   227
 Kodres, L.   227
 Sharma, S.   227
Engerman, S.   99
Engerman, S. L.   42

Fernandez, R.   50
Folkerts-Landau, D.   225(n27)
Fujimori, A. K.   51
Fujita, M., *et al.* (1999)   132(n3)
 Krugman, P.   132(n3)
 Venables, A. J.   132(n3)

Gang, F.   271
Gates, B.   112(n12)
Gelb, A.   249
Genghis Khan   103
Genicot, G.   98
Ghosh, A. R.   199(n15)
Giovannini, A.   222(n1)

Goetzmann, W. N.   207
Goldin, C.   36
Gomez, E. T.   162
Goodman, R., *et al.* (1998)   171, 175
 Kwon, H.-J.   175
 White, G.   175
Gorbachov, M. S.   247(n16)
Govinda, R.   114
Graham, G.   225(n28)
Greenberg, M.   213, 225(n21)
Greenspan, A.   36(n10), 221,
    224(n16, n18), 224–5(n20)
Grilli, V.   32
Gros, D.,   222(n1)
Grossman, G.   148, 149–50

Haber, S.   49
Habibie, B. J.   157, 167
Haggard, S.   x, **6–7**, 50–1, 155, 159
Hai, W.   271
Hale, D. D.   223(n14)
Hall, R.   46
Harberger, A. C.   48, 49, 54
Hayami, Y.   242, 250
Helpman, E.   148, 149–50
Hennessee, L.   222(n1), 223(n4)
Hoff, K.   36(n7)
Hughes, P.   58(n1)
Hunter, S. T.   247(n12)

Ickes B. W.   247(n5)
Imaoka, H.   139
International Monetary Fund   74, 76,
    77n, 223(n6), 224(n17)
Ishikawa, S.   136

Jacoby, S. M.   23
Jansen, A.   227
Jefferson, G. H.   270(n12, n17)
Jiang Zemin   265
Jin, Y.   271
Johnson, C.   162
Johnson, S.   35(n6), 59
Jomo, K. S.   155, 162
Jones, C. I.   46
Jones, L.   269(n1)
Jones, R. W.   132(n2)

Kalirajan, K. P.   114
Kalyuzhnova, Y.   247(n12)

Subject Index

Sierra Leone: quintile incomes   109,
109t
Singapore   58(n3), 131, 132(n1), 162,
173, 255, 269(n3)
customs duty as
percentage of import value
(1988–98)   128f
per capita income (PPP,
1960–2000)   67f
relative per capita real income (PPP,
1960–2000)   68f
Singapore: Central Provident Fund
156, 173
SK   188t
skill   52
political   265
technical   265
slavery   43
Slovak Republic   232
Slovenia   232
small
businesses   171
countries   28
economies   131
markets   205
social
adjustment loans   172
capital   231
conflict   17, 19, 25
contract   79, **170–4**
costs   58(n5), 165, 172
decay   91
group   5
insurance   13, 14, **23–4**, 25, 34,
156, 171–2, 173–4
investment funds   172
norms   112(n7)
policy   174
security   23, 26, 80
services   171
system   8
tension   179, 180
welfare   79, 106, 156
socialist system   84(n9)
socialists   26
soft budgets   8, 260, 261, 262,
270(n11)
South America   15
South Asia   16
globalization indicators (1989–99)   89t

per capita income (PPP,
1960–2000)   67f
relative per capita
real income (PPP, 1960–2000)   68f
share of world trade
(1960–99)   65f
South Korea
see Korea
Southeast Asia (SEA)   171, 254, 255
competition from China   117t, 118
current agenda   129–31
definition   **132(n1)**
development pattern   116
economic slump (mid-1980s)   123
FDI for import substitution   119–23
FDI and international commercial
policy   **115–33**
industrialization strategies   5
Japanese official development
assistance   128
lessons for LDCs in other
regions   131–2
as model   116–19
response to Asian
financial crisis (slower than
Korea)   159
Soviet Union   13, 231, 235
sovkhozes (state farms)   234–5
'space' (city planning concept)   125
Spain   43, 45
specialization   69
specialization patterns   **140–1**
speculation   210
'speculators' (Mahathir)   160
spot market
244, 245
SPS-related regulations   131
Sri Lanka   34
stabilization   25, 47, 49,
58(n2, n4), 233
stagnation   268, 269
state   4, 9–10, 13, 235, 260
role in OORs   **54**
roll-back   14
strong and competent   10
'strong' or 'developmental'   162
state farms   234–5, 242(n22)
state functions   3, 82
state intervention   84(n8)
state monopolies   257

Vietnamese Communist Party   262
voters   20, 170
voting costs   58(n10)

wage controls   17
wage levels   137, 147
wage rate   95, 96f
wages   95f, 96–7, 99–100, 100f, 101,
      112(n5), 193, 234, 245
   real   17, 51, 170
   real growth (Korea, 1996–2000)   198t
war   90
   civil war   247(n6)
   military action   91, 111(n2)
Washington Consensus   xi, 13, 27,
      41–2, 47, 58(n2), 80
   alternative industrialization strategies
      in Southeast Asia   5
   augmented/new/revised   28, 29
   and beyond   **1–10**
   building market system from
      scratch   8–9
   development strategies under
      globalization   4–6, **85–152**
   discontent about the orthodoxy   14
   getting policy intervention right   5–6
   hedge funds (how to tame)   7–8
   increasing roles of government under
      globalization   4
   inequality and globalization   4–5
   lessons from twentieth century   3
   markets, governments and
      institutions   2–4, **11–84**
   onset and management of Asian crisis
      (political view)   6–7
   policy reforms and Asian crisis   6–8,
      155–228
   regime transition in Korea (economic
      view)   7
   state and development strategy   1–2
   strategic choices for China and
      Vietnam   8–9
   strategies for reforms and regime
      change   3
   transition to market economy   8–9,
      229–71
welfare state   23–4, 36(n8), 171, 172
   capitalist   2–3, 82, 83–4(n8–9)
   Keynesian-type discretionary
      policies   83–4(n8)

West Virginia   102
Western Europe   13, 34, 72
   per capita GDP (1000–1998)   104t
   merchandise exports
      as percentage of GDP
      (1870–1995)   88t
Western hemisphere
   capital flows (1970–99)   75f
   capital account liberalization
      (1970–98)   77f
wheat farmers   232, 241–6,
      248(n26, n29)
   isoprofit curve   244
wheat price   243–4, 245
wheat production   8
   exports   234
   government procurement system   236
   Kazakhstan   **231–50**
   institutional and organizational
      evolution of input
      procurement   **240–6**, 248(n25–31)
   land productivity   245, 246, 247(n15),
      248(n31)
   production and productivity
      of private farms   236–40,
      247–8(n18–24)
   TFP   238–9, 239f
   yields   242
wheat traders   232, 241–6
   isoprofit curve   244
wholesale trade   126f, 257
winners   48, 50, 58(n2)
women   88, 90, 94, 171
workers   23, 45, 51, 52, 80,
      92, 93, 95, 96–7, 98, 102,
      172, 173, 233, 245, 261, 262
   skilled   93, 129
   unskilled   129
   see also labour
workforce quality   173
working capital   240
working conditions   93
working hours: statutory limits   **93–101**,
      112(n6–11)
world
   merchandise exports as percentage of
      GDP (1870–1995)   88t
   per capita income (PPP, 1960–2000) 67f
   relative per capita real income
      (PPP, 1960–2000)   68f

World Bank   30, 110, 137–8, 172,
    268, 270(n7)
world economy   7, 19, 64, 73
    governance   **28–9**
    integration   80, 82, 137
    new rules of game   9
    optimistic view   4
world markets   30, 35, 142
world trade   28, 138, 142f
World Trade Organization (WTO)   87,
    102, 110, 115
    China's entry   264, 267
    framework   5
    General Agreement on Tariffs and
        Trade (GATT)   252

'greenroom effect'   102
membership conditions   267
rules   269
system   177
Uruguay Round   28
world wars   90
    inter-war era (1918–39)   88
    post-war era (1945–)   24, 64, 72,
        83–4(n8)
    World War II
        (1939–45)   24

yen   207, 223(n8)

Zaire   15